ST. MARY'S
ST. MARY'S CITY, MARYLAND 20686

Eduardo De Filippo

Twayne's World Authors Series
Italian Literature

Anthony Oldcorn, Editor
Brown University

TWAS 733

Eduardo De Filippo in the role of Pulcinella
Photograph reprinted with the permission of Eduardo De Filippo

Eduardo De Filippo

By Mario B. Mignone
State University of New York at Stony Brook

Twayne Publishers • Boston

Eduardo De Filippo

Mario B. Mignone

Copyright © 1984 by G. K. Hall & Company
All Rights Reserved
Published by Twayne Publishers
A Division of G. K. Hall & Company
70 Lincoln Street
Boston, Massachusetts 02111

Printed on permanent/durable acid-
free paper and bound in the United
States of America.

Library of Congress Cataloging in Publication Data

Mignone, Mario B.
  Eduardo De Filippo.

  (Twayne's world authors series ; TWAS 733)
  Bibliography: p.
  Includes index.
  1. De Filippo, Eduardo, 1900–   —Criticism
and interpretation. I. Title. II. Series.
PQ4815.I48Z77   1984   852'.912   84-583
ISBN 0-8057-6580-8

To my parents

Contents

About the Author
Preface
Chronology

Chapter One
Eduardo De Filippo, Naples,
and the Neapolitan Popular Theater   1

Chapter Two
De Filippo's Inspiration and Creative Process   20

Chapter Three
Early Works: Range and Versatility   37

Chapter Four
Neorealism   67

Chapter Five
Reality vs. Illusion   91

Chapter Six
Family Drama   119

Chapter Seven
Theater: The Art of Social Awareness   138

Chapter Eight
Plays of Social Protest   147

Chapter Nine
Conclusion   179

Notes and References   183
Selected Bibliography   191
Index   194

About the Author

Mario B. Mignone was born and raised in Italy. He earned his B.A. degree at the City College of New York and his M.A. and Ph.D. degrees at Rutgers University while holding a three-year National Defense Education Act Scholarship. In 1970 he joined the faculty of the State University of New York at Stony Brook where he has been teaching contemporary Italian literature, theater, and film. He has contributed a number of articles to journals such as Forum Italicum, Italian Quarterly, Players, and the NEMLA Italian Studies, and has written several essays for the Encyclopedia of World Literature in the 20th Century. He is the author of two other books: Il teatro di Eduardo De Filippo (1974) and Anormalità e angoscia nella narrativa di Dino Buzzati (1981).

Preface

The names of Torquato Tasso (1544-1595), Gianbattista Vico (1668-1744), Vincenzo Bellini (1801-1835), Luigi Pirandello (1867-1936), and Benedetto Croce are among the many that testify to the remarkable intellectual and cultural contribution nourished by Italy's South. That this nourishment continues is proved by the artistic achievements of Eduardo De Filippo, born in Naples in 1900 and incontestably the greatest living Italian playwright, actor, and theatrical producer. By this fertile combination of activities, he continues a very old Italian tradition and has become a beloved national institution.

In his many years of theatrical activity Eduardo De Filippo has written about forty-five plays. All have been performed by De Filippo's own theater company, Il teatro di Eduardo, which he founded in 1945. Many have been performed abroad, in at least thirty countries, and some have been published in translation.

In recognition of his high artistic achievements, De Filippo has been awarded the Croce di Commendatore, first by King Victor Emmanuel III, then by his son King Umberto, and then by the first President of Italy. He was made Grande Ufficiale and Cavaliere di Gran Croce dell'Ordine al Merito della Repubblica, thus receiving the highest honor that the Italian establishment can offer. He has been awarded the French Legion of Honor and the degree of Doctor of Letters, honoris causa, by the University of Birmingham; he has received various decorations in U.S.S.R. and has been nominated for the Nobel Prize.

That the creative talents of Eduardo De Filippo should be esteemed by such distinguished American men of the theater as Eric Bentley and Thornton Wilder is not surprising. In 1951, when De Filippo had written very few major works, Bentley called him one of the three or four most original figures in the contemporary theater. Wilder often said that De Filippo was his favorite living playwright.

De Filippo emerged in the mid-1940s as one of Italy's

EDUARDO DE FILIPPO

most creative playwrights. Since 1945, his distinctive genre of dialect comedy has become familiar throughout Italy simply as "The Theater of Eduardo," and he himself as "Eduardo." Most of his plays are set in his native Naples and portray the vicissitudes of an extremely wide range of characters from lower middle class Neapolitan society and covering a broad emotional and social spectrum. As an actor-playwright, Eduardo has frequently been compared to Molière, while his works, being in dialect, have been ranked with those of Synge and O'Casey, and, in his own country's tradition of dialect theater, with those of (Angelo Beolco) Ruzzante (1502-1542) and Carlo Goldoni (1707-1793). Some of the ingredients of his plays, including the main character he portrays, are in direct line of descent from the commedia dell'arte. The frontispiece to this volume portrays the actor Eduardo in the costume of the Neapolitan maschera, Pulcinella. Indeed, De Filippo is the twentieth-century Pulcinella and, beyond this, a symbol of the age, the twentieth-century Everyman.

Although De Filippo's goal is to amuse, he also follows Hamlet's suggestion to the players, "to hold, as 'twere, the mirror up to nature!" He has worked out a common denominator of fun and feeling that accords with something in everyone. To common, underprivileged little men, he is their representative. To aesthetes he is a dreamer ever searching for beauty in an often ugly and cruel world. In women he appeals to the maternal or feminine instinct. To Freudians, he personifies our frustrations. To leftists, his plays protest the crushing of the individual by social forces.

Many critics, however, have wrongly defined Eduardo's theater with neat, restrictive labels. Unquestionably, he was influenced by Pirandello and by the Neapolitan dialect theater. We cannot disregard, however, additional formative influences: his acquaintance with other forms of popular theater, the unique character of the city in which he was born and where he lived all his life, his professional experience on the stage, the interaction with his family, all of whom were also actors. His theater provides a link between native Neapolitan traditions and the vaster intellectual currents of Europe, all developed by De Filippo according to his own personal style.

De Filippo has known great national and international success. In England his company performed at the Aldwych

Preface

Theater, in the World Theater repertoire, in 1973-74; subsequently it moved to the West End for a very successful run. His 1977 production of Filumena Marturano and 1972 production of Millionaires' Naples! were highly acclaimed, and The Big Magic was performed twice on Radio 3 in 1975. In the United States, however, De Filippo is almost unknown. Filumena Marturano failed twice on Broadway, in 1956 and 1980; and in 1973 Saturday, Sunday and Monday was also a flop. Criticism in English is limited to no more than a few articles.

The purpose of this study, therefore, is two fold: to introduce the Italian playwright to an English-speaking audience and to present a more global view of his art by evaluating all his works in the light of his formative experience in Naples and tradition of the Neapolitan dialect theater. To this end, De Filippo's plays are addressed more or less chronologically, in the belief that such a presentation is best suited to a study of the playwright's artistic evolution. The book is divided into nine chapters. The first two are arranged as a mosaic of brief topics intended to open discussion rather than complete it. I realize that these analytic fragments may tease and frustrate the reader, but if they also whet the appetite, I feel that my purpose has been served. Chapter 3 analyzes the works of his youth, written between the two World Wars. The next five chapters deal with two phases of his artistic development and analyze the works written since World War II. The conclusion assesses his significance to Italian and world literature. I have avoided dry analysis in favor of a clear, comprehensive approach that will not segregate the various components of De Filippo's theater, but instead will make them recognizable when they are clothed in flesh and viewed in motion. Thus, I have tried to recapture the impression made by the play in performance or in an imaginative reading. The result may not be as neat as a rigid analysis component by component, but I trust it is more lively. Furthermore, it has been easier this way to show not merely how the playwright's intimate involvement with production has made properties, set, costume, dialogue, and action all contribute to our understanding of character, but also how through them he develops and projects a theatricality all his own.

Because only a very few of De Filippo's plays have been translated into English, plot summaries provide the reader with the background necessary to make the critical comments relevant.

I would like to express my deep-felt appreciation to Professor Anthony Oldcorn, editor of the Italian series of Twayne's World Authors. His thoughtful advice and careful, critical reading were a big contribution to the completion of this book. I also wish to thank my friend Mark Heumann for his editorial help and his wise counsel; my mother and father Mr. and Mrs. Roberto Mignone for their encouragement; and, of course, my wife and my three daughters for their understanding and patience.

Mario B. Mignone

State University of New York at Stony Brook

Chronology

1900   Birth of Eduardo De Filippo on May 24 in Naples.

1904   First appearance on stage as a crying infant. Begins to appear in the theatrical company of his natural father Eduardo Scarpetta.

1914   Becomes a member of Vincenzo Scarpetta's company, remaining until 1921.

1921   Writes his first one-act play, Pharmacy on Call. Member of the theatrical company of Peppino Villani.

1925   Eduardo Scarpetta dies without acknowledging his three illegitimate children in his will.

1928   Marries the American actress Dorothy Pennington. The union lasts only a few months.

1929   In the summer, together with his brother Peppino and his sister Titina, Eduardo performs in the vaudeville-style review of Kokasse and Tricot (pseudonyms of Mario Mangini and Eduardo) for the Molinari company. His one-act Sik-Sik, the Incomparable Magician gives him the first big success as playwright.

1931   Forms the company Teatro Umoristico i De Filippo with his brother and sister.

1932   Pirandello, impressed with the excellence of the De Filippo company, asks to have his Liolà staged in a Neapolitan version.

1934   The De Filippo company stages Liolà.

1935   After the success of Liolà, Pirandello asks the company to stage his Cap and Bells in a Neapolitan version. Eduardo takes the role of the protagonist Ciampa.

1937 The New Suit, written by Eduardo and Pirandello from a short story by Pirandello, is staged, but flops.

1941 Titina, who had temporarily left the De Filippo company to work for the company of Nino Taranto, rejoins her brothers.

1944 Peppino De Filippo leaves the company, bringing about its dissolution.

1945 With Titina, Eduardo forms the company Il teatro di Eduardo. On March 25, debut of Millionaires' Naples! at the San Carlo theater, Naples. From now on, his company performs both in Italy and abroad.

1946 Eduardo writes and stages Filumena Marturano, which most critics consider his masterpiece.

1952 Marriage to Dorothy Pennington is annulled in the Republic of San Marino. The annulment is recognized in Italy in 1956.

1954 On January 21 inaugurates the rebuilt San Ferdinando theater in Naples, which he had bought after the war.

1956 Marries Thea Prandi, with whom he has already had two children. Enormous success of Filumena Marturano in Moscow.

1959 Separates from Thea Prandi.

1960 Ten-year-old daughter dies of a cerebral hemorrhage.

1961 Death of his wife.

1962 On tour in Austria, Belgium, Poland, Hungary, and Russia.

1972 Participates in the World Theatre Season at the

Chronology

Aldwych Theatre, London, with Millionaires' Naples!

1973 Saturday, Sunday and Monday is staged at the Old Vic Theatre, London, Sir Laurence Olivier in the leading role.

1974 Undergoes heart surgery to have a pacemaker implanted.

1977 Marries longtime friend Isabella Quarantotti. Filumena Marturano staged at the Lyric Theatre, London, starring Joan Plowright and Colin Blakely.

1980 Filumena Marturano again a flop on Broadway.

1981 Nominated senator for life to the Italian Parliament by Italian President Sandro Pertini.

Chapter One
Eduardo De Filippo, Naples, and the Neapolitan Popular Theater

The explanation of De Filippo's success with critics and audiences must be sought first of all in the essentially theatrical character of his art, which has its roots in the popular theater. No one has expressed this character better than the American playwright Thornton Wilder: "To love De Filippo's theater one must truly love theater— not the well-shaped play, not the picture of relatively superficial customs and manners, not the heated unfoldment of patterns of idealized heroism and villainy—but the 'show,' 'of the people, by the people, for the people'—absurd, extravagant, often preposterous, but close to life and stage" (1). De Filippo's art is bound to the best Italian theater tradition, the nonliterary tradition, with its emphasis on the actor and on stage spectacle. In fact, De Filippo is one of the very few playwrights who can also claim greatness as an actor and director:

> He is an incomparable dramatist, an incomparable metteur-en-scène, an incomparable actor.
> How sad his plays are—the weight of humanity.
> How controlled his acting has become—that powerful quiet.
> How superb his management of group score—everyone in his company is a faultless actor. (2)

Indisputably, De Filippo is an impeccable showman, a rarity in the world theater today.
Audiences throughout Italy have constantly accorded him well-deserved recognition over the years for his merits both as an actor and as a playwright. Yet critics virtually ignored him until the years immediately following World War II. This neglect was mainly due to the Fascist government, which imposed a single national language on the Italian people and, to this end, banned

1

all books and plays written and performed in any dialect. De Filippo escaped the worst consequences of such a policy because of his immense popularity, but the official literary critics ignored him, hoping that if they gave the impression that he was insignificant, his popularity would eventually fade away. It was not until 1945, with the staging of Millionaires' Naples!, that he received his first significant critical acclaim.

One of the first reviewers to give positive appraisal of De Filippo's artistic worth was the well-known theater critic Silvio D'Amico, who was also one of the first to take cognizance of both the actor and the author and to note the influence of the great Luigi Pirandello (1867-1936) on the Neapolitan playwright. D'Amico felt that the comedy in De Filippo's plays transforms the Sicilian author's pirandellismo, accentuating the innate tragedy of the individual situations and rendering them, as a result, all the more pitiful (3). Thus, he rightly affirms that Pirandello's literary influence is finally of marginal importance to De Filippo's finished product.

Another critic who has examined the impact of Pirandello on De Filippo's works is Vito Pandolfi. He too correctly indicates that De Filippo's roots are to be found above all in authors such as Giovanni Verga (1840-1922) and Raffaele Viviani (1888-1950). However, he proposes that, rather than talk about influence, one should consider the process from Verga to De Filippo an evolution of thought and even of point of view (4). Pandolfi shows that De Filippo represents the latest phase in the linguistic evolution of the dialect theater and that he develops traditional themes of the Neapolitan theater, particularly ones evident in the works of Eduardo Scarpetta: poverty as the mother of inventiveness, the desperate sense of humor peculiar to Naples, and the freewheeling mimic skits that made up the genre of the pulcinellata. This development occurs, as Pandolfi points out, because of the growing moral commitment that De Filippo feels toward society, a commitment revealed in his increasing emphasis on the psychology of his characters as they appear in their environment.

Indeed, no study of De Filippo's work is complete without an examination of the Neapolitan component: not only the accidents of his birth, family background, and early experience, but also his beginnings as actor and playwright in the Neapolitan dialect-theater tradition. In many works, the Neapolitan component appears in the undistinguished documentary reality of the social and psychological situation; in many others, it is attenuated and generalized, no more than a coloring or afterglow that points back through analogy to facts and circumstances actually or potentially experienced.

The Neapolitan Theater at the Turn of the Century

The life of Naples and the theater of the turn of the century constitute less the limits for De Filippo's artistic expression than their circumstances of its earliest development and inspiration. In 1900, the year of his birth, Naples still suffered from the difficulties that had plagued it under foreign domination up until the Unification of Italy forty years before: a decadent aristocracy, a politically entrenched bourgeoisie, the masses ill housed and ill fed. Whole neighborhoods were unemployed; the underworld spread.

The Neapolitan theater reflected the social upheaval of the time. The plays staged at the Teatro San Carlino —the Neapolitan theater of the masses, Giulio Trevisani justly notes—were characterized by social and, at times, political criticism that dwelt upon the deteriorating economic conditions (5). Remaining faithful to its comic tradition, it nonetheless presented bitter, sorrowful truths. The parodies, the farces, the commedia dell'arte caricatures of manners—all had at least a veneer of social satire and moral intent.

This change in the Neapolitan theater began with Pasquale Altavilla (1806-1872). His plays provided a new measure of realism: they were rich in local color, faithful to the language of the common people, and often amazingly sensitive in their satire and social comment. In Altavilla's pulcinellate in particular laughter is evoked by the same events as make up daily life. Any exaggeration can usually be overlooked, for, to the Neapolitan, life itself is absurd, an endless pulcinellata. In other respects, however, Altavilla's pulcinellate are essentially the same as those that preceded them. The subjects are the same: theft, trickery, innocence beguiled, discord, catastrophe, jealousy, triumph, and, eternally, the quid pro quo. And the characters are equally numerous: fanatics, philosophers, servants, widows, rivals, lovers, madmen, and feigned madmen, cuckolds, and, of course, the ghosts and false ghosts so especially popular in the Neapolitan theater, up to and including De Filippo's own apparitions in Those Ghosts!

A certain degree of indignation is apparent in the works of Antonio Petito (1822-1876), a grotesque and satirical actor who tried to dignify the masses—represented up to then as foolish, servile, ridiculous, and humiliated—by imputing to them the bourgeois values of the honest and courageous citizen, the good father of the family, the industrious worker. When Petito realized that the mask of the traditional character hindered his message, he began alternating Pulcinella with Pascariello, a real Neapolitan, a free and comically serious citizen embodying the virtues and misfortunes of the Neapolitan people. Deemphasis of the mask did not, however, bring with it a change in the repertory. To the detriment of his social criticism, Petito remained in the realm of the commedia dell'arte, depending on improvisation to let the company and the individual actors display their comic talents.

The reform was continued by De Filippo's natural father, Eduardo Scarpetta (1853-1929). He created Sciosciamocca, a semi-mask with more humanity and naturalness, representing the Neapolitan citizen in his day-to-day struggle with hunger, poverty, and the tyranny of the upper class. Scarpetta focused on the life of lower-class Naples, portraying the darkness of moral misfortune and, often, social impoverishment. Hunger is a continuing protagonist, overcome, as in the early comedies of Chaplin, after many grave vicissitudes and with heroic zeal. But even if the comedy of hunger, which becomes obsessive, hides a tragic bitterness and sorrowful skepticism, Scarpetta presented it nonetheless in a farcical spirit, with a decidedly comic technique. Avoiding melodrama and sentimentality, Scarpetta tended to stir his audience's pity through wistful buffoonery. His criticism of the middle class, whom he blamed for manias, vices, misfortunes, and disillusionment, he conducted as De Filippo does sometimes, by placing a wretched, melancholy protagonist in a crowd of comical characters. And in this protagonist, as in many of De Filippo's characters, there is a spirit that first resists misfortune, then lapses into a resignation punctuated with intermittent hopes.

Succeeding Scarpetta was the crudely realistic and naturalistic theater of Raffaele Viviani (1888-1950), which presented a depressing portrait of the Naples of the alleyways and the hovels. The subject matter of his plays—the anxieties, fears, hopes, and misfortunes of the lower class—was the living material of the large social movements of the time. A more indirect influence on De Filippo was the realistic theater of Salvatore Di Giàcomo (1862-1934). Di Giàcomo's plays reflected the life of the Neapolitan lower class very closely. Populating his Naples with criminals, delinquents, prostitutes, and the indigent, setting his plays in prisons, poorhouses, and the streets, he nonetheless tempered the grimness with compassion. It is typical of Di Giàcomo, and of Neapolitans in general, to soften the stark reality of daily life with pity and poetic fantasy. His dramaturgy is distinguished by powerful scenes and strong act climaxes. In his turn, De Filippo has made these features characteristic of his own playwriting.

Certain notes of De Filippo's music may be heard in the works of other Neapolitan playwrights and actors: Ernesto Mùrolo (1876-1939), Ferdinando Russo (1866-1927), and Federico Stella (1835-1930). Mùrolo wrote better than fifteen plays and reviews, some of them touched with melancholy like Se dice . . . (So they say . . . , 1913), some of them sentimental like Addio bella Napoli (Farewell, my beautiful Naples!, 1909). The nostalgia for the old order, the sense of irony, and the resignation pervading Mùrolo find occasional expression in De Filippo's later plays; like Mùrolo, De Filippo looks to the streets and alleyways of Naples for his subjects. Russo too expressed the fiber of Naples in his plays. Luciella Catena (1920), his best work, is a drama of unrequited love which evolves with intense romantic passion and concludes melodramatically; it may have suggested to De Filippo the theme of Filumena Marturano, though in that play Russo's violence is replaced with a more practical stratagem. Stella's theatrical company staged popular plays and chronicles representing the passions and pleasures of lower-class Naples. The people crowded into the San Ferndinando theater to see his performances because they identified with the protagonists: men who struggled for a living, women who defended their honor at the price of their lives.

Although De Filippo does not take his characteristic tone from any of these playwrights, nonetheless they have had an indisputable effect on his artistic career. It seems especially likely that, early on, De Filippo was impressed with the effective use Mùrolo, Russo, and Di Giàcomo made of local color. The cramped rooms, the shabby clothes, the street shrines, the ebb and flow of Neapolitan low life inevitably left their mark on the young De Filippo as he performed in these plays. However, in observing his later theatrical practice, one finds this attention to local color applied rather differently. Eduardo's world is made up of members of the lower bourgeoisie, of humble businessmen, streetcar conductors, postage stamp dealers, and boardinghouse keepers. We normally find them not in the streets, but in their lower-class homes, at the dinner table, at a family ritual or skirmish. Like Scarpetta and Viviani, De Filippo places the sordid, often disillusioning facts of life in a comic or absurd frame. Some of his realistic techniques and his moral concern for the plight of the lower classes may have been inspired by Roberto Bracco (1862-1943). Yet De Filippo avoids the sentimentality of Mùrolo, the Romantic passion of Russo, the passionate melodrama of Di Giàcomo.

Even during the period from 1945 to 1948, when De Filippo tended most strongly toward naturalism in setting and primary dramatic development, his naturalism was never pure, but always muted and directed to a purpose. Indeed, more than Di Giàcomo and other Neapolitan playwrights, De Filippo has tended to suppress the uncompromising starkness of naturalism in favor of a whimsical, even lyrical quality. The "ghosts" in <u>Those Ghosts!</u>, the "magic" in <u>The Big Magic</u>, and the "fireworks" in <u>The Voices Within</u> are typical—and quite unrealistic—conductors of De Filippo's main thought. Nonetheless, the resolutions of these plays, and of De Filippo's dramas in general, have the same impulse toward naturalistic inevitability, if not the same intensity, as the works of Di Giàcomo and Viviani.

De Filippo's theatrical experience included acting in vaudeville and curtain-raising <u>avanspettacolo</u>, until World War II the two most common forms of entertainment for the masses and the lower-middle-class audience; many of their elements figure in his artistic development. Vaudeville and <u>avanspettacolo</u>—the latter term describes the stage shows which frequently accompanied movies up to the end of World War II—both consisted of a series of comedy sketches interspersed with lively musical numbers and variety acts by ventriloquists, magicians, and impressionists. Especially in the <u>avanspettacolo</u> one found quick-fire humorous dialogue between two interlocutors, a comic and a straight man, frequent verbal and visual gags, a wide variety of slapstick routines involving energetic, mock-violent physical contact, clownish facial expressions, exaggerated, semi-acrobatic movement, simple and down-to-earth language occasionally punctuated by vulgarity and double entendre, and, of course, an extremely concise structure and rapid succession of episodes. These shows created an atmosphere of open, continuous, almost aggressive rapport between performers and audience. The actors made a deliberate effort to destroy the artificial barriers between the stage and the audience, thus restoring the immediate contact between the two that characterized semipopular comic theater. Although the cultivated elite regarded such shows as vulgar and artistically mediocre, they attracted huge numbers of working-class and lower-middle-class spectators, who thoroughly enjoyed their uninhibited, flamboyant humor.

De Filippo's Artistic Itinerary

It is not easy to say which author or theatrical tendency had the strongest influence on the young De Filippo; but, whichever one it was, the influences were weak and exterior. In his first works one inevitably discovers the mark of Scarpetta, with whom he worked until 1910, and of Viviani, who remained the dominant figure in Neapolitan theater until the end of World War II. But his own brand of humorous pathos is quite distinct from Scarpetta's farce and Viviani's violent realism. From them, as Pandolfi says so well, De Filippo learned above all his "theatricality," the ability to translate into scenes the world which he was beginning to know. But while he keeps their popular vigor, their expressive vivacity, the freshness and simplicity of their scenic movement, he does not linger on the comic slapstick or the bawdry of the Neapolitan farce, but proceeds through them to analyze the world of the little man, of the masses, and the lower middle class in their suffering. Though elements of farce are still present, De Filippo departs from pure farce and from the play of contrived tricks to scrutinize the feelings of the Neapolitan; and thus he turns folkloric characteristics into a vision of the human condition. Blending the farcical comedy of Scarpetta, who seems to elude reality, with the tragi-

comedy of everyday life, he presents a world with its
own characters moving within real plots; their farcical
exterior does not suffocate the interior drama of the
characters, but instead underlines their value.

From his very childhood, Eduardo De Filippo participated in the theatrical life of Naples. In a certain
sense, he was born in the theater. His father was the
actor-playwright Eduardo Scarpetta, his mother a niece of
Rosa De Filippo, Scarpetta's legitimate wife. She bore
him three children during their extended extramarital
relationship, and Scarpetta never left her or them.

At the age of four Eduardo De Filippo made his first
stage appearance in his natural father's theatrical
company; and he made sporadic appearances in the company's productions until 1909, when he played the role of
Peppeniello in Viviani's Miseria e nobilità (Misery
and nobility, 1887). Although Scarpetta's repertory
consisted mainly of adaptations of French farces, the
real essence of his theater was the farcical tradition of
the San Carlino theater, directly descended from the
commedia dell'arte, which he updated and disciplined.
Under Scarpetta's tutelage, De Filippo learned "to a T"
the difficult techniques of improvisation. He learned
how to support the other actors; and in particular he
learned the importance of accurate observation, imitation, and caricature, essential elements of Scarpetta's
farces and those of the San Carlino theater. When
Scarpetta died in 1925, his son Vincenzo took his place
as head of the Teatro Nuovo. Eduardo De Filippo, with
his brother Peppino and sister Titina, continued to work
on and off with the company. By 1916 Titina had become
the leading actress and Eduardo was the company's second
leading actor.

In 1911-12 Eduardo attended a boarding school between
Rome and Naples, but he continued to perform in the summer. During the summers of 1913 and 1914 Eduardo worked
with the theater company of Enrico Altieri, a particular
success at the time, performing classical Neapolitan
plays and a vast and disparate repertory ranging from
Pulcinella farces to melodramas, from socio-historical
dramas to starkly tragic plays. The sensitive young
actor had absorbed the Neapolitan comic and dramatic
authors who were to be the roots of his own theater, a
theater nonetheless based upon the attentive observation
of real life. The work was very hard. He spent entire
days at the theater, rehearsing in the morning from ten

Naples and the Neapolitan Popular Theater

until about twelve, when he would eat; at three o'clock he began performances, usually presenting two shows a day and three on Sundays. Fridays were reserved for comic shows in which the plays of Scarpetta or similar authors were staged. In the tragic plays Eduardo played very small parts, while in the comedies good comic roles were entrusted to him because he was already superb as a comic actor. After his great success in Di Giàcomo's Assunta Spina (1910), Eduardo gave indication of becoming a great Neapolitan actor. On stage he lived the sorrows of his characters, and his complete identification with them brought him into closer contact with the social reality of his city.

During the winters, from 1913 until 1920, Eduardo stayed with the Vincenzo Scarpetta troupe, except for an interruption of several months in 1918 for military service. Summers he worked with the various companies of seratanti ("evening players") in the Naples area. In 1920 he was again called into the army. In the barracks he successfully organized numerous shows; whenever he could, he performed at the Manzoni theater in Rome. With the end of his military service in 1922, he entered the company of Corbinci and made his debut at the Partenope Theater with Titina and several members of the Carloni family in Enzo L. Mùrolo's Wonderful Sorrento: it was his first production in the full sense of the word. During this period the impresario Vincenzo di Napoli, who had seen him and been extremely impressed with his acting, engaged him in his company. Eduardo was put in charge of updating the review and thus given the opportunity to exercise his writing skills for the company. His realistic, yet often satirical portrayals of Neapolitans were so successful that he was soon promoted to leading actor of the company. With the troupe Eduardo went to Palermo, to the Olimpia Theater, where the company stayed until 1923, staging Guido Di Napoli's variety review 4+4=8.

Back with Vincenzo Scarpetta from 1923 to 1927, Eduardo produced several plays and was well on his way to becoming the most beloved actor in the company. In the summer of 1924 he joined the company of Peppino Villani and revived the review 4+4=8, now entitled 8+8=16. Scheduled to run for a month at most, it ran for a year; and the young actor, besides gaining noteworthy personal success, continually updated the review, writing topical satirical sketches reflecting real-life events of the day. During the summers of 1925 and 1927, he worked at the Fiorentini Theater in La rivista che non piacerà (This review is not going to be liked) by Michele Galdieri. His brother Peppino at his side, Eduardo was the director and main actor. By this time he had already written noteworthy one-acts like Farmacia di turno (Pharmacy on duty, 1921) and comedies in three acts like Ho fatto il guaio? Riparerò (Did I make a mess of things? I'll make it up, 1922), later renamed Uomo e galantuomo (Men and gentlemen, 1926).

In 1929 the three De Filippos found themselves reunited in the Molinari review company, where they remained for two years. Under the pseudonyms of M. Molise, Tricot, and V. Maglini, Eduardo began to collaborate with other writers—among them, Galdieri, Mangini, and Nelli—in composing short, mostly farcical sketches. In 1930, with Sik-Sik, the Incomparable Magician, Eduardo's career as an author reached a turning point. He was so successful that in the summer of 1931 he proposed to his brother and sister that they form a theater company of their own, La Compagnia del Teatro Umoristico i De Filippo. The new company played in Rome and Naples, and in 1933 it opened at the Sannazzaro Theater to great public acclaim with Eduardo's Chi è cchiù felice 'e me! (Who is happier than I!, 1928). Even the critics noticed that the De Filippos' plays were more substantial than the frivolous repertoire they had become accustomed to. Pirandello went to see them, and he was so impressed that he asked Eduardo to adapt some of his own short stories and stage them with his company.

The De Filippos' greatest strength was their ensemble playing. Presenting most of their performances in the Neapolitan dialect, the actors avoided the exaggeration, buffoonery, and tricks of many other companies and produced plays that had a polished, modern quality. In 1933 the critic Alberto Consiglio wrote about the acting of the family:

> Their art has nothing in common, either in form or in spirit, with regionalism. Their most vital force derives, first of all, from the fact that they draw their every inspiration from a worldly wise vision, rooted in the suffering of life. . . . They show neither respect for tradition nor concern for originality. In fact, their repertory does not include many

authors: a few comedies by Gino Rocca, deftly adapted; a play by Paola Riccora, and then, many, more than a dozen, by Mr. Molise and Mr. Bertucci—shy pseudonyms of Eduardo and Peppino. Their quality, therefore, cannot be attributed simply to their virtuosity as actors: the effectiveness of their pantomime, of their scenic organization, of their speech, comes, above all, from the unfettered freedom of the poetic soul. . . . Theater becomes for them nothing less than life itself: not life in its grotesque, symbolic, or exceptional aspects, but human life, seen and felt with intelligent humanity and perfect accuracy. Is this not perhaps the eternal formula of the theater? (6)

At the Sannazzaro, in addition to works by Pirandello and Eduardo, Rocca and Riccora, the "Humoristic Company of the De Filippos" presented works by Peppino and Titina, by Lucio D'Ambra, Luigi Antonelli, D. Falconi, Ugo Betti, F. M. Martini, and A. Curcio. Eduardo's popularity was by now indisputable.

For a long time, unfortunately, while honoring Eduardo the actor, critics continued to have doubts about Eduardo the playwright. Even when excited about the acting ability of the family, they considered the texts little more than plots at the service of the acting; often they downplayed the intrinsic vitality of Eduardo's theater by binding it indissolubly to his talent as an actor. But this talent if anything enriches the very human poetry of his theater, just as that poetry finds its most perfect expression in his performances. And the critics did him a still graver wrong in thinking his talent limited by his thoroughgoing education in the dialect theater.

Although the Fascist regime used every means to discourage dialect theater, the "Humoristic Company of the De Filippos" was left in peace because of its great popularity and success. With the money he earned with his first film, Tre uomini in frac (Three men in tails), Eduardo formed a larger company and with it toured Rome, San Remo, Milan, Turin, Genoa, conquering audiences wherever he went. In 1938 the "Humoristic Company," disappointing its large following, lost Titina, who joined another company.

In the development of De Filippo as a playwright 1945 was a key year. Historically, it was the end of the war, the monarchy, and Fascism, the beginning of democracy and free artistic expression. It was also the end of Peppino De Filippo's cooperation with his older brother. The separation came about because of the growing difference in theatrical philosophy between the two brothers. After many years of complementing each other in performance, they had developed different ideas about the type of plays they should stage. As he gained experience, Eduardo came to lean toward plays that expressed his social and moral concerns; Peppino, on the other hand, was devoted to the farces which had played so successfully since the early days in Naples. The resulting rift led Peppino and Eduardo to form separate companies. Eduardo formed Il teatro di Eduardo, which he has directed ever since. These events, combined with Eduardo's nearly twenty-five years as an author-actor, provided the catalyst to bring him to maturity as a dramatist. There began the period of masterpieces, as De Filippo abandoned the farcical vein for a more morally impassioned presentation of contemporary social reality.

Titina had returned to the company in 1942, and she remained there even after the war had ended in the south; but in 1945 she too left temporarily. Peppino's departure was significant for Eduardo's theatrical production; with the loss of the great comic actor, Eduardo no longer felt compelled to write farcical roles, but now felt free to present his own world, by nature more dramatic than comic.

Eduardo's ripening social commitment led him to buy Naples' old San Ferdinando Theater, much in need of repair after World War II bombings. In his inaugural speech Eduardo made it quite clear that the theater was to belong to the people, to reflect their problems and to entertain them. Its purpose was to represent daily reality in all its political, social, and cultural aspects.
The theater became a springboard for the works of its owner and gave him repeated successes.

Eduardo's public success became more frequent and resounding with the years, one high point being the 1962 tour to Russia, Poland, Hungary, Austria, and Belgium.
In translation, a number of plays have been successful in many more countries. It could be said that, with Eduardo (and it is indicative of his popularity that his first name alone is enough to identify him), Neapolitan theater has become a citizen of the world.

The Actor

As an actor-author, De Filippo is in many ways comparable to Chaplin. He has created a recurrent character for himself, the name varying from play to play: Sik-Sik, Luca Cupiello, Gennaro Jovine, Pasquale Lojacono—all variations of the Eduardo mask. Consequently, the rhythm and much of the detail of his plays have been governed by his style as an actor. Indeed, for many critics, Eduardo's stage experience has not only enriched his writings inestimably, but has been the precondition of their success. As early as 1946 Silvio D'Amico recognized the compatibility of actor and playwright in De Filippo:

> The constant quarrel in the theater between author and actor is settled in one case only: when the author is also the chief actor. In such a situation, the theatrical production only attains excellence when the actor's individuality, instead of functioning uneasily in the alien role, is spontaneously in harmony with his own personality. This happens when the character is born within the actor; when, in short, he completely creates himself. In our more recent experience, it has been the case with many performers in dialect whom we have known, from Ferravilla to Petrolini. Today it is the case with Eduardo De Filippo. (7)

D'Amico was speaking of Eduardo's work in Filumena Marturano, written in the period from 1945 to 1948 which critics have regarded as his most creative. However, in 1953, following the appearance of The Big Magic and Fear Number One, Vito Pandolfi saw a conflict between the two aspects of Eduardo's art: "Has Eduardo created a type, a countenance, and a recurrent character? Or has he created a series of personages? It is rather unclear, he seems to be at a crossroads: and this, perhaps, constitutes one of the major limitations. He cannot bring himself to sacrifice everything to the actor or everything to the author, thereby weakening both the comedian and the script by not investigating them and penetrating beyond their usual limits" (8). By 1959 Pandolfi's misgivings had crystallized. The playwright, he said, "too often violates the nature of his characters because of his absorption in intellectual abstractions, which in him often appear over-ambitious, regardless of his admittedly good intentions" (9). It cannot be denied that Eduardo the actor placed his own demands as an actor on Eduardo the playwright; however, the advantages of this stage experience for the playwright outweigh the disadvantages.

Physically, Eduardo lacks the attractions of youth or beauty or sexual presence or an ingratiating aspect. Medium in height and lean in build, he often presents a preoccupied air. His smile, rarely seen, is a wry one. His slightly grotesque face, with its long, sunken cheeks, is inscrutable. His face is like a corrugated mask of careworn comedy pierced by smoldering, heavy-lidded eyes. It is the last surviving mask of the commedia dell'arte: that of Pulcinella grown older, sadder, and wiser.

Eduardo's relationship to the commedia is not that of a self-conscious artist re-creating a style, but that of a popular regionalist working in a realistic vein for the people of his own area. In his acting he is removed from the comic mask. Probably the greatest difference in technique lies in their styles of physical movement. Pulcinella's role is an inherently acrobatic one. His very costume seems to call for large movements. Whether he is ripping the bedclothes off, jumping from roof to roof, or stumbling over a concealed bag of money, Pulcinella's is a physically dynamic role. Eduardo's style of performance is quite the opposite. His acting is immensely subtle and restrained. To quote Eric Bentley:

> Eduardo on the stage is an astonishment. For five minutes or so he may be a complete let-down. This is not acting at all, we cry, above all it is not Italian acting! Voice and body are so quiet. Pianissimo. No glamour, no effusion of brilliance. . . . Rather, a series of statements, vocal and corporeal. When the feeling of anticlimax has passed we realize that these statements are beautiful in themselves—beautiful in their clean economy, their rightness—and beautiful in relation to each other and to the whole: there are differentiations, sharp of shifting, between one speech and the next: there is a carefully gauged relationship between beginning, middle and end. . . . Eduardo is an actor and more likely . . . to be the heir of Commedia dell'arte than any other important performer now living and . . . his style is distinctly

different from anything one expected. It is a realistic style. It makes few departures from life. The "art" consists in the skill of the imitation, the careful registering of detail and nuance, and a considered underlining of the effects—the outline is firmer, the shape more sure. (10)

Gestures are of the utmost importance, as are vocal technique, facial expressions, and alteration of rhythms. By merely raising a single eyebrow or tentatively gesturing with a hand, Eduardo achieves great effect. Even the silent pauses are eloquent discourse. He has explained his debts in this way: "The main influences on my work as an actor have been life, humanity, nature, and the commedia dell'arte tradition. Although very much admiring the major theorists of the modern theater, I have always preferred to seek my inspiration from the natural source of art, life" (11).

For De Filippo, theater and life are indivisible, the man and the actor are one (12). On stage, De Filippo does not overwhelm the product of the playwright, but gives it completion: "My work as an actor and as a playwright, has been interrelated in the same way in which rapport develops, or ought to, between an author and his interpreter: by means of a certain distance and reciprocal respect. Author and actor ought to complete each other, not compete with each other, and each ought to respect the limits of his task." The role is created in symbiosis with the author:

> I approach the creation of a role by trying to understand the thinking and the essence of the character, with the help of the author's words. Even though—or perhaps because—I am an author, I know that a real intimacy can exist only between character and actor. The author creates the character, but the actor must give the character life. Besides the word, the actor has at his disposition gestures, glances, movements, and the audience, which by way of its reaction can little by little let him know the true theatrical nature of the character. I am convinced that despite reflection and rehearsals, the real study begins above all upon contact with the audience, and, in effect, such a study continues until one is acting the character. Perhaps the study never really ends at all. (13)

For Eduardo, acting exists to bring life on the stage a
character created by the author in the pages of the text;
and this animation, achieved through the identification
of actor and character, acquires meaning only if the
actor-character succeeds in establishing an intimate rapport with the spectator. All his life as an actor
Eduardo has aimed at the role in which he would reach perfection, all the time knowing that such perfection is
unattainable:

> The real "method" of learning how to act is to do
> theater with those who know how to do theater. This
> is how tradition is formed, and tradition renders all
> theories superfluous.
> The actor dies without being able to say he has
> reached perfection; he gives to the public the results
> of his continuous artistic experience, but that experience is superseded at the very moment in which it is
> acquired. (14)

In these words Eduardo reveals three qualities of his
personality: his lack of fear in the face of difficulties and the enthusiasm with which he accepts the challenge, his innate humility, and his lifelong quest for
perfection.

The Director

Equally important in De Filippo's artistic development is his long experience as director. His first full
production as director goes back to 1922 at the Teatro
Partenope, with Mùrolo's Wonderful Sorrento. During
the period of the Teatro Umoristico i De Filippo, he
directed his own plays and those of others, such as
Pirandello, D'Ambra, Riccora, and Rocca. With Il Teatro
di Eduardo he produces and directs mostly his own plays;
however, over the years he has presented works by
Pirandello, Rocca, Betti, Altavilla, Petito, Scarpetta,
and Viviani. He has also successfully directed productions of operas by Rossini, Donizetti, Paisiello, Verdi,
and Shostakovich, as well as movies and television films.

As director, De Filippo exercises a firm discipline.
Whoever works for him knows well the rigid rules to abide
by: punctuality, unsentimental involvement with the
other actors of the company, maximum reserve, and abso-

Naples and the Neapolitan Popular Theater

lute silence during rehearsals. He praises his coworkers infrequently, expecting that his silence will show his satisfaction. When a new member of the company has been selected, De Filippo demands three things: "first time, then patience, and then impatience." The new actor is hired for a term of either two or three years. During the first year or so, he is instructed to observe, to watch his would-be colleagues perform their craft. Then he will be given a small part. But in this first period, De Filippo is rigorous and demanding: the actor is forced to strive mightily to survive in the role assigned. For the maestro "the theater is made up of great actors and good actors, of big actors and small actors. All are necessary to the health of the theater" (15). De Filippo, however, is not a dictator on the stage. He recognizes that "a theatrical production is the creative work of the author, the actor, the director, the scene designer, etc. Only when this work is carried out with the enthusiastic and humble contribution of everyone can theater be achieved. When one of the elements prevails over the others, it makes a spectacle of itself" (16). In the theatrical creation, however, the director takes on himself a weighty responsibility: to coordinate the acting and blend it with the various theatrical elements into a whole. His approach to directing calls for intense preparation—a startling contrast to the seemingly improvised results: "he will rehearse his actors in a new play around a table continuously until lines are learned, then set them on stage and provide gestures and movements to fit their words. After twenty to thirty rehearsals the play will be ready for performance" (17). De Filippo gives his actors a high degree of creative freedom: "I believe that the function of the director, with regard to the actor, is not to impose his own vision of how the role ought to be acted, but rather to stimulate the actor's creation of the role, and then to help perfect that creation, combining it with that of the others with the pace of the show. In general, I pay much more attention to a creative actor than to one who awaits orders. The former is a collaborator, the latter a hireling" (18). Though he fosters creative freedom, he carefully guards against any possibility of acting that is too tangential and threatens to veer off into something alien to the character the actor is portraying or to become untrue to the particular scene or the overall theme of the play.

No method deprives De Filippo of his individual creative freedom; no rule is so restrictive as to prevent him from being an experimenter and innovator. He believes that for the imaginative craftsman of the theater there are no artistic boundaries that cannot be crossed without some benefit to the adventurer. In his many years as director, Eduardo has gone from the realistic representation of life in an almost Stanislavsky style to the quasi-Brechtian analytical approach of his most recent play, Gli esami non finiscono mai (The exams are never over). Basically, however, he is a realist.

Indeed, most of De Filippo's stage productions, like the majority of his plays, create the illusion of being true to life without necessarily being a simple photographic copy of reality. De Filippo aims at realities below the surface; he probes much deeper and farther than the stylized "spontaneity" that Stanislavsky loved for so much of his life. The external reality of the stage set functions to complement the inner reality of the play, for the basis of that reality are the characters.

De Filippo is not interested in representing the individual with his unique problem. To him it is the predominant type that is all-important—not merely the simple stereotype, but one that categorizes vast numbers of persons. His is a kind of archetype that combines and embodies the qualities of large masses of human beings and their collective sentiments.

The point of departure, then, is the reality of Naples and Neapolitans. But that reality serves also to capture, easily and naturally, the attention of the spectators. The spectators realize that they are facing a theatrical reality that is not divorced from real life; for De Filippo, real life is theatrical, and Neapolitan life is the most theatrical of all. Eduardo combines this reality with his fantasy, his own theatricality, his own eclectic sense of artistic showmanship, to make his own stage creations as distinctive a trademark as those of any other great director. The mark of his craftsmanship is an emphasis on physical activity, gesture, and mime because he considers them the most essential tools of the actor; they amplify a spoken idea or feeling visually and kinesthetically, while at the same time intensifying the ideas and feelings by condensing time and space. This does not mean that Eduardo is not concerned with speech. On the contrary, he monitors the speech of his actors very carefully for inflection, tempo, rhythm, and

Naples and the Neapolitan Popular Theater

movement, since these elements always have to be coordinated with visual elements to achieve the best theatrical show.

This view is not new in De Filippo's art. What he injects in acting, directing, and writing about his works is a cleverly devised, unmistakably modern recapitulation of the commedia dell'arte tradition framed in the sociopolitical environment of contemporary Naples. Lodovico Zorzi has aptly described this link: "Underneath the varnish of stage technique, jokes, gambolizing masks, dialect, baroque production, joy, and marvelous improvisation, the commedia shows the marks of an unhealed ideological crisis, of an ethical and social void. . . . The reasons for such a void are known: political and economic chaos, a multitude of local restrictions, and the linguistic label which commedia documents" (19). The early plays De Filippo wrote and acted in were very much like Chaplin shorts. Almost all were designed to represent incidents in the life of the little man, the povero diavolo or poor devil. As his drama developed and his concern with the family became more and more pronounced, De Filippo subsumed the image of the "poor devil" and fashioned the pathetically reluctant hero who is forced by circumstances to muster his long-abandoned manhood and come to the rescue of his family. Imbuing him with the last vestige of the Pulcinella mask, De Filippo made his Neapolitan anti-hero a classic character of Neapolitan dialect theater, the Italian popular theater, and, indeed, the world stage.

Chapter Two
De Filippo's Inspiration and Creative Process

Naples: De Filippo's Major Inspiration

Eric Bentley has put well the need for examining De Filippo's art in the context of his city: "It is sometimes debated how far we need to know an author's background in order to judge his work. I should think we need to know it whenever we would otherwise be in danger of taking something as his personal contribution when it is a representative product of his time and place. Thus some of Eduardo's attitudes . . . may seem forced when we take them as an assertion of his will, whereas as an expression of a social tradition we might let them pass" (1). To the mind of a foreign spectator, the attitude of Gennaro in Millionaires' Naples!—the husband who disapproves of, yet cooperates in his wife's illegal business—may appear inconsistent. However, his actions, like those of other De Filippo characters, are consistent with the world view of the people of Naples. To Eduardo's people, the state is the enemy. The Fascist suppression of Neapolitan regionalism was only the most recent episode in their long history of oppression. When Matteo Generoso, the protagonist of Fear Number One, says, "If twelve wars broke out one after the other, they'd make no impression on me," this is not some absurd idea of the author's, but rather an expression of a fundamental Neapolitan attitude. Getting on with the business of day-to-day living, regardless of what happens in the newspapers, is the people's concern.

Naples is a city of paradoxes: poor in industries, rich in the sun, suffering, and song. It is a city that venerates the innocent charm of children and a city where children lose their innocence very early. Naples reflects the practice of dolce far niente ("sweet idleness") and hums day and night with the kinetic energy of human beings working, selling, arguing, singing, cursing.

Neapolitans can cry and laugh at the same time. They are gay, ruthless, life-loving, cynical, superstitious, kindly, and extremely patient. For them life is lived from day to day; luck in the next lottery may be just across the piazza.

De Filippo's Naples is not the stereotyped tourist panorama of Vesuvius and the bay, as it is idealized on postcards, but a complex, volcanic city, full of contradictions, absurdities, and extravagance, reflecting the full spectrum of the human condition. It is the Naples that Thornton Wilder characterized as an "anthill of vitality—cynical yet religious—religious yet superstitious—shadowed by the volcano and the thought of death—always aboil with one passion or another, yet abounding in courtesy and charm. Above all, profoundly knit by the ties of the family, parent and child" (2). De Filippo's attention is focused above all on the masses and lower middle class of Naples, on that part of the population for whom the tests of life are harder but not necessarily more tragic than for those "better off," because they have an innate flair for life. In lower-class Naples the duality of social relations is very evident. People are close to one another, aware of one another, ready to defend one another; but this same closeness provides opportunities for exploitation as well as protection and aid. In short, as Bentley notes, "the lower depths of Naples form as fantastic a society of adventurers and desperadoes as can well be imagined. Living by the skin of their teeth, a dreary past behind and a blank future ahead, they accept the present with peculiar vehemence. Familiar with death, they do not take life too seriously. They are willing to see it as a joke, a paradox, a fantasy, a show, a game" (3). Neapolitans of the lower classes run the gamut of human life:

> It is because of their capacity for community and individuality at once that the Neapolitan situation is tragic and not merely pathetic. For they are a people who have perfected the art of <u>communitas</u> while at the same time celebrating the human personality for the riches it contains. Could they fashion a utopia of their own, I am certain it would be anti-platonic— a social organization for diversity and maximal self-expression. Just as Plato would have cast out actors and playwrights as subversives, the Neapolitans would

give these a central role, for they represent the full range of human feelings and catch all the rays that shine from the prism that is man. (4)

For De Filippo, Naples is not just a city or his city, but a magnifying glass through which he contemplates humanity in its myriad manifestations.

Even the less keen and sensitive observers are struck by the pulsation of life in this city. And life is an event to be celebrated because existence is a movable, continuing feast. Its living soul is as Belmonte observes:

> . . . resolute and passionate, but it is also unconscious, and insensate to the prod of awareness and reason. As such it can emerge, or it becomes hypnotic. The movement in Naples—the traffic jams, the pushy, shoving crowds, the absence of lines forming for anything, the endless barrage of shouts falling like arrows on ears, the simultaneous clash of a million destinations and petty opposed intentions— combine into a devastating assault on the senses. Or else the entire scene retreats, slowing and settling finally into a brilliantly colored frieze depicting a grand, if raucous, commedia. (5)

In Naples, behavior is charged with a meaning that may either reveal the truth or mask it, and spontaneity and artifice blend into one another like the tints of a watercolor. Much of Neapolitan life, especially its more passionate side, has a basic and undeniable theatricality. It is not accidental that one of the greatest moments in Naples's theater history is its improvisational commedia dell'arte, with its emphasis on spontaneity, immediacy, and broad physical actions. Anyone who watches Neapolitans in conversation soon realizes that the hands, and indeed the entire body, often communicate as much as the accompanying words. The outsider can easily mistake a simple conversation for a heated argument, since many Neapolitans converse with a commitment and excitement that is often not commensurate with the importance of the subject matter under discussion. This gesticulation and the spirit it expresses are theatrical, if not operatic, suggesting a performance even when none is intended.

Indeed, in the poor quarters of Naples even the most

banal events can be elevated to the level of drama. Action is a vehicle of communication, and "in the language of symbolic action, a rage might be a plea, a kiss an economic stratagem." The tonalities are theatrical. In the poor quarters of Naples every person becomes a playwright and an actor, seeking to determine and organize the reactions of an audience—but a critic too, more than ready to demolish the transparent devices and weaker props of his fellows. In the words of Thomas Belmonte, "if drama was originally invented as a metaphor for life, in Naples the metaphor has overwhelmed the referent, and society presents itself as a series of plays within plays" (6).

To love and understand De Filippo's theater one has to love and understand the theater performed on the vast stage of Naples. Because he could capture it in its fullness, De Filippo achieved a high degree of drama and theatricality even in dealing with seemingly cerebral themes. For example, the philosophy of the absurd, very evident in his plays, is not so much the subject matter of his characters' discussions as the Neapolitan way of living. As Bentley says, "There is a philosophy of the absurd, after all, in plebeian humor in general: your life is hopeless but you laugh, you are cheerful and morally positive, against all reason" (7). But Neapolitans are believers. In spite of their cynicism about most aspects of life, they give themselves to religion with unconditional fervor. They preserve a facade of Catholic ritual, but prefer their Madonna-goddesses to Christ and maintain an active belief in a myriad local house-spirits, reminiscent of the pre-Christian epoch. Similarly, De Filippo's characters are Christian-pagans for whom God, Christ, the Madonna, and all the saints are little more than agencies on hand for the purpose of healing and punishing, as they are, for example, in I Won't Pay You, Filumena Marturano, and many other plays.

Among the manifold components of this Neapolitan life, De Filippo focuses his attention very often on the family. Pushing aside the mythology of sentimental "familism" that pervades Italian culture, he shows the contradictions of family life, the violent clash of motives, and the tangled web of longings, jealousies, and long-nurtured resentments that form the substrata of so much family interaction. He commonly notes that the individual behaves differently within the family circle than in other social arenas. The home is not a stage for presenting hypocritical spectacles to others. Whatever a person may appear to be elsewhere, the family knows better. The secret weaknesses of the individual, the shame of sins long hidden from the world, the family assimilates and keeps to itself. If the honesty of the family is often cruel, it may also be redemptive and sometimes therapeutic, as in Millionaires' Naples! and My Family! The Neapolitan family remains at the core of De Filippo's art, and he is a keen observer of its minute particularities. Indeed, it is extraordinary what subtle variations he can play on this perennial theme—in Christmas at the Cupiello's, Filumena Marturano, My Love and My Heart, Saturday, Sunday, and Monday, and many others.

In portraying Naples, De Filippo writes of the very society from which Pulcinella grew and to which Pulcinella has most meaning. Like him, De Filippo's characters move rather hopelessly around the fringe of life; like him, they possess an indomitable will to live in spite of everything (8). However, in contrast to the Pulcinella of the commedia dell'arte, De Filippo's protagonist possesses an activated social conscience. As Mario Stefanile has said:

> De Filippo's Pulcinella is made up of Molière and Goldoni, a bit of Shakespeare and a lot of Viviani, almost all of Scarpetta, and most of Petrolini, and even certain formulas of the mature Jouvet. This is because, through Pulcinella, what is expressed is the morality of Naples, the desire typical of the Parthenopean, to correct the social aspects of life in his own favor and to reduce everything to his own image and likeness—splendor and misery, nobility and indignity, racketeers and honest men, the rich and the poor, men and women. (9)

De Filippo's characters are neither heroes nor clowns. They are men—more often than not part hero and part clown, each one having his own personality, his own nature, and stamped with the character of the land in which he was born and lives. They live in a world that man still values. In it they can continue to live, struggle, hope; they continue to cheat and love each other, to despise and pity one another. And, above all, in spite of everything, they continue to delude themselves in the search for truth. Theirs is not a confused search for abstract truth, but a search based on total suspicion and mistrust—yet tempered with a constant, naive hope for something better, with the same hope that animates the lower-middle-class Neapolitans to live and survive day by day. Illusion and reality are fused, as if man needed to create an unreal world which is all his own, while at the same time keeping close watch on reality. Perhaps some day things will change, but meanwhile life has to go on: "Eventually the night has to pass . . .," says the protagonist in the closing line of Millionaires' Naples!

In the plays De Filippo wrote during and immediately after World War II, Naples represents both the human and the economic destruction of a particular city and the fate of the many countries that had experienced the same devastation, the same anguish and existential boredom that dominated the life of those years. In the plays written in the 1960s and 1970s Naples is a city at the mercy of the selfishness, hypocrisy, corruption, and violence of the materialistic society which evolved in those years. Eduardo's attachment to Naples, then, is not merely sentimental. Although his suppositions seem to be those of an earlier breed of popular Neapolitan playwrights with old-fashioned notions, it must not be supposed that Eduardo is a producer of locally acceptable social drama, on a different wavelength from the avantgarde and from modern European comedy in general. On the contrary, while nourishing himself on the rich humus of Neapolitan life and theater, he shows himself perfectly familiar with the comedy of European intellectuals, for the most part born of mistrust, its ethos repeatedly one of meaninglessness and isolation in an absurd world, in which language has ceased to convey meaning and the structures of society are mocked. Yet De Filippo only partially accepts this legacy of Pirandello, Jarry, and their successors, with its special kind of liberating irony which allows the spectator to dismiss, for the duration of a play, the demands of everyday life. The world of these playwrights—socially hollow, reeling, having no center of traditional bourgeois gravity, where one has to be off-center if he is to escape the void, where the heroes are individualists, nonconformists, eccentric, and way-out—De Filippo can accept only for the crisis it presents, not for its nihilistic content.

For De Filippo the world is not hollow. Life has a meaning; when things go wrong it matters; and that meaning and matter may be adequately conveyed by language.

However, elements of relativistic and existentialist thinking as well as the idea of a disintegrating world are recurring themes in his plays, explicitly so in Millionaires' Naples!, Those Ghosts, My Family!, The Voices Within, and The Local Authority. These plays are the products not only of a postwar setting but also of a relativistic age, of a world falling apart both physically and metaphysically. The children in My Family! strive for existential freedom no less than the characters of Sartre, and the dialogue echoes, more intimately, less portentously, the same dilemmas faced by the French philosopher. The Cimmaruta family in The Voices Within is fragmented by conflicting versions of nonexistent truth; truth is chimerical in Those Ghosts! and The Big Magic. De Filippo's sophistication extends to a canny understanding of voguish attitudes, and he finds the voguish attitudes wanting.

De Filippo's Encounter with Pirandello

Many critics have long assumed that Luigi Pirandello served as a key literary influence on Eduardo De Filippo. Eduardo was very young and still unknown when he began to experience the fascination of Pirandello's art and thought. The Pirandellian quality of some plays of De Filippo could be, therefore, a consequence of a youthful infatuation.

De Filippo first saw Pirandello's Six Characters in Search of an Author in 1921. Two years later he had read everything Pirandello had written, and he remained very impressed with his art. In 1933, when De Filippo had reached a certain degree of popularity, he met the older playwright who asked him to produce Liolà (10). After twenty-five rehearsals, all of which Pirandello attended, Liolà opened at the Teatro Odeon in Milan, with Peppino De Filippo in the title role. The performance received twenty-two curtain calls. Sometime later they met again in Naples, and Pirandello asked De Filippo about the possibility of adapting his short story L'abito nuovo (The new suit) for the stage, overwhelming him with the suggestion that they write the play together. For fifteen days during December 1935, from 5 to 8 P.M., the two playwrights worked together in Rome, where De Filippo's company was performing. Pirandello wrote a prose outline of ideas and action. From time to time he

De Filippo's Inspiration and Creative Process

would hand sheets of paper to De Filippo, seated at a desk next to him, who would write the dialogue. During one of the last evenings Pirandello asked De Filippo to adapt his Cap and Bells. Only a month later this play opened in Naples at the Fiorentini Theater, with Eduardo in the leading role, and played twenty-two sold-out performances.

While performing this comedy in Milan, De Filippo received a telegram from Pirandello asking him to produce The New Suit. He answered that the production of Cap and Bells had exhausted him and that he would prefer to wait a year before staging the work. Pirandello was hurt and did not reply. About four months later Eduardo saw Pirandello during an intermission of Cap and Bells, which he was performing at the Quirino Theater in Rome. To Eduardo, the old and famous playwright resembled a young author eager for his first production, and Eduardo told him so. Pirandello replied, "But you, my dear Eduardo, can afford to wait; I cannot!" A month later, rehearsals started, but Pirandello was dead of pneumonia before the play opened.

This very close contact with Pirandello and his theater inevitably left an imprint on De Filippo which is evident in his view of life and the way he gives it theatrical expression. Corrado Alvaro points out the influence in negative terms: "Eduardo De Filippo, believing himself to be far removed from modern life and the life common to all, tries to exceed his limits by attempting the style of Pirandello, the form least suited to Eduardo and which Pirandello himself finally dropped uneasily" (11). But Eduardo has been less ready to admit that he has been significantly influenced by Pirandello. When asked about it, he replied:

> When I began to write my plays, I did not know of Pirandello. In 1928 I wrote Chi è cchiù felice 'e me! [Who is happier than I!] and made my debut with this play in 1931. Thus I began to write before I began to associate with him. . . . The conclusions about life which I have come to are not, in fact, Pirandello-like conclusions. We are close in our mentality: Neapolitans are sophisticated in the same way Sicilians are. The characters of Non ti pago [I won't pay you] win out at all costs and actually conquer by their will power, by their stubbornness which is similar to that of the Sicilians. (12)

Eric Bentley has also maintained that, except in The Big Magic, Pirandello's influence on De Filippo is only superficial. Certainly, many affinities with Pirandello's theater can be found: in the way De Filippo celebrates maternal love, in his metaphysical speculation on the nature of reality and illusion, in his emphasis on the drama of fear and compassion. However, as Bentley points out, while Pirandello deals with abstract concepts, never revealing the truth on any given matter because truth is relative and definite judgment is impossible, De Filippo concerns himself with specific personal traumas. In many plays he deals with the Pirandellian theme that illusions are needed because life is more than we can stand; in some cases the conclusions of the plays recall those of the great master in that the intrusion of reality, which had threatened to shatter the illusion, instead ironically reinforces it and makes it permanent. At times, too, their characters show similarities. It is difficult to establish to what degree these affinities are due to influence because, as De Filippo himself has said, at the base of their art there is a common denominator: the Southern Italian outlook on life. Long traditions bind together the mainland and the island Kingdom of the Two Sicilies. Unable to live freely under centuries of Spanish domination, the people of Sicily and those of Naples learned to cope in the same manner, by meditating and philosophizing. But for the dialectical Sicilian fury of Pirandello, De Filippo substitutes Neapolitan cynicism. Even the pessimism of De Filippo's characters, which makes one think of the nihilism of Pirandello's, is a mocking negativism which, while it has the flavor of paradox, has its origin in the traditional popular attitude of "goldbricking."

Moreover, alike as their plays might appear, they differ greatly in tone. Pirandello's bleak, pessimistic outlook becomes less dreary with De Filippo. No matter how much De Filippo's characters suffer in the play, the endings are often resolved happily. Furthermore, the truth is discoverable to those who wish to find it. Illusions are never allowed to remain ambiguous; if one man has an illusion, others recognize it as such.

De Filippo's plays are not drama in the Pirandellian sense, nor comedies in the sense that English-speaking audiences—and especially the Broadway audience—understand the term. As Bentley observes:

Naples is a different place, and Neapolitan folk drama is a different art; one enjoys it not least for its difference. . . . One enjoys, above all, the fine blend of comedy and drama, the naive pathos, the almost noble seriousness of what might easily become ludicrous. Some non-Italians are surprised, even displeased, by this last feature. "Why don't they play comedy as comedy?" Fully to answer the question would be to explain and justify a simpler, but also more delicate, realism than our own stage at present has to show. (13)

There is a wide spectrum of humor in a De Filippo play. The laughter he elicits ranges from chuckles to belly laughs. But there is also a central fiber, a sense of the tragedy of life. For his propensity for the tragicomic, De Filippo could be called the Italian Gogol. This blend of comedy and pathos also recalls some moments in Chaplin's works.

It is the blend of comedy and pathos that lends the work of De Filippo its special tone. His plays may be both realistic and fantastic, both comic and moralistic, both sentimental and grotesque. It is a blend that De Filippo achieves through his examination of the bittersweet plebeian life of Naples.

The Playwright in His Creative Process

De Filippo has occasionally spoken about the content and form of his art. In a 1956 interview he said: "The theater is neither a book nor a literary work: it must always be lively, and thus for one-and-a-half to two hours it must always have elements of surprise. That's why the public comes to see my plays, because it enjoys itself and takes something home as well" (14). In December 1972, upon receiving the Feltrinelli International Prize for the Theater, he pointed out the elements that contribute to the creation of his plays. Except for a few works written in his youth, at the base of his art "lies always the conflict between individual and society."

In general, if an idea does not have social meaning or social application, I'm not interested in developing it. It's clear that I'm aware that what is true for me might not be true for others, but I'm here to speak to you about myself, and since pity, indignation, love, and emotions in general, are felt in the heart, this much I can affirm—that ideas spring first from my heart and then from my brain. (15)

De Filippo points out that it is easy for him to have an idea, difficult, on the other hand, to give it form and communicate it. He has been successful mainly because, as he says, "I was able to absorb avidly and with pity the life of so many people, and I have been able to create a language which, although theatrically elaborate, becomes the means of expression of the various characters and not of their author" (16). He explains:

In most cases, the creative process is long. The germinal idea undergoes the seasoning of time to test the degree of its validity: after having had the idea and given it a sketchy form, there begins the long and laborious period during which, for months and more often for years, I keep the idea enclosed in me. . . . If an idea is not valid, little by little it fades away, disappears, and does not obsess the mind any longer; but if it is valid, with time it ripens and improves and consequently the comedy develops both as text and as theater, as a complete show, staged and acted down to the smallest detail, exactly the way I wanted it seen and felt. In a way this is unfortunate, as I will never feel it again once it has become a theatrical reality. (17)

Then the play staged in his mind and carried with him for so long is fixed in the pages of the script: "Only when the beginning and the end of the 'action' are clear to me and I know to perfection the life, death and miracles of every character, even the secondary ones, do I begin to write" (18). He writes the play, staging it in his mind's eye as he goes along. True, this is the practice of every playwright; but De Filippo does it by fusing the writing process to the acting and directing experiences. Such fusion is evident not only in the fluidity, spontaneity, and naturalness of the dialogue, but also in the numerous and often detailed stage directions.

Early in his artistic career De Filippo made a statement that has remained true up to the present:

De Filippo's Inspiration and Creative Process 31

> Our purpose in coming forward on the stage has never been to hold conferences, to conduct discussions about grave problems, or to teach courses in philosophy. We are truly people of the theater, free from every bond and bias, and we are theater people in the sense of being both actors and audience; that is why we concern ourselves with reproducing in our plays life as people see it and feel it, with its elements of comedy and sentiment, poetry and the grotesque, with its contrasts of suffering and buffoonery, and nothing more. To sum up, every day we are more strongly convinced that this is exactly what the public seeks from us, and for this they applaud us generously as actors and as authors. (19)

De Filippo writes a play basing it not on the presentation of lofty philosophical abstractions, but as a part of life, to make it live in its own right as a work of drama. Every character, like every life, however minor, always has something to say, comic or serious, emotionally or intellectually, and De Filippo aims to create characters who reflect in varying degrees sentiments and ideas possessed of a certain universality.

When the curtain rises on an Eduardo De Filippo play, the audience is not apt to receive a scenic surprise. For over fifty years, the settings of his comedies have been remarkably consistent. One sees the interior of a lower-middle-class apartment. Seldom does Eduardo write a play which, like <u>De Pretore Vincenzo</u> or <u>Tommaso D'Amalfi</u>, moves out into the streets and alleys of Naples. The playwright's choice of the interior setting shows his interest in exploring the motives, values, and plight of the poor and the struggling. Although the strain of naturalism in De Filippo is not of Strindbergian intensity, it is strong enough in this essentially realistic playwright to cause him to examine people in the environment where they are most likely to be themselves. For Eduardo is committed to exposing the hypocrisy of human beings, and their financial, physical, or spiritual destitution:

> Except for a few works I wrote when I was young, . . . at the base of my theater there is always the conflict between the individual and society. I mean to say that everything always starts from an emotive stimulus: reaction to an injustice, scorn for hypocrisy,

mine and others', solidarity with and human sympathy for a person or a group of people, rebellion against outdated and anachronistic laws, fear in the face of events, such as wars, which disrupt the life of the people. (20)

De Filippo finds drama particularly in the life and language of those living in poverty and suffering social injustice. From the early works—light farces, yet already sensitive to human value—to the great neorealist plays of the immediate postwar period, which explore the drama of humanity ravaged by war, to the most recent works cast in the form of "parables" and some strongly critical of our present-day society. De Filippo shows a continuous effort to reach his audience with his commitment to mitigating the absurdities and incongruities of life through the correction of social ills. By his own admission, he writes in reaction to the injustices perpetrated against the weak in society: the illegitimate, the unhappily married, the poor, the oppressed. From his passionate identification with the socially deprived arises the plays' moral protest, which attempts to produce awareness of the human predicament and to compel reflection. Yet his theater is not political propaganda. De Filippo himself rejected this label: "I am not Brecht, and for that matter I would not like to be him. I do not approve of political speeches in the theater. However, I certainly am in favor of pointing out [social] wounds" (21).

Neither can his theater be labeled "social theater," since it does not, for instance, concern itself so much with the class struggle or with the social and economic condition of the deprived classes, as with moral failure and its social consequences. He focuses his attention on such themes as hypocrisy, evil masquerading as good, egoism disguised as charity, the alienating influence on the individual of a demoralized society, the oppressive condition arising from lack of tolerance and respect for human dignity, the arbitrariness of society, the absurdities and inadequacies of the judicial system. Only a very few plays fail because of De Filippo's commitment to social betterment. Usually, this very commitment accounts for the depth of inspiration, the thematic richness, the authenticity in character and dialogue, the balance of irony and humor, and thus the sense of perspective in his dramatization of social issues. He writes

play after play exposing one wrong after another, spurred
on by the conviction that the only way to remedy the ills
of society is to prompt public reaction to them. He is
not always successful in arousing this reaction and often
overstates his point, but he is always faithful to his
vision of the playwright as society's moral guide. Over
the years he has maintained this interest and has increasingly confirmed the importance that he attaches to the
involvement of the public, for it is this public that
must fulfill the moral function of his work.

Language

Part of De Filippo's artistic achievement is undoubtedly due to his successful working solution to the problems
of finding, or inventing, a form of spoken Italian suitable for use on the stage. This is an accomplishment
because literary Italian, and above all stage Italian, is
essentially an artificial language. While standard
English, standard French, or standard American is spoken,
if not by the whole population at least by important
sections of it, standard Italian only exists on paper.
In ordinary life even the most educated Italians have
their clearly defined regional accent and vocabulary. It
is therefore far more difficult in Italian to write dramatic dialogue which sounds like real speech, yet free
from local overtones and the limitations on intelligibility imposed by the use of a dialect. Only during the
1960s, for a variety of reasons—mass communications, the
urbanization of large numbers of former agricultural
workers and their families, geographical migration,
travel for pleasure—did a generalized form of spoken
Italian start to assert itself on a wider scale. Theater
has mostly used the Italian literary language, an abstraction usually bombastic or stilted, incomprehensible to
the majority of Italians, and therefore necessarily
restricted both socially and in its range of expressive
possibilities. As Pier Paolo Pasolini commented, "traditional theater has accepted . . . an Italian which does
not exist. Upon such a convention—that is, upon
nothing, upon what is nonexistent, dead—it has based the
conventionality of diction. The result is repugnant" (22).
Side by side with literary theater exists a tradition of regional theater, richer in expressiveness, but
very limited, by reason of the mutual incomprehensibility

of Italy's many dialects, in its potential for reaching
people beyond the local area. De Filippo is the one playwright who has resolved the division between these two
kinds of theatrical language. To overcome the linguistic
conventionality of bourgeois theater, he invented a new
vehicle of oral expression which has the spontaneity and
immediacy of popular dialect while still retaining that
minimum of conventional abstraction necessary to reach a
wide audience.

In his early works De Filippo used almost exclusively
a pure Neapolitan dialect, which was not only appropriate
for his characters, who had affinities with those of the
cabaret theater and the avanspettacolo, but also reflected with almost obsessive rigor the life of the Neapolitan masses and lower middle class. At the beginning of
their careers, the use of the dialect was also unavoidable for Eduardo and his brother and sister, since they
saw themselves as continuing the tradition inherited from
Scarpetta. But as De Filippo's repertory changed, due to
his desire to appeal to an audience all over the peninsula, his means of expression changed too. The Neapolitan
vernacular went through a process of Italianization,
following the lead of the "half-Neapolitan" already
spoken by middle-class Neapolitans and becoming more
understandable to other Italians. Since the war, De
Filippo has developed a dramatic dialogue that comes very
close to the everyday spoken vernacular employed throughout southern Italy, but with the particular inflection
and cadence characteristic of Naples. It is, moreover, a
language which has a "common denominator" with spoken
Italian and is readily understood in other regions.

De Filippo's texts reproduce the rhythm and flow of
ordinary conversational Italian as faithfully as possible. They are characterized by run-on sentences, with
pauses in the form of dots (. . .) dividing each clause,
instead of carefully constructed, grammatically selfcontained periodic sentences. Although in the later
works dialect expressions appear only rarely, his scripts
are colored with expressive idioms, popular slang, and
frequent, sometimes outlandish puns. Sometimes the
author inserts a few words in Neapolitan dialect at the
end of a punchline, to enrich the local "flavor" and
maintain the immediacy of geographical setting. However,
dialect never serves merely to add charm or mere local
color to his characters' speech, or to give an air of
"scholarly" authenticity, as an aesthetic device for its

own sake. Rather, it serves to heighten either their plight or their overflowing excitement. With most of the characters, De Filippo mingles dialect with Italian, alternating the pungency of the one with the suavity of the other and extracting all the flavor and fun he can from the rich tonality of their utterance.

The result is a collection of plays free of intellectual abstractions, rhetorical figures, and learned metaphors. It is unfailingly expressive, rich in comic elements, and full of the spontaneous, colorful epithets of "street language." Thornton Wilder made a particular point of admiring Eduardo's language: "To know and love his plays one must have a relish for dialect and regional speech, for that color and immediacy of the language, used for a longtime by a portion of the society little touched by the over-sophisticated and cultivated 'polite' world" (23). For this same reason Bentley hails Eduardo's theater as "popular": "It is a popular theater as against an art theater. This means . . . that it is a dialect theater and not an 'Italian' one. It uses a popularly spoken language and not an official, national, bourgeois language—in this respect resembling Synge and O'Casey rather than Pinero and Galsworthy. The lack of a national theatrical repertoire in Italy may be deplorable, but the quality of the defect is—the regional theater" (24). Indeed, with De Filippo as with the Irishman John Millington Synge, half of the effect of the play lies in the dialect. The language of The Playboy of the Western World serves to turn a potentially tragic situation into a richly comic one. Similarly, Filumena Marturano's Neapolitan dialect dispels any lugubrious potentialities of the plot—the old story of the prostitute with the heart of gold—and makes her a truly heroic plebeian. Just as a Synge play would lose much of its value if it were rewritten in American English, so do the Neapolitan comedies of De Filippo seem essentially untranslatable (25).

Moreover, in addition to the language, his comedies depend for much of their effect upon the gestures used by the characters. Although the Italian stage does not have an Oriental "gesturology," different regions, and Naples in particular, have virtually a system of gestures with accepted meanings. The side of one's hand repeatedly jabbed at one's ribs indicates hunger; pulling the lower eyelid down with one finger is the nonverbal way to describe shrewdness in another person. One must, indeed, study beforehand the meaning of Neapolitan gestures to derive the full flavor from a De Filippo performance (26). With gestures and dialect both lost in foreign performances, Eduardo's plays in translation hardly approximate the original works.

Chapter Three
Early Works: Range and Versatility

From Farce to Satire

De Filippo's theatrical works of the first phase, written before World War II and collected under the title Cantata dei giorni pari (Cantata for even days), are usually neglected by critics. In 1945 De Filippo himself characterized them as "plays of the old theater":

> In those plays I wanted to show the world of plot and intrigue and interest: the adulterers, the gambler, the superstitious, the slothful, the fraudulent. All part of a recognizable, definable Neapolitan way of life, but a way of life belonging to the nineteenth century. In those plays I kept alive a Naples which was already dead in part, and in part was covered up and hidden by the "paternalistic" care of the Fascist regime, and which, if it should revive today, would be seen in a different way, under a different aspect. (1)

But De Filippo's judgment on his work is too severe, for many of these plays have been restaged since 1945 with great success because of their relevancy and their theatricality.

The early works cannot be discarded, not only because they have documentary value, but also because, despite the influence of earlier Neapolitan playwrights, they introduce some of the themes that will become characteristic of him. Focused on the problems of contemporary Neapolitan society, these plays have a satirical bite, a tinge of irony. They reflect "even days" in appearance only; fascism wanted to project Italy as a country with its dreams fulfilled, but even the farces convey the desolate condition of the masses and lower middle class in the 1920s and 1930s.

While apparently simple, though obviously put together

by a skilled actor, these first works are not pure experiment, sketches, or "pretexts" for acting. In their preference for jest and movement over words, in the lively action, the comical situation full of surprises and misunderstandings, in the quick lines studied to seem natural and full of the spirit of the spoken language, they echo the pulcinellata (2); however, they already manifest a humor which verges on the grotesque, a dramatic tension at times approaching the tragic, a tendency to psychological intimacy, and a moral sensitivity to social conditions. The vivacity of the action is sustained by the many minor characters, at times mere caricatures, who carry with them an inexhaustible mimic potential. Seldom are they solidly fitted into the overall structure; rather, they remain accessories, tending to predictability because they have the fixed, generic characteristics of types. They appear, then just as suddenly disappear, the laughter of the audience trailing after them. The farcical situations do not, however, arise from accident and chance, as in the commedia dell'arte and traditional Neapolitan dialect theater, but from a human condition that is basically dramatic; and the lazzi, or comic business, while they make us laugh, at the same time exteriorize the pain of that state, rendering it sensible, immediate, and visible. At the center of this world is the main character, part of everyday reality, whose vitality stems from the absurdity of humble life observed from a new angle.

    The theatrical strength of these characters lies not merely in their mimicry, but also in their language. The dialogue, at times rudimentary, at times abrupt and excited, never becomes monotonous or colorless, but always maintains its spontaneity and the fluidity necessary to remain theatrical. Although the Neapolitan linguistic texture gradually absorbs Italian forms, colored so as to indicate the characters' social levels, De Filippo sustains his artistic preference for dialect even when complying with the prohibition of dialects during the last years of Fascism. And at the base of the farcical situations and the language, there is always Naples itself, with its tragicomic, its humble and desolate reality, its scarcity of sustenance and human resources.

    The one-act Farmacia di turno (Pharmacy on duty), the first work in Cantata for Even Days, was written in 1920 for Peppino Villani's company, but never staged. While an actor in the company, De Filippo had begun

Early Works: Range and Versatility

writing his own monologue. But this play is no product of a tyro's enthusiasm and ebullience. Though only twenty, De Filippo had sixteen years of acting experience behind him, and the play bears the mark of a skilled actor who knows the language of mimicry, movement, pauses, and nuances. Little more than a sketch, it nonetheless contains early versions of later themes: the isolation of the individual, the injustice of the law, the plight of the poor. Moreover, it shows De Filippo's dissatisfaction with the condescension implicit in "picturesque" representation and local caricature. Approaching writing from both his stage experience and his experience in living, he invests familiar comic types with a bitter humanity.

This first work is certainly naive in its use of theatrical conventions and stock types, but the earthiness and spontaneity of the dialogue are arresting. The scenes show no divergence between study and invention, theory and practice. The Neapolitan dialect theater, direct descendant of the commedia dell'arte, acquires a new complexion when filtered through De Filippo's sensibility. The result is a realistic world, with its own characters, and a credible plot which in its comicalness evinces suffering. The work is characteristic of De Filippo's early theater in its focus on characterization. Each character, however sketchy, has some personal story to tell.

The play centers on the pharmacist Don Saverio, a proud man who despite his rational approach to life, is compelled to endure an evil fate. He had approached marriage pragmatically, first making sure that his business was a success. But his wife in the meantime has left him for a richer man, and now he is alone, ridiculed by the neighbors; his inward pain at lacking a family is reflected in his refusal to assent to an annulment on the grounds of childlessness. So, at once resigned and humiliated, he spends his day serving the poor customers of his area, often in the company of his doctor and friend Don Teodoro, who comes in to chat, to take a nap in the cozy armchair, or to ask advice on the best way to get rid of the mice in his house. The play begins realistically, but the plot twists soon recall the pulcinellata. One of the first customers is Carmela, maid to Don Saverio's ex-wife, who comes in to buy some aspirin for her mistress; distracted by the unexpected appearance of her suitor Enrico, she leaves instead with an envelope containing Don Teodoro's rat poison. A wretched couple arrives looking for the doctor. The wife is clearly suffering from malnutrition, but no one would dare diagnose it as such because to do so would reflect on their economic status and deal a severe blow to their pride. Don Teodoro's diagnosis is no different from earlier doctors', and the couple cannot pay for the consultation. Finally, the doorman Gregorio arrives, his face swollen, and Don Saverio is happy to be able to show off his skill in extracting a tooth. But his satisfaction is short-lived: the next visitor is the policeman who has come to arrest him for attempting to poison his ex-wife. Don Saverio is led away with such despatch that the drugstore is locked with the doorman inside. Gregorio's plight, however, is a temporary inconvenience and, coming upon the heels of Don Saverio's arrest, it provides dramatic relief, minimizing the seriousness of the pharmacist's predicament.

Pharmacy on Duty alternates between the bitter reality of poverty borne with pride and the farce of the pulcinellata, over all of which hovers the author's own sense of irony. De Filippo's fatalistic vision of the irony present in everyday life will not allow any of the characters to triumph. Saverio's ex-wife is herself a victim, fatally ill, while Gregorio's temporary imprisonment provides a physical symbol of the common state of the characters, each imprisoned in his private situation and powerless to change it. From his first appearance as an author, without over-insistence, De Filippo shows the moralistic intentions that characterize his most famous plays. Nonetheless, watching this play, one has the impression of being still in the mainstream of the San Carlino theater tradition. The stuff of farce, for example, is the doctor's haste in changing chairs when the pharmacist tells him that his father died sitting in that very chair, Enrico's flirting with Carmela in the presence of Don Saverio, who has no choice but to go along with the love affair, the accidental substitution of rat poison for medicine.

The vis comica is the result not just of unexpected situations, but also of the unexpected and naively witty punchlines, as for example when Vincenzo brings in his young wife Rafilina who has reluctantly consented to be examined by Don Teodoro, the doctor:

    Teodoro.   Sit down, please. (Rafilina sits down and starts to take off her shoes.) Wait a

Early Works: Range and Versatility 41

> minute! . . . Wait a minute! . . . Leave your shoes alone! . . . Just undo your blouse a bit.
> Rafilina. [To her husband Vincenzo] And you made me change my stockings!
> Teodoro. You thought you were taking her out to buy a pair of shoes?
> Vincenzo. O.K., forget it . . . When we go home you can put the ones with holes back on.
> Teodoro. Well, now, how do you feel, young woman?
> Rafilina. How do I feel?! Oh! Nobody knows how I feel!
> Teodoro. But I'm the doctor. I have to know! (3)

Here the whole situation is comical, building to an explosion of laughter as the meaning of the expression "Nobody knows how I feel!" ("'O saccio sul' io"), a common Neapolitan exclamation, is transferred from the idiomatic to the literal level. No less comic are Vincenzo and Enrico's gimmicks, which nonetheless at the same time evince their suffering. As soon as the spectator stops laughing, he feels the bitterness of the situation.

Dominated by a crepuscular, Chekhovian atmosphere, the play seems only a moment in a faded, melancholic life. De Filippo's way of making the characters speak and move in chiaroscuro goes back to the Neapolitan playwright Lìbero Bòvio. But as Robert G. Bander writes,

> The melancholy strain which Eduardo has introduced into the farcical tradition of Italian dialect theater is a measure of his difference from Ruzzante, Goldoni, and Gallina; his comic inventiveness sharply differentiates him from Di Giàcomo, Bracco, Russo, Mùrolo, and most of the other Neapolitan vernacular dramatists of an earlier period. De Filippo's sense of spiritual unrest, and his ability to dramatize it in a colloquial manner with which his audience can empathize, is his mark of individuality as a playwright. (4)

Most important, even at this early point in his artistic career, De Filippo had already begun to create a mythic, universal character. At the very outset he struck a rich vein of comedy, a vein that led deep into humanity and could therefore be appreciated and understood by all. Incidents in the life of poor Neapolitans come to represent the comic-pathetic condition of the universal "little man."

The problems of the "little man" are chiefly economic in the one-act Filosoficamente (Philosophically, 1928). Gaetano Piscopo seems at first to be a stereotypical Neapolitan, believing passionately in the power of dreams to give him winning numbers in the weekly lottery and refusing to take responsibility for his obsession, preferring to blame his dead wife. But beneath the humor is real pain. Gaetano's primary worry is not his gambling, or even his perennial losses, but his two unmarried daughters, Maria and Margherita. The first part of the act shows the family trying to scrape together the money to buy pizzas and fruit for one of the modest parties that are Gaetano's way of introducing his daughters to well-intentioned young men. They are under threat of eviction, and to throw the party they have to go hungry for a few days. Gaetano's efforts to keep up appearances despite his poverty show the superficiality, but also the endurance, of the Neapolitan lower bourgeoisie. The party is a failure. Despite the jokes, the conversation between the old and the young comes to nothing, and even in the young people's conversation there is a certain rancor and envy. The characters are united in a lifeless, pathetic attitude, and everything seems placed on the same plane, portrayed with analytical objectivity.

Evident in these early works is De Filippo's ability to turn traditional farce in whatever direction he wants —toward pathos or toward social criticism. Nonetheless, most are dominated by humor for the pure enjoyment of it. The complicated three-act Uomo e galantuomo (Men and gentlemen, 1922), about the interactions of traveling actors with provincial nobility, shows De Filippo's total assimilation of the comic effects of the Neapolitan popular theater. The influence of the pulcinellata shows in the vivacity, freshness, and wit of the spoken language, the fanciful, exuberant dialogue, and the lazzi pulcinelleschi or comic "bits." The pompous exuberance comes from the plays of Pasquale Altavilla, while from Scarpetta comes the overall scheme, the types, the inner movement of the action, the comical expedients, and the use of social background. The essential elements of De Filippo's comedy—the traditional chase of love and treachery, the slapstick, the craziness and tricks, mistaken identity and misunderstandings, gossip and buffoonery—as well as his skills at interweaving plots

Early Works: Range and Versatility

and using dialect realistically are all here in this one play.

Quei figuri di trent'anni fa (The old gang of thirty years ago, 1929) is a comic farce; at the same time, however, it criticizes the Italy of the "golden times" of Fascism, showing the misery beneath its alleged heroic grandeur. In this play De Filippo leaves the familiar lower-middle-class setting and turns to another corner of Neapolitan life, to a clandestine gambling house operated by a certain Gennaro Ferri. Gennaro hires Luigi as a shill in a gambling game; and as Luigi is schooled in the secrets of the trade, he shows comic slowness in understanding just what trade he is learning, what is expected of him, and consequently what will be the outcome of his involvement. Luigi's ingenuousness is the source of all the jokes in this play, so obviously rooted in the pulcinellata of Scarpetta and the commedia. As in Men and Gentlemen, here there is none of the pity and desperation expressed in Pharmacy on Duty and especially in Philosophically. The dialogue and funny situations keep the spectators detached from the stage action, so they can better understand De Filippo's implicit criticism of Fascism. In fact, the intent of the play did not escape the censor, Leopoldo Zurlo, who made De Filippo change the title, originally Le bische (The gambling-house), and forced him to set it thirty years earlier, prior to the coming of Fascism, under the pretense that the regime had abolished such illicit practices. Under Fascism there could be no aberrations, only "even days."

No such political implications are apparent in Pericolosamente (Dangerously, 1938), a modernized pulcinellata on the theme of the taming of the shrew. In the San Carlino theater, as in the Punch-and-Judy show, Pulcinella, a coward outside the house, always used a stick when teaching wisdom to his wife. The twentieth-century Pulcinella uses a gun loaded with blanks, which, like the cardboard slapstick, makes a lot of noise but does no harm.

In most of De Filippo's early works farce serves to veil the wretchedness of the characters as they resort to precarious stratagems in order to save face or to survive. At times, the grotesque situations become pathetic because of the protagonist's inability to establish communications with the surrounding world. From such a world of misery and loneliness emerges Sik-Sik, De Filippo's first major character, who exhibits a hopeless will to survive even as he sorrowfully resigns himself to the squalor around him—the same squalor that will face the protagonists in many of the postwar plays. Sik-Sik, l'artefice magico (Sik-Sik, the Incomparable Magician, 1929), written for Mario Mangini's Pulcinella principe in sogno and interpreted by the three De Filippos, was the first work in which Eduardo wrote a part for himself; his first big success, it became a hallmark of his style of humor and the first clear sign of his future greatness. The stage directions describe the magician as follows:

> Sik-Sik is a man of about 40, with a thick black moustache. He is wearing a light-colored jacket that is none too clean; his black pants belong with the tail-coat he will put on during his performance. He wears a soft hat. In one hand he carries a small suitcase and in the other a cage containing two identical pigeons. He has a cigar stump between his teeth. Sik-Sik is the typical traditional strolling actor: poor, tormented, and . . . a philosopher. Giorgetta, his wife, follows him. She wears no hat and has a threadbare coat over her shoulders. Her untidy dress clearly shows her to be pregnant. Like her husband, she looks tired and discouraged. [p. 121]

The protagonist might almost be the author himself as he was at the time of his association with the Kokasse company: so thin as to be almost emaciated, sicco sicco in Neapolitan. Sik-Sik and Giorgetta are presented as somewhat lacking in talent, very poor, discouraged to the point of futility, but nonetheless dedicated to their profession. Their magic act reveals their destitution in terms of the magician-actor's belief in his art, in terms of the hunger that forces him to use his pregnant wife in the act, even down to locking her in a trunk, and in terms of the stage on which what amounts to a real contest takes place between him and the audience.

Arriving late one evening Sik-Sik misses his regular assistant Nicola. After scolding his wife, he desperately latches onto Rafele, a "shabby and wretched man" who asks him for a light and whom he asks to be his partner in the act. There follows a dialogue reminiscent of Abbott and Costello's "Who's on first?":

> Sik-Sik. I'll do very easy tricks tonight because you

Early Works: Range and Versatility

                 are new at the job . . . O.K.,; the curtain rises. You'll know the minute I'm supposed to come on, because the music will go like this: Pe...pepe, pe...pepe, pe...pepe, pe...pepe. Got it? (The tune Sik-Sik hums is the trumpet motif from <u>Mephistophele</u>.)
Rafele.   And he makes his entrance.
Sik-Sik. Who makes his entrance?
Rafele.   Peppe.
Sik-Sik. Who's Peppe?
Rafele.   The fellow you just told me about.
Sik-Sik. No. Pepe is the trumpet.
Rafele.   Oh, the trumpeter is called Peppe.
Sik-Sik. No, no, no, no, no. That's the noise the trumpet makes. Don't confuse the issue. Then, after the blare of the trumpet, I make my entrance. You'll recognize me at once. I'll be wearing a genuine Chinese kimono, you know, so I look more important. When you see me enter, you say: This guy really looks Chinese. The audience will already be impressed because, as you know, the Chinese are past masters of this kind of show. Their skill and patience are endless. You ought to see how patient the Chinese are. [pp. 123-24]

    Robert Corrigan's statement that "Eduardo De Filippo . . . is unquestionably the fullest contemporary embodiment of the <u>commedia</u> spirit" finds justification especially in plays like this, where <u>commedia</u> elements are easily identifiable in the linguistic devices, line exchanges, and slapstick visual comedy (5). Sik-Sik suggests a combination of Pulcinella and Bragadoccio, Giorgetta a combination of Columbina and Speraldina, Rafele the <u>zanni</u> (<u>commedia</u> clowns), but with a twentieth-century twist. Rafele makes the audience laugh, but he also increases Sik-Sik's desperation to an almost tragic intensity as he gives away the secrets of the three basic tricks that make up the show: the water-drinking trick, the trunk escape, and the trick of the disappearing dove.
    At the last moment before the performance, Sik-Sik's usual assistant Nicola arrives and wants his part back. Rafele is aware of his own limitations, but he needs the money and, besides, he needs to prove himself superior to

the equally foolish Nicola. In the ensuing scuffle
Rafele loses the fake padlock used for the trunk escape,
as well as his pigeon, which, however, he is able to
replace with a chicken. When during the performance Sik-
Sik asks for a volunteer from the audience, he is faced
with two. Predictably, the three tricks are disasters.
But Sik-Sik's resourcefulness is limitless. When each of
the partners testifies that the water went down his
gullet, Sik-Sik announces that he has materialized half
of the glassful for each of them. There is no padlock
for either partner to substitute; to free his wife
Sik-Sik has to break the good one. When, finally, a
chicken comes out of Rafele's hat instead of a pigeon,
Sik-Sik concludes triumphantly that not only has he
translated the pigeon from the cage to the hat, but also
changed it into a chicken. Though the spectator can
laugh at the failure of the tricks, nonetheless he cannot
laugh at Sik-Sik and his wife, victims of events over
which they have no control. Mechanically, the orchestra
breaks into a fanfare, ironically emphasizing the failure
of Sik-Sik's act; "the curtain, however, is more
compassionate, and it falls to end the play."

    Sik-Sik, the Incomparable Magician might seem no
more than the dodges of a second-rate magician capable of
extraordinary mimicry, juxtaposed with the pulcinellesque
improvisations of a very stupid foil. But it is also the
drama of a wretched man forced to make ends meet. Sik-
Sik is a character on the edges of society, clinging to
life by means of his poor tricks; to convince himself of
their adequacy, he often repeats to Rafele that when he
comes on stage and performs, "it will bring the house
down." His thirst for applause almost equals the hunger
of his stomach; and if his illusion, that he can impose
himself on the audience by his appearance alone, crumbles
bit by bit when he is actually on stage, nonetheless he
resists and finds a way to save at least the illusion of
not being wholly beaten.

    In De Filippo's work tragic humor is defined by the
destruction of illusions, the collapse of ideals, the
irony of fate, and, sometimes, the ability to bear it
all. One notes a foretaste of the attitude of the characters of the mature dramas—Pasquale Lojacono of Those
Ghosts!, Calogero Di Spelta of The Big Magic, Pasquale
Cimmaruta of The Voices Within—as Sik-Sik tenaciously
refuses to recognize his failure in order to preserve the
authenticity of his art, as he stubbornly fights to

remain "the incomparable magician" by enclosing himself in illusions. In fact, when Defilippian characters cannot otherwise escape the sad reality that traps them, they often flee into dreams or magic. The difference being that, good or deceitful, dreams come from outside, as a supernatural intervention, supplying, let's say, a winning number in the lottery (Philosophically, I Won't Pay You), or revealing a distressing situation (The Voices Within). Magic, on the other hand, is entirely in the hands of man, who must succeed by his own resourcefulness (The Big Magic, The Top Hat). Gennaro Magliulo put it quite well when he observed that in this short drama we find both "the Defilippian intuition of an oppressing human and social condition and also the intuition of the attitude which the homo Neapolitanus is accustomed to assume in facing that condition" (6). The knockabout comedy is qualified by a subtle, painful humor, the "sorrowful humor" that Pandolfi observes as the dominant note of De Filippo's mature plays (7).

Much of the serious note is conveyed in the stage directions, which, kept to a minimum up to this work, now increase in number and elaborateness. De Filippo describes in great detail not only the scene but the prelude to it, defining an emotional atmosphere that assures identification with the character:

> Once again he draws back the curtain, but the trunk remains inexorably closed. What will the audience say? What will they do? But the magician is thinking of his wife Giorgetta, about to become a mother, and locked inside! The trick, the theater, the audience, everything else vanishes from Sik-Sik's mind. He has an idea, the only way he can help her. He goes off into the wings and comes back with a hammer. He slips behind the curtain, and soon we hear muffled desperate strokes of the hammer, with Sik-Sik's panting voice counting aloud above the hammering: "And a one! and a two!" [p. 136]

Clearly, the author has also assumed a narrative distance from his creation. His stage directions are no longer merely instructions to the actors. Instead, they articulate the vision of a man who wants to go beyond the limits of theatrical language and comment on suffering humanity. Sik-Sik is enmeshed in a situation which an ambiguous Pirandellian humor addresses with laughter though aware of the tragic undertones of the situation. By this direct intervention De Filippo wants to make us feel the complete, inexpressible drama of Sik-Sik in this moment of surprise, strain, discouragement, and dejection, all of which must be interpreted by an actor in a gesture, in intense and prolonged mimicry. The stage directions are thus like musical cadences, hinted at but not fixed in a definite way and therefore capable of later development and new interpretations, according to the ability of the actor and the receptiveness of the audience. Words thus express only one, partial aspect of De Filippo's artistic personality; along with his linguistic ability goes his acting and directing sense. As the years pass, the significance of the stage directions increases, and in the postwar plays they often are concerned with portraying custom and reiterating satirical social criticism.

Though not added to the text until about 1934-35, the first stage direction of the play nonetheless sheds light on De Filippo's growing consciousness of himself as an artist and commentator on his own works:

> It is nine-thirty.
> The public is gathering in front of the ticket office. In fifteen minutes the show will start. This is the moment when I am most aware of the awesome responsibility facing me: the crowd is anonymous, all strangers; one enormous question mark. Never more than at this moment am I so completely outside the fiction of my role. I'm not yet convinced of the character I shall become in a few minutes, on the stage. I feel that I'm part of the crowd; it's as if I was going to go up to the ticket office and ask for an orchestra seat to see the show too. Not until the moment when the spotlights blind me with their stars of light and the curtain rises on the dark theater pit, can I possibly take up my part in the fiction. The minutes pursue me inexorably. They sweep me on in their rush, they overwhelm me, they push me toward the little stage door, which closes ominously, with a hollow sound, behind me. [p. 121]

It is clear that here we are in the presence not merely of stage directions, but of a man addressing his own methods of expression. De Filippo wants to maintain not only the "fictitious character of the stage, but also

Early Works: Range and Versatility

that degree of freedom of the imagination, that unforeseeable suggestion of the stage—the engulfing stage with its blinding lights," the extraordinary rapport with the audience which he must constantly enliven and renew, and the deep desire to understand, to interpret, to give a significance to every encounter (8). The conception of the nature of theater first suggested in Sik-Sik marks the beginning of De Filippo's interest in the theoretical aspects of the theater, an interest which finds its fullest expression in The Art of Comedy and The Top Hat.

De Filippo's first six plays demonstrate his debt to commedia dell'arte and to the Neapolitan theatrical tradition. And, albeit in germinal form, they establish those features that will later come to characterize his theater: the importance of acceptance by the audience, the emphasis on characterization, the mixture of humor and pathos, the development of a recognizably Defilippian protagonist, and the necessity to theorize on human nature, the dramatic situation, and, of course, the role and status of the theater.

Interior Vacillation and Intimate Drama

The combination of pain and humor evident in De Filippo's early works is conveyed less in action, more in mood, in some of the plays that follow. Of significance to De Filippo is what is sensed and fleeting, transmitted indirectly through glances, sighs, and subtle crises: a panoply of feelings, from remorse to hatred. The plays' expressive realism reflects the influence of Neapolitan playwrights like Rocco Galdieri, Libero Bovio, Enzo Mùrolo, and Eduardo Nicolardi, and, from outside Italy, Anton Chekhov, whose plays were very popular in Italy during the late 1920s and the 1930s.

It seems logical and perhaps inevitable that De Filippo should follow this course, for he treats characters who live according to outmoded ideals, once cherished, but potentially destructive in a world that no longer honors them. Some people are so sentimentally attached to their ideals that they become blind to reality and to the needs of those around them, even to the extent of destroying their families. Their happiness proves to be naive; and when it crumbles, it leaves a malancholy sense of loss. All in all, the plays are informed with irony, humor, and the playwright's growing pessimism.

In the two-act Chi è cchiù felice 'e me! . . . (Who is happier than I! . . . , 1928), the protagonist Vincenzo is a sensible, prudent, discreet man who avoids everything that might disrupt his quiet life. He lives on a small monthly income which is enough to ensure his contentment despite the little sacrifices he must make to afford an occasional luxury: a more expensive pipe tobacco, for instance, means fewer cartridges for his biweekly hunting trips. Happiness means order; there can be no risks, no unknown factors. His day includes at least one meal, an afternoon walk, and a card game with friends; he retires every night at twelve o'clock sharp. With his beautiful young wife, Margherita, and a carefully circumscribed life, Vincenzo thinks himself the happiest man in the world. But one day a local dandy, who has killed in self-defense, takes refuge in Vincenzo's home, as if to warn him that his happiness is precarious and that any external intervention could destroy it. Riccardo, the young man, falls in love with Margherita, who, feeling her femininity reawakening after years of boring "happiness," accepts his attentions. But the neighbors' gossip cannot disturb Vincenzo's peace or compromise his idealism. Realizing that his wife no longer treats him as she used to, he tries to reaffirm his happiness and prove his wife's fidelity to himself and his neighbors by calling them to witness as she begs Riccardo to leave, declaring that she will never give herself to him. Vincenzo is thrilled at these words, then disheartened when Margherita gives Riccardo a passionate good-bye embrace that shows how much she loves him.

In this play the traditional themes of farce—conjugal misfortune, the betrayed and unaware husband—are invested with a new spirit, to become intimate drama. The strength of the play is in its caricatured types set in the realistic context of Neapolitan customs. The betrayed husband appears both comical and humiliated; and events are treated with a bitter sarcasm. Behind the comedy of character, behind the caricatures, the lively dialogue, the sarcasm and farcical episodes, lies a middle-class psychological drama on the theme of conjugal happiness which will be developed more subtly in Those Ghosts!

Vincenzo is something of a negative character. By being content with what he has, he becomes in fact "a

Early Works: Range and Versatility

priest of the isolated happiness, stubbornly pursuing it with a faith which leaves no room for even modest uncertainties!" (9). He is a deserter in the struggle of life, and from his suffering stems an ambivalent tension between tragedy and comedy. On the other hand, Margherita is the first of many positive women in De Filippo's plays. Though she tries to go along with her husband's kind of forced happiness, she can find no lasting personal satisfaction. She is unable to repress her feeling for Riccardo despite her will to remain faithful and preserve the family honor. She thus unconsciously rebels against those conventional attitudes that often define the housewife's domesticity as merely a form of resignation. In this respect she is the first in a long line of De Filippo's women who take an active role in determining their destinies. As its ironic title indicates, with this play De Filippo begins developing paradoxes of the Pirandellian sort. To the unreflecting illusions of the blinkered optimist, he juxtaposes the vulnerability of human certitude in the face of chance, which so easily dissolves conventional beliefs and promises; what dominates, more or less vainly opposed by laws and moral norms, is the sweeping force of passion and carnal desire. The situations thus are more complex and dramatic than in the previous works.

In his concern for characterization De Filippo does not wholly abandon social criticism. In Vincenzo one may easily see the typical attitude of the middle-class Italian of those years: passive submission to the comfortable socioeconomic ambiance provided by a political system—Fascism—which frees the individual from every responsibility while lulling him into self-satisfied optimistic apathy. Moreover, as Scornavacca notes, one may easily see in the treatment of the minor characters an anticipation of De Filippo's later satire of manners:

> The hypocritical maneuvers and the fictitious ingenuousness with which Vincenzo's neighbors and so-called friends proceed to stir up suspicion in his brain, instilling it drop by drop, with minced phrases, treating him with malicious compassion, underline the love for the satire of manners which has remained a characteristic of Eduardo's theater. (10)

The satire of the earlier plays here is more refined,

underlying not merely an action or scene, but the whole play.

In most of the plays to this point the main character has consistent features: a weak will and the inability to separate reality from fantasy. In the plays that follow the protagonists often ruin their lives because they are unable to assert their "selves." Ironically, they are anti-heroes in the supposedly heroic era of Fascism. They do not transcend themselves, though at least they overcome their immaturity. At this point, the drama functions to criticize Fascism implicitly, the middle class explicitly. Later, with the fall of the regime, this kind of protagonist is criticized in order to emancipate him from the past, its moral codes, its doctrines, its atavistic ways of thinking.

Gennariniello (1932) is another variation on the situation of the characters trapped because one of them is unable to face reality. Gennaro, the head of the family, though his authority is somewhat undermined by the double diminutive on the end of his name, is incapable of a decisive, serious act of will; that is, though he can act decisively, he cannot will seriously. Instead of worrying about his son's stupidity, he worries that he does not pursue girls; instead of worrying about his spinster sister's psychological problems, he worries about marrying her off. He makes his living creating and selling foolish inventions and dreaming of others that will make him rich. Deeply discontented with his modest lot in life, he aspires to a higher social station. An attractive neighbor comes to symbolize for Gennaro a life beyond his reach; but when he makes advances to her, she responds by teasing him in front of everyone, causing serious domestic quarrels and finally exposing him to the silent pity of his family, neighbors, and onlookers.
This character exhibits the senile sensuality of the poor man who inevitably must make a bitter, grotesque return to the truth and to his gray and advanced autumn. The play presents a picture, at once pathetic and funny, of Neapolitan life as well as a portrait of a human type very dear to De Filippo: the man who seems generally ignorant of the wretchedness around him, and who aspires to a dignity that because of his very ignorance is unbecoming to him.

As in all the prewar plays with similar situations, De Filippo never shows how the character will deal with the discovery that he has been living a lie. The playwright

Early Works: Range and Versatility

suggests, however, that in those years of strong Fascist control the masses and the lower middle class, exemplified in Gennariniello, had no chance. Implicit criticism of Fascism may be seen in Gennariniello's gallismo—his boasting of his sexual prowess, typical of the current machismo. Gallismo was encouraged by the Fascist regime as an expression of strength and defiance, and Gennariniello's unconscious acceptance of it shows the Italian inability to rebel against anachronistic ideas. Ranged against the male character's empty illusions is the practical world of the female character, Concetta, who plods through the day working as a housemaid to make a few lire and save the family from starvation. She fills the void left by her husband; and though she whines somewhat when he is off in his dream world, she comes to his defense in moments of crisis. Add to these two characters the only son, an adolescent coddled by his parents, yet ready to give them his affection in their worst moments, and the husband's sentimental spinster sister, in other plays often replaced by a bachelor brother, and we see the pattern for the Neapolitan family of many of De Filippo's later works. From the family life portrayed here flows an intimacy strong to the point of sentimentality, but corrected with the same kind of grotesque twist at which De Filippo aims in Sik-Sik (11).

More and more, De Filippo seems attracted to a protagonist who lacks any heroic potential, who drifts wherever he is led by his failure to take life seriously. He is a tragicomic character: whereas heroes insist on the truth, he avoids it, and instead of being the protagonist in a conflict between truth and illusion, he, often unwittingly, exposes the conflict between truth and self-deception. His dreams frequently help him evade the future and regress permanently. All this usually occurs against the backdrop of the family, which the protagonist often needs to idealize despite its actual state of degeneration. Nowhere is this situation more evident than in Natale in casa Cupiello (Christmas at the Cupiellos', 1931), which De Filippo himself has called one of his most significant works. The high point of his first creative phase and, for many reasons, a key work in his artistic development, it still enjoys success with audiences and critics; in 1966 it was produced at the Malyj Theater in Moscow, directed by Leonid Varpokhovsky, and for Russian television in 1973, again under his direction, with the well-known Vladimir Doronin in the lead.

The action swings between farce and drama, between naturalistic realism and spiritual investigation, between comedy and irony, all given a balance exceptional for De Filippo in this period. The opening scene is a normal one in the everyday life of the Neapolitan lower middle class. Concetta, patient, calm, a cup in her hand, tries to wake her husband, the monotony of her voice reflecting her resignation:

> Concetta. (With the monotonous tone of someone who knows beforehand that she will have to call many times before being heard) Luca . . . Luca . . . Wake up, it's nine o'clock.
> Pause. Luca continues to sleep.
> (As before, but a little louder) Luca . . . Luca . . . Wake up, it's nine o'clock.
> Luca grunts under the blankets as he turns over. Pause.
> (As before, in the same tone) . . . Luca . . . Wake up, it's nine o'clock. Here's your coffee.
> Luca. (Without understanding, still half asleep) Oh? . . . The coffee? (Murmuring something incoherent, he sticks his head out, completely swathed in a woolen shawl, then he sits up in bed, stretches out an arm as if he were about to take the cup of coffee, but then slowly lets his arm fall down again; his head sinks back and he falls asleep again. All of this is done with his eyes closed.) [pp. 221-22]

De Filippo's scenes and stage directions deserve accurate reconstruction, since he presents his characters not only through dialogue but also suggestive visual details. The opening action really tells us nothing that could not be deduced from the words, but it does emphasize the eternal lethargy of the characters and the fact that they live worlds apart from one another. It presents them visually and therefore more cogently than words can, particularly when words must create the illusion of everyday speech. And it becomes particularly revealing when the protagonist does not speak much. In the scene there is a perfect harmony between the atmosphere created by the stage business and that created by the words and tone of voice; indeed, in this expressive Defilippian language,

Early Works: Range and Versatility

there is meaning even in the pauses, rich in their interior tonalities.

Luca Cupiello wants to keep alive the joy of earlier years, when the children were small and the family was all united. In a glow of nostalgia he builds the traditional Nativity scene, oblivious to his children's cynicism and his family's struggle against poverty and the threat of dissolution (12). Only when the family conflict reaches a climax, at the end of act 2, does Luca peep out from behind his paper toys. Ninuccia, his daughter, is surprised by her husband in the arms of another man. Insults are hurled, the rivals rush outside to fight, mother and daughter are left fainting and hysterical. This is the moment Luca chooses for his entrance as one of the three Wise Men of the Nativity story, a long rug draped over his shoulder, a gold paper crown on his head, a sparkler in one hand and an umbrella in the other as a Christmas present for his wife. With his son and brother behind him, dressed in similar fashion, he kneels before his appalled wife and sings a carol as the curtain falls. Three days later, with the opening of act 3, he lies in bed again, paralyzed by his encounter with reality; and in the end he dies, unable to come to grips with the grown-up world. His eyes are filled with the vision of a vast, world-sized manger in which a giant newborn baby Jesus howls; as he breathes his last, he cries, "What a beautiful crèche!" and, as an added touch of irony, he asks forgiveness for his daughter as he joins her hand with her lover's, mistaking him for her husband.

In the very setting of the first act, the Cupiellos' master bedroom, we are faced with abject poverty. Luca, his wife, and their son Nennillo must all share the one bedroom. The house is obviously unheated: Concetta wears a shawl about her shoulders. Luca's head is wrapped in a woolen scarf, and Nennillo is buried under the bedcovers. A similar setting will be seen in Millionaires' Naples! and Filumena Marturano. The protagonist, despite his advanced age, personifies innate simplicity, purity, and traditional values as he insists on using his Christmas manger to communicate his world to others. Luca is hardly a new character for De Filippo; there were glimpses of him in Vincenzo of Who is Happier than I!, who pursued happiness, if not as naively as Luca, just as unrealistically. There is, however, a marked difference. More than merely a simple, naive person who does not want to grow, Luca also wants to keep the world around him the way it was. With his manger he pays homage to a very old and not exclusively Neapolitan tradition, motivated by the childlike residue of uncorrupted goodness lying more or less hidden in every man. Convinced of Christ's benevolence, he would like to find that same genuine love among men. But it is a vain desire. He and his manger are rejected by all; and in that rejection is the rejection of the spirit of Christmas—its joy, hope, love, and family unity—and all humanity's rejection of the mystery of love expressed in Christ's incarnation. The manger is on stage for the audience too. More than a way of telling us what is going on in the characters' minds, it forces us to reflect on the contrast between apparent joy and actual misery. In a materialistic world—De Filippo seems to suggest—only innocent and perhaps naive people like Luca are capable of such love.

However, Luca's stubbornness in building the Nativity scene also demonstrates his immaturity and irresponsibility; it is a way of fleeing into a world of illusion. He does not exercise the necessary paternal authority and guidance, either by helping his lazy son make a life for himself or by persuading his libertine daughter to remain faithful to her husband; his family goes to pieces, and he must suffer for his unconscious escapism. Through the attending physician, De Filippo comments bitterly and sadly: "Luca Cupiello has always been a big child who thought of the world as an enormous toy . . . when he realized that the toy should be played with, not as a child, but as a big man . . . he couldn't do it. The man in Luca Cupiello is missing." "Luca dies and must die, even if he arouses pity," De Filippo told me in an interview. "He is a victim of his own addiction to the game of childish illusions. The manger he builds is a kind of drug which paralyzes his imagination and distracts him from daily living." In fact, Eduardo concluded that "the manger also symbolizes anything which does not have any relation to the real problems of a man or a class of people, anything which is encouraged by the authorities." It is a kind of Homeric lotus, a soporific, like soccer, television, or whatever else is used to put the conscience to sleep.

This implicit social criticism, so characteristic of De Filippo's postwar theater, comes through most clearly in the structural elements which will become basic in

Early Works: Range and Versatility

those later plays. In the majority of the mature works the action centers around a tormented, disillusioned character who suffers from alienation and lack of communication with the surrounding world, particularly the family. On stage, Luca is always shown somewhat isolated from others, often in confrontation with them. But the others do not constitute a solid opposition. They have differing opinions, but, in their own way, they too lack any balanced, realistic approach to life, living their lives in absurd pettiness, busy with concerns important for appearances only. In them one sees the historical condition of Italian society in that period, and one recognizes in particular the spirit of the Neapolitan lower middle class—their desires, resourcefulness, ardor and extravagance, goodness and impulsiveness, misery and will to live—and at the same time their unawareness of their social and political plight. Luca, his neighbors, and their whole class lack the courage to look beyond Fascism's facades and discover the reality; they represent an irresponsible society which, by continuing to play with toys, indirectly indulges the wishes of the political power. In the postwar plays De Filippo tries to show how his characters can deal with a crumbling world by achieving solidarity as a family (witness the Jovine family in Millionaires' Naples!). However, this solidarity is as frequently betrayed within the family as in the society it reflects. This betrayal is developed most poignantly in De Filippo's treatment of World War II, and it is visible in less blatant injustices like the exploitation of the poor and the oppression of the weak through regressive, suffocating social institutions and the indifference of society as a whole.

But even when dealing with such complex themes, De Filippo does not abandon his comic vein. Christmas at the Cupiellos' gets its humanity from its Neapolitan atmosphere and its vivacious comedy from its structure, a series of blunders reminiscent of the pulcinellata. The unsuspecting Luca first delivers to his son-in-law his daughter's confession that she is running away with her lover, then insists that the lover stay for Christmas dinner. But in his Pulcinellesque mistake of uniting the lovers at his deathbed, he imparts a lesson on the importance of love, be it extramarital or not. Like every Pulcinella, he is unaware that he pronounces truths that society would prefer to ignore. And so it is that the farcical elements have a serious side. There are reminiscences of the lazzi of the commedia in the confrontation between the weak father and his stubborn son, in the uncle who is always being robbed and mocked by his nephew, in the boy's persistence in finding the manger ugly. Nennillo and his uncle are still tied to the fixed types of the tradition, but they point toward more individualized characters later on. The one serious character is again a woman. While her husband builds the manger, Concetta must take care of the details of everyday life and even prepare the glue and provide the nails for his project. Like the wife in Gennariniello, she must bear the family responsibility alone and, like her too, she genuinely loves her husband.

Toward the Theater of the Grotesque

In an era that Pirandello characterized as grandiose in the worst sense—"Italians all living the life of the senses, intoxicated by sun, light, color, exulting in song, each one playing some easy musical instrument . . . fanciful men of letters speaking a grandiloquent tongue, magnificient adorners, and evokers of past glories"—De Filippo portrayed the humble and even the degenerated aspects of life. Inherent in his writing is an essentially ethical purpose: to castigate the moral failure of the men of his times and to condemn dissolute or immoral customs, evil masquerading as good, egoism in the guise of charity. Although his ethical position has a social basis, his interest in social issues is less urgent than his concern for moral or existential issues. With moral themes, his sarcasm and irony are accentuated. However, the reduction of men to puppets elicits pity as well. While openly attacking the games of pretense which convention compels people to play, while demolishing the facade of bourgeois respectability, De Filippo nonetheless takes a sympathetic attitude toward the individual victim, showing genuine feelings crumbling under the pressure of an inflexible code of conduct.

De Filippo brings to these themes his own understanding of the popular theater and the theater of the grotesque. Luigi Ferrante remarks that De Filippo's "grotesque is expressed by means of an irony of popular origin which operates in his plays as a means of demystifying hypocrisies and clichés" (13). By ironically decomposing reality, De Filippo reveals the factitious nature of what is taken for reality, displaying in his characters the behavior of man in a post-heroic age. Irony also derives from the playwright's awareness that the values of that period, the age of Fascism, have themselves been shown to be fragile and hollow. The result is a drama of emptiness, of people who have no future.

In the two-act Ditegli sempre di sì (Always say yes!, 1932) the hero Michele is the victim of a conflict between an "idiotic" self-effacement and the practical need for self-assertion. The dominant signifiers here are the "fool" and the "wise man" juxtaposed humorously to suggest that wisdom and madness are not always distinguishable. "Foolish," like "crazy," is a label other people impose on someone who threatens their conventional, rigidly prescribed view of reality, and Michele earns both qualifiers as he returns from "a long business trip" —actually a period in a mental asylum—and starts naively revealing everyone's secrets. Out of the "madness" of social relationships—so De Filippo paradoxically suggests—arises the protagonist's personal history. His is the kind of madness described by Roland Barthes in a review of Foucault, a madness which no longer demands a substantive definition as a disease, or a functional definition as antisocial behavior, but a structural definition as the discourse of reason about nonsense. The madman's derangement derives from his belief that others perceive the same reality as he does, and from his failure to recognize that each person must find the truth for himself. Michele speaks with the voice of madness as he rebels against conventional roles and behavior. But his madness is no mere comic resolution to a funny situation, as it was in Men and Gentlemen; rather, it is a paradoxical twisting of social reality by a man who takes euphemisms and clichés seriously and thus judges the "wise" speakers insane. His position therefore is not farcical, but grotesque. In renewing the old theme of the "madman" who reveals the craziness of sane people, De Filippo relates himself to Pirandello, Dostoievski, and the literature of Decadence in general, but with a Neapolitan spirit.

In these works written during De Filippo's association with Pirandello, the master's evident influence never distorts the essentially popular nature of De Filippo's theater; the solid realism at their base saves them from the dry intellectualism and abstraction that often plague the grotesque theater. Uno coi capelli bianchi (A fellow with white hair, 1935) fails for a different reason: the dialectic of being and appearance, face and mask, and the relativity of truth, is never adequately connected to the other motifs, in particular the conflict between the older generation and the younger. This conflict was of great contemporary concern, however, because of the Fascist regime's reactionary doctrine and praxis, and the play was well received by the Fascist public despite its faults.

With this three-act play De Filippo sets aside the lower-middle-class milieu for the arrogant, well-to-do upper middle class. His growing polemical tendency manifests itself as he turns the grotesque to the task of denouncing a specific bourgeois type, the man of privilege who thinks he has the right to impose his views on others and judge them with an air of superiority. Thus, he creates his first wholly negative character—one who nevertheless deserves our pity. The title of the play is a phrase used to describe an older person who acts in a manner unbefitting his age. Old Battista Grossi should be disinterested, serene, indulgent, and trustworthy. Instead, he is hypocritical, impulsive, and irresponsible. He feigns modesty, but is deeply self-centered. He pretends support for youth, but would be the first to blame them. Simulating innocence, he is flagrantly culpable of inadequacy as a human being.

Battista is obviously a caricature; and, as Freud observes, caricature is a means of rejecting those who stand for "authority and respect and who are exalted in some sense" (14). Nonetheless, De Filippo does not make Battista a pathological case. The character does not act wholly out of malice, but because, after so many years of hard work, he refuses to accept being replaced by his son-in-law as head of the family business. Because everyone respects the wisdom of someone with white hair, Battista can involve himself again in the life around him; but he does so by creating intrigues, suspicion, and discord, perhaps feeling that only in this way can he regain a measure of power and keep up the illusion of youth. Unfortunately, the more he wants to be part of the family and feel important, the more he forces himself on them and the more he is isolated. Through a protagonist like Battista, living an existential drama in a hostile world, the grotesque situation becomes Pirandellian tragicomedy. The protagonist is a victim, his oppressor Time; and, as

Early Works: Range and Versatility

always, Time wins. What seems at first a private tragedy thus becomes a profoundly human drama of universal importance.

Battista suggests a more deeply explored Luca Cupiello. However, he lacks Luca's poetry, remaining an aged child, one who does not understand the cycle of life. In him there is the hypocrisy of Molière's Tartuffe and the slander of Don Marcio in Goldoni's La bottega del caffè. De Filippo has suggested that Battista is a product of capitalism: his father and grandfather created wealth, but he himself has accomplished little, living on what others have done and envying whoever replaces him in the world of work. But, however well drawn, he cannot guarantee a good play, and this one lacks the theatricality that one expects from De Filippo and the cohesion needed for it to live on stage. The contrast between life and form—obviously Pirandellian—is not given an adequate problematic suspense, and the play ends up confused in tone, satirical and documentary at the same time.

A Pirandello short story that De Filippo and Pirandello dramatized together, "L'abito nuovo" (The new suit, 1936) rewards attention by showing how De Filippo could bring his theatrical and thematic abilities to bear on a structure not his own (15). As with other Pirandello short stories, the world of this story is permeated by a bitter sadness that expresses itself in the grotesque deformation of a man's life. The down-at-heel Michele Crispucci has had to suffer the shame of his wife's desertion and now, on top of that, the indignity of the wealth, of suspicious origin, he has inherited at her death. His colleagues, who mocked him as the betrayed husband, envy his newfound wealth. Michele would like nothing more than to give it away to them, but his mother and daughter are opposed to his wish. It is emblematic of his decision to accept the legacy when he comes home wearing a new suit. More than simply a sketch awaiting broader development, the story is perfect in itself, with its own life. In sharp, concentrated language, Pirandello had created a dramatic work which could easily have been expanded as it was and divided into highly effective theatrical scenes.

But when De Filippo transformed it into a play, he did not merely adapt it; the final three-act work is quite different from the original. While the short story concentrates exclusively on the central character and "the difficulty and the pain of lifting his voice out of that abyss of silence in which his soul had been submerged for so long," the play fuses realistic, grotesque, and absurd elements to develop a wider significance and a new spirit. The themes remain Pirandellian: an honest man succumbs because he cannot bear to continue wearing the mask that society imposes on him, or perhaps because he realizes that he is not the person others see in him. But De Filippo continues to develop his own drama, the drama of the man attached to a fictitious reality which he has made for himself and which he does not want to see destroyed by others, but who nonetheless—like Luca, Battista, or Vincenzo—is finally defeated. The abstractly allusive surrealistic tone of the short story is not to De Filippo's taste; accordingly he fills the play with characters of a Neapolitan cast and color.

The New Suit is a satire on the bourgeois mentality which values only money and appearances. It is a bitter play, intended to convey a certain warning to a world in which men of moral scruples like Crispucci are getting fewer, while people like Concettino and the greedy neighbors multiply, infinitely multiplying offenses to conscience. The characters are thus larger in the play than in the story, especially the ex-wife, who from a modest prostitute becomes a new Aphrodite and a symbol of lust. The strongest effects—dramatic, ironic, harsh, and irritating—come from the theater of the grotesque, the vivacity comes from the popular theater. The protagonist is obviously Pirandellian, but his existential suffering is typically Defilippian, a suffering that will become more pronounced in postwar plays like Those Ghosts! and The Big Magic.

In Non ti pago (I won't pay you, 1940), as in The New Suit, De Filippo casts Neapolitan milieu and elements from the popular theater in a Pirandellian mold. Again, the focus is on the paradoxes of everyday life, expressed in a protagonist whose innate stubbornness recalls Pirandello, but whose characteristic habits are Neapolitan: the ancient passion for the lottery, the superstitious belief in the power of dreams, and the dependence on a palliative religion—all illusory antidotes for an incurable poverty. As Carlo Filosa has pointed out, in I Won't Pay You De Filippo makes perfect use of two essential methods of Pirandello's theater: the initial static one of giving the basic paradox a striking but apparently realistic context; and the

Early Works: Range and Versatility

second dynamic one of demonstrating the paradox through an insistent and ultimately sophistic dialectic (16). However, here the similarity ends, for De Filippo is most interested in the moral implications of the situation, and he reserves his most powerful condemnation for ignorance, superstition, and the unscrupulous clergymen who exploit them.

The play centers on Ferdinando Quagliulo, the manager of a lotto office, and his paradoxical refusal to pay off on a four-million lire jackpot. He contends that the winner, his dependent and his daughter's fiancé Mario Bertolini, accidentally intercepted numbers that Ferdinando's dead father had intended to reveal to Ferdinando himself. Unbeknown to his father, Ferdinando had changed addresses, and Mario instead was on hand to dream the prophetic dream! After many quarrels, Ferdinando finally pays; but he calls on the realm of the dead to burden Mario with a problem for every lira. And, indeed, Mario faces so many troubles that he is in the end compelled to renounce the money to free himself from the curse.

Ferdinando's strange refusal to honor a legitimate winning ticket reflects lower- and middle-class Neapolitans' belief in dreams and their connection to the numbers game of lotto, a belief so strong that the Book of Dreams, which assigns numbers to dream objects and events, becomes almost a new Gospel, and superstition becomes a faith inseparably fused with religion. Mario's actions too are reactions to a reality created wholly out of his credulity. Thus, in a Pirandellian way, illusions, desires, and fact become one indivisible reality. However, unlike Pirandello, De Filippo indirectly shows the social nature of the illusions. In his view, superstition is a bow to the fearful and inexorable power that the poor people unconsciously feel lies behind the misfortunes of life. Behind the comedy is thus a bitter reality which justifies De Filippo's sarcastic tone when Ferdinando confronts the priest, the one wanting to know about the life beyond and the reason for his father's mistake, the other defining everything as a "mystery" because he is comfortable with other people's superstition. But De Filippo anticipates the solutions devised by the protagonists of his mature plays, especially Those Ghosts! and The Big Magic, in making Ferdinando —still victimized, still trapped by superstition—defend himself by a bold, realistic-fantastic stratagem. Thus, as much as certain situations or attitudes may suggest Pirandello, the influence is on again, off again, often external—sometimes a matter of plot only. Don Ferdinando's "proofs" for his contention, which tend toward the absurd and surreal, never detract in the slightest from the joyful involvement of the spectator; they are staged with rare comicalness, rendered with an able, relaxed attention to dialogue, and moved by a spirit of excitement.

I Won't Pay You marks the climax of the first phase of De Filippo's career as a playwright and, in its portrayal of the central character, a major step in his artistic development. In this play his special brand of paradoxical fantasy is at its freshest. His unbreakable attachment to the San Carlino theater—its types, manners, and traditional subjects—is evident in the swift pace of the scenes, constantly governed by a logic which makes fantasy and reality work naturally together, and in the lively speech, its style ironic but glib and easy. Nonetheless, the deep seriousness of his comedy shows unequivocally that he entertains a more profound purpose and draws his motives from feeling. The play thus has the playfulness of a joke, but is enriched by human excitement and satirical jabs. Italian audiences responded heartily to Eduardo's ironic messages, chief of which was that to gain a little one must work hard, but to gain a great deal one need do nothing at all.

In the postwar plays corruption, misery, and existential desperation are clearly connected to their social causes, and De Filippo often gives his central character a subsidiary function as his spokesman in condemning social evils. In the early 1940s such criticism, however peripheral, had to be disguised because of the Fascist censorship. Nonetheless, Io, l'erede (I'm the heir, 1942), the last of the early works, points toward things to come. Through yet another Pirandellian plot, De Filippo shows how philanthropy can at times be destructive to both giver and receiver. Once again he exploits a situation dear to the popular Neapolitan theater: Ludovico, a sly sponger, manages to trick his way into a household and live without working. Characteristically, the old theme acquires a new value as a vehicle for criticizing the middle class for its unscrupulous charities and—recalling Brecht's Rise and Fall of the City of Mahagonny—commenting on the generally negative effect that philanthropy has had on social progress. A great success abroad, especially in London and Russia, it was revived in April 1968 at the Valle theater in Rome under the title The Heir and was more successful than it had been a quarter century earlier.

Through the protagonist, Prospero Ribera, De Filippo expresses his contempt for the hypocritical gestures of wealthy landowners who attempt to consolidate their power under the guise of charity. Ludovico would like to live according to a human code, and he therefore proposes a new article to be added to the Code of Civil Law:

> Any person who, in order to sleep in peace at night and to reserve a place for himself in Paradise, commits an abnormal act of kindness against a fellow citizen, thereby removing from circulation and rendering unproductive a portion of our human capital, and who, to justify this same act of egotistical profiteering, attributes it to Christian charity, shall be punished by so many years imprisonment. [p. 527]

Ludovico is no simple sponger, but, rather, a living reproach to the world which had made his wronged father its dependent; and he submits to it only in order to take his revenge on it. This society cannot take hold of its conscience by itself; he must shake it loose from ingrained customs by exaggerated, absurd behavior. In De Filippo's mature plays the main character develops beyond Ludovico's kind of self-critical reaction against the system; in demonstrating his thesis, Ludovico does not really succeed as a human character, though he does manage to bring a certain dramatic force to a situation initially stagnant.

In these last plays De Filippo presents a main character who attempts to free himself from a suffocating existence. However, he gives such painstaking attention to the comic-grotesque chorus, in order to portray the moral and social misfortunes of the lower classes, that the humor becomes painful, the irony too biting, the dialogue sometimes too stylized and even pedantic. But, notwithstanding these defects, De Filippo shows a new sureness of structure. The scenes are always functional, ending neatly either with a cap line or with a dramatic turn of events that gives the action new development. The main characters, in the early works mere sketches, maintain the vivacity of their theatrical antecedents and receive more attention, have more purpose. The early works depend on clownish gimmicks, slapstick, surprise, misunderstandings, double entendre, and comic lines that indirectly underline the main character's interior drama. In the last works the comedy is a higher comedy which usually stems not from the lines themselves, but from the more studied situations in which the main character is put. The secondary characters are almost free of the limitations of type; often they function to increase the main character's desperation or to create an atmosphere that contrasts with that desperation and lets us feel it more.

Chapter Four
Neorealism

The End of the War and New Hopes

Italy was devastated by the 1943 defeat, the agony of the ensuing civil war, and the damage to its physical resources. Paradoxically, however, these setbacks proved less destructive in their effects than the "mutilated" victory of 1918. Indeed, in Italy at the end of 1945 there was an extraordinary moment of real hope. After the many years under Fascism a euphoria of freedom gripped the nation. The great event of 1945 was not so much the disappearance of dictatorship, Fascism, and the monarchy, but rather the affirmation of those principles that animated the Resistance movement: the sudden awakening of the Italians from the long nightmare of war, the rebirth of the nation and its immediate encounter with the struggle for survival, the restoration of individual dignity. Many Italians saw the Resistance as a new Risorgimento because of its struggle against the oppressor, its principles of liberty, justice, and solidarity. It was the Resistance that restored faith in man and his ability to change his own destiny; and it gave rise to the conviction that cultural values could be saved through concrete social and political actions.

For the creative artist, the war seemed to be a period of stasis, but it brought forth the possibility of meditating on the horrors of war and on the socially precarious condition of much of the population. When the conflict finally ended in 1945 and a new democratic government was installed, many artists and writers emerged with a reborn sense of civic commitment. Once the strict censorship of the Fascist regime had fallen, they could turn their eyes freely to the observation of reality. The poverty, social disorder, and suffering that Fascism had forbidden to be represented, and the humanity ravaged by the war, became their subject matter. The attitude of the post-World War II artist was best summarized by film director Alberto Lattuada:

So we are in rags? Then let us show our rags to the
world. So we are defeated? Then let us contemplate
our disaster. So we owe them to the Mafia? To hypocrisy? To conformism? To irresponsibility? To
faulty education? Then let us pay all our debts with
a fierce love of honesty, and the world will be moved
to participate in this great combat with truth. This
confession will throw light on our hidden virtues, our
faith in life, our immense Christian brotherhood. We
will meet at least with comprehension and esteem.(1)

Once again the artist takes up a civic position and functions within society. The theater, the novel, and the
movies were the chief means by which contemporary society
was placed under investigation. Thus, in their masterpieces, De Sica, Visconti, Zavattini, and Rossellini
dealt with the themes of real life, expressing them with
deep emotional involvement and consuming lyricism. The
intensity and fervor of the discovery rendered the artist
inseparable from the man.

Neorealist theater, like neorealist film and fiction,
generally took an instinctively populist or leftist viewpoint, espousing a more or less explicit faith both in
the irresistible power of collective action and in
Marxist dialectical conflict and the inevitability of
historical progress—all supported by a somewhat mystical
notion of Christian brotherhood. However, it did not
necessarily share the doctrinaire optimism of socialist
realism, with its voluntaristic faith in an ultimate,
inescapable positive solution to social problems. The
lower-class characters who are often the protagonists of
neorealistic works lack the conviction that they can
achieve collectively a better status.

De Filippo's theater of the immediate postwar period
reflects such neorealist tendencies. Indeed, De Filippo
had already touched on the themes and ways of neorealism
in some of his early plays. In the thirties, despite the
restrictions imposed by the Fascist regime, he had given
melancholic representation to the humble and the lonely,
to the scarcity both of means of subsistence and of human
resources among the lower middle class and Neapolitan
masses. The experience of the world conflict did, however, affect his ethic and his realism. In 1945 he commented:

The new century, this twentieth century, did not reach

Naples until the arrival of the Allies; here in
Naples, it seems to me, the second world war made
a hundred years pass overnight. And if that much
time has gone by, then I need to write about different things. . . . I feel this need to change, to meet
the challenge to today; if I don't, I'll feel I've
become useless. The type of theatre which attracts me
now would reduce to a minimum the usual plot, intrigue, and mechanical elements, in an effort to get
at the facts of life, everyday life. It would also
allow me, whenever I felt like it, to throw in something new every night, anything that had made sufficient impression upon me during the day. In this
sense, <u>Millionaires' Naples!</u> is my first step in a
new direction. (2)

As the result of the war, De Filippo acquired a more
universal sense of history; he began to view his vocation
as a man of the theater as even more humanly and socially
committed, and he began to express his judgment on his
time with greater authenticity. He no longer merely
toyed with sentimental involvement and commiseration, but
took upon himself a moral task with fervor and moral
indignation. He softened the farcical mood in favor of a
more morally passionate presentation of contemporary
social reality. His engagé theater became a dialogue
with the reader and the spectator, as he called on the
audience to meditate on the meaning of human suffering
beyond the comic dramatic occasion. From this deeply
involved human and social mission sprang a new humanism,
an implicit call to brotherhood, generosity, equality,
and justice.

Like many artists of the period, De Filippo was guided
by a renewed commitment to human solidarity and justice.
Solidarity, or rather the lack of it, is seen within the
context of the family and its extension, society, while
war is considered to epitomize the most treacherous
betrayal of solidarity. Justice, or its betrayal, is
treated mainly in terms of social injustice: the plight
and exploitation of the poor, the meaninglessness of
certain conventions and established institutions, the
abuse of women, and the victimization of illegitimate
children in Italian society. Social commitment is accompanied very often by the denunciation of hypocrisy and
egoism, two destructive elements that the war had merely
intensified.

In most of his postwar plays De Filippo represents resolute, just-minded individuals devoted to a cause and possessing enough strength of conviction to achieve their purpose. Such is the case with Gennaro Jovine in *Millionaires' Naples!*, Alberto Stigliano in *My Family!*, Fabio Della Ragione in *The Local Authority*, and, most of all, Filumena Marturano in the play of the same name. At times, the protagonist serves to observe and comment upon the action and thus acts as a bridge between the other characters and the audience; such is the case with Gennaro. At other times, as with Filumena Marturano, the protagonist expresses the call to a human code—or simply moral indignation—directly, in words and deeds. But, however, reduced by misfortune, this character always finds a way to make his/her choice and act upon it; it is only on the surface that he/she seems to accept his/her condition as inevitable. Such characters are victorious because they are firmly rooted in reality; they have an acute perception of the situation around them, and they do not shirk their responsibility to act in the face of opposition and wrongdoing.

These characters, however, constitute a minority in De Filippo's works. Much more often, the characters at least initially take refuge in illusion, either because they are oblivious to reality or because they lack the ability to cope with it. This is the case with Pasquale Lojacono in *Those Ghosts!*, Calogero Di Spelta in *The Big Magic*, and Ascanio Penna in *The War Memorial*. These characters, however, are never treated by the author with contempt, rather they are depicted with compassion, for they dream Everyman's dream of a perfect world with perfect human beings. Moreover, their vision seldom harms anyone but themselves, since almost inevitably they must face the reality around them and see their ideals mercilessly unmasked as illusions.

Out of the contrast between the protagonist and the comic-grotesque chorus, who represent the blinkered view of the middle class, De Filippo develops a tragic tension and thus the drama of a suffering humanity. Except in *Filumena Marturano*, *My Love and My Heart*, and *The Contract*, where the action begins in medias res, the first scenes generally present a picture of the Naples of misery, superstition, and prying inquisitiveness. The anecdotal episodes and the details emblematic of the hardships of daily life, expressed in the costumes, picturesque gossip, and comic types, create an atmosphere that

Neorealism

clearly portrays the circumstances from which the dramatic situation will emerge. Obviously De Filippo did not completely reject the technique of the late nineteenth-century bourgeois theater. The first act prepares and convincingly develops the situation as the actors see it, providing a dramatic premise that will interest the average spectator. In the second and third acts the development of the premise or premises is toned down, and the author proceeds by allusions and innuendos which convey moral sentiments. At the outset of the play the premise is generally some past event which is responsible for the present situation; the first act lets the audience in on it, and thus the act is like the prelude to the play, preparing for the crisis and ending in a moment of complication and high tension. The second act develops toward another moment of crisis and the revelation of the characters' guilt; and the third act presents the exposure of the characters and the situation, followed by clarification and, sometimes, redemption.

But bourgeois comedy had presented itself as lived experience, substantially faithful to reality in emotional facts, psychological reactions, and dramatic tension. In Defilippian comedy the language of experience, of suffering, is replaced by the language of confrontation. Thus, the drama no longer seems an unfolding of lived events, but a process to be experienced in itself, a process in which the secondary characters, pressed by the main character, generally find themselves confronted with their errors and their responsibilities.

Millionaires' Naples!

Undoubtedly, the turning point in De Filippo's career came in 1945 with the production of Napoli milionaria! (Millionaires' Naples!). With this play, his theater enters a second and more significant phase, for it clearly shows the development of his theatrical abilities and the intensification of his moral purpose. Beginning with this work, the playwright's comical whimsy is balanced in each play against his propensity for moral comment.

Written while Italy was still at war, Millionaires' Naples! is the pulsating dramatic portrait of a city which, though disrupted by war, manages to survive. Here De Filippo exercised an unprecedented artistic courage, becoming at the moment of the Liberation one of the very first artists to use images and materials from contemporary reality; then, with a moral courage no less remarkable, he confronted the Italian audience with their own inner degradation, denying them the alibi of a merely military defeat. Thus, the play also marks a revolutionary moment in the development of the Italian artistic panorama. De Filippo precedes the directors of such films as Open City, Paisan, Bicycle Thief, and The Gold of Naples and in fact points the way along the new road of neorealism. The surrounding world is not just presented and interpreted, but for the first time judged, observed from a polemical perspective, even commented on openly by a character at once both inside and outside the action. De Filippo does not, however, create a piece of socialist realism or dogmatic party propaganda. Although he intends serious social criticism and calls for humanitarian solidarity and social change, he refuses to define political answers.

Millionaires' Naples! is a story of defeat, in particular the defeat of a family in a city thrown off balance by war, afflicted with deprivation and corruption, facing the strain of living with unemployment, shortages, and overcrowding. Here there is no cult of heroism, no false utopia, no pride or exaltation of power. In the title itself, reinforced by the exclamation mark, De Filippo underlines with irony the tragic-realistic inspiration of the play and its sad representaion of the war's ridiculous aspects to which so many of the poor fell victim. Displaying in ironic, hilarious colors the shrewdness that Neapolitans summon in moments of desperation, the play becomes an act of accusal. The vis comica and the farcical effects, imbued with sarcasm, are counterbalanced by a profound anguish, which in the later half of act 2 gives way to pity for the helpless victims of injustice, violence, and other such games of the powerful.

The drama of the Jovine family is typical of that of so many Neapolitan families during the difficult war and postwar years, typical of the drama of so many families of the whole nation and so many other nations of the world. The crack-up of the Jovines is well on the way when the action begins in 1942: black-market coffee and other rations are being delivered to their home by Fascist section leaders, and the family is drowning in illicit goodies. The entrepreneur behind this thriving trade is Amalia Jovine; finding herself in economic straits, with three children, Amedeo, Maria Rosaria, and Rita, and an unemployed husband, Gennaro, she has taken the reins of the family and fights with every trick to support those who depend on her. Her rebellion against poverty thus stands in contrast to the resigned submission and self-sacrifice of earlier Defilippian women. Swearing that she is selling the food at cost, pouring cups of coffee for people who behave more like friends than clients, Amalia runs her profitable black-market business despite her husband's strong disapproval.

The first act develops an atmosphere layer by layer, in a way comparable to the naturalistic theater of Di Giàcomo's The Vow (O' voto), Verga's Cavalleria rusticana, or, above all, Sean O'Casey's Juno and the Paycock—an atmosphere which accounts for the circumstances of the action. It could stand by itself as a complete one-act play; and, indeed, it is quite different from the other two acts. It is a pulcinellata in a naturalistic setting. The curtain rises on the squalid interior of a first-floor slum dwelling, a basso, which testifies mutely to the poverty of Naples. "The confused murmur of people arguing" in the alley and the comments inside the house immediately show how humiliating is the struggle to survive in war-troubled Naples. Amedeo, "physically weak," comes on stage yawning and stretching his stiff arms and legs; "putting on a T-shirt patched and riddled with holes," carrying a ragged towel in his hand, he presents an immediate image of human degradation; and the same effect is created by his poorly dressed sister, wearily washing cups and answering him with an indifference almost equal to his own.

In the first act Gennaro recalls the passive characters of earlier works. At the beginning he limits himself to commenting with veiled bitterness on the present situation. However, the passivity of his humiliating position as one of the unemployed soon becomes his mode of active collaboration. In the midst of a terrifying air raid a police officer comes to inspect the premises, and Gennaro must play a corpse laid out on the bed which hides his wife's black-market goods. Gennaro plays the Pulcinella role is a situation that has all the ingredients of the old commedia. The hovel is transformed in the twinkling of an eye into a house of mourning, and the former customers suddenly become praying nuns, weeping and wailing, and thereby giving a degree of authenticity to the scene as they try to keep the officer from getting close enough to touch the body. The bombardment intensifies, and most of the mourners run for safety, leaving Gennaro and the policeman alone to continue their duel. Humor and pathos are so balanced that they maintain a certain tension even as the situation moves toward its own relaxation and resolution. As the bombs fall ever closer, the officer is forced to admit that, though perspiring desperately, the "corpse" knows how to stay impassive. He thus concludes that he is in the presence of an unusual dead man, and, when he discovers the black-market goods under the bed, he cannot help expressing to Gennaro his admiration for the man's willingness to sacrifice himself for his family. When he promises not to arrest him, Amalia and the children abandon their pretense of mourning and pay their grateful respects to the generous officer, recognizing with the supreme Neapolitan compliment that he "is no fool." The act thus ends with the spectator suspended between amused participation in the theatrical solution and sorrowful awareness that the truce cannot last: Gennaro and the policeman have reached a temporary understanding, a sense of mutual respect, but have not resolved the problem.

Openly farcical, the first act is De Filippo's farewell to his former theatrical style. With the second act there is no change in the classical structure of the play, but there are fewer farcical elements and an increase in realistic portrayal, sarcasm, and anguish. This act too begins with a choral scene which presents the background. The Liberation has come, and foodstuffs are being sold in abundance. The confused voices of the street vendors reflect the intoxication with living which is exploding after so many years of Fascist oppression. Young women in flashy makeup, wearing short, loud-colored dresses and using a language of unusual liberty, indicate the kind of change taking place. The Jovine family shares in the general euphoria. Without Gennaro, who has been deported by the Nazis to a forced labor camp, Amalia is incontestably at the center of the family's illicit traffic. She carries on her business expanded with unallayed determination, with the help of her suitor Settebellizze. But though she may be making millions, she has become a ruthless profiteer and has acquired an insensibility worthy of the worst heartless capitalist. The gap between Amalia and her customers has widened proportionately. The humble but friendly living room has taken on anonymous respectability: now the women are making cigarette deals and trying to catch American husbands, while Amalia has just concluded a deal evicting a late-paying client from his house. All this business has left her no time for motherhood, and her children are drifting toward prostitution and robbery. It is clear that the war has destroyed this family's solidarity along with that of society at large.

But the rendering of accounts must come, above all with Maria Rosaria, who has been seduced and abandoned. The youngest daughter, another victim of maternal neglect, becomes gravely ill. Into this critical situation, suddenly, after a year of imprisonment, Gennaro returns. He is greasy, tattered, old-looking, gaunt, dressed in clothes he has picked up from dead soldiers. He no longer recognizes the place or the people: the "hovel" has been renovated and redecorated, and Amalia is richly dressed. Dazed by what he sees, he hesitates. His wife is thunderstruck. All at once she guesses what he has been through. Each stammers toward an embrace, with Gennaro muttering, "A century, Ama', a century . . .," words which express both the physical and the interior suffering of his odyssey.

Gennaro would like to begin to tell his story to his family, whose spiritual fall he has sensed in their ostentatious life-style. But it is difficult for him to be heard. Oppressed for centuries by the rich, the nobles, the priests, by viceroys and kings, most recently by the Fascists, the Neapolitans now enjoy a fleeting wealth. Rather than evil human beings, they are poor people who have regained a measure of freedom in a chaotic situation. They do not want to listen to Gennaro who by now has learned that the "war is not finished . . . Nothing is finished." Gennaro is a new version of the father figure in De Filippo's theater: he abandons the customary passivity of the other male characters and acts, in order to bring about the family's redemption.

In the third act his attempts to communicate seem to be working. Even Amalia realizes the abyss into which she has fallen. Weary from the pain and shame, she asks her husband, "What happened?", with some discomfort recalling the simple, honest life of their past and seeking the reason for the change that has taken place. What a price to pay for the millions accumulated! This reflection is the origin of the bitter, ironic title: Naples full of millions. Gennaro does not condemn her—indeed, he consoles her, saying that it was all due to the war:

"And it's not just in Naples. It's all over! Everywhere. . . . All we can do now is wait, Ama'. We must wait. Like the doctor said . . . We must wait out the night" (3). In the end compassion replaces condemnation, and despair seems balanced by hope. Gennaro's faith is justified, especially because his message of mutual aid and tolerance is echoed elsewhere in the play. The accountant Riccardo, driven to destitution through the inflated prices Amalia charges, nonetheless provides the medicine needed to cure the youngest daughter. This action proves to Gennaro that solidarity must extend beyond the family to society as a whole.

Gennaro shares the idealism and purity of earlier characters, especially Luca Cupiello; and, like him, he is alienated from his family. But, unlike Luca, he does not take refuge in the past. On the contrary, he is aware of the world around him and of his own responsibilities—above all, toward suffering humanity. His conscience has been sharpened by the experience of two wars. He understands that man must die and that, lacking the assurance of God's help, he must forgive and help others. Luca Cupiello lacks this kind of conscience, and he continues to play at life, oblivious of the looming shadow of death. Gennaro's experience of the war, more than anything else, has given him a renewed moral and humanitarian sense, which in the long run will prevail over the facile cynicism of the rich. Thus, the play's final note of faith in men and their future is no more rhetorical optimism, but a faith in a time when the present disorder will be recognized for what it is: the beginning of a renaissance of the individual's will to free himself from want and poverty, and a sign of new life, substantial, concrete, and vital.

For such achievements, solidarity is essential, and it can be achieved if the government fosters it. But De Filippo sees government as the primary cause of disunity. Since the government has no regard for the interests of the people, it follows that the people themselves have no regard for each other. From the first act, the corruption which will involve Gennaro's family is established as, above all, the corruption of a society founded on selfishness and exploitation. For this reason, and because of the economic problems it has been forced to face along with the rest of wartime Italy, the Jovine family may be partially excused its errors. Their corruption was motivated by the sheer need to survive famine

and destitution. The detailed attention given in act 1
to the effects of the war on the lives of Neapolitans,
already stripped of resources by the authorities and the
classes in power, also points toward this conclusion.
The war has thrown the city into misery and chaos; abandoned to themselves, the people manage somehow to survive. It is not so much that the characters cause their
adverse conditions, but that the conditions motivate the
characters.

The play is thus a profound condemnation of war and a
deep expression of hope that the world will return to
peace and brotherhood. Individual mercy, born in the
members of the Jovine family, becomes social, universal,
extended mercy to the human family. And even the historical moment of World War II is only an image of every
absurd international catastrophe. Out of the history
that it tells, the milieu it conveys, and the humanity of
its characters, the play releases profound and universal
truths and an ever-living and real message. Giorgio
Prosperi came to this same conclusion when he reviewed
the 1971 production:

> How does a war play, written and presented before the
> war was over, achieve now, twenty-six years later, a
> success even greater than that of the highly (and
> rightly) praised first performance? Like every true
> artist, Eduardo had in fact already succeeded in seeing history between the lines of the day-to-day chronicle, and this fact re-emerges a whole generation later, as today's audiences discover, in a play already
> famous, a new play, a play that is their own. (4)

For this same reason the play was a success with public
and critics when it was performed in 1972 at the Aldwych
in London.

Millionaires' Naples! reveals a poet of living and
felt humanity. De Filippo dispenses with journalistic
language, moralistic preaching, facile polemic, and rhetoric. If there is polemic vigor, it comes through in a
drama in which the characters suffer more than they talk
about suffering. Social themes, characters, and events
are placed in perfect balance, so that they are never
overpowering. Perhaps the only weakness in the play is
the character of Riccardo, the representative of the middle class, who, in trying to keep up appearances, has
only suffered more intensely in the cataclysm. Riccardo

is different from the very successful, if one-dimensional, figure of Gennaro, who articulates both the experience of the war veteran and an ancient, totally Neapolitan wisdom, passive and moralistic, sententious and resigned. Riccardo is an ad hoc character, who comes onstage under a pretext, first to be established as a victim and then to make moralistic comments, and he makes a prime contribution to the bitter, painful tone of the play.

The comic elements of the first act, and to some extent the second, blending in the manner of folklore with the ancient popular wisdom, never really relieve the pain of the dramatic situation; and that situation is simply made more painful by Gennaro's experiences, told in sorrowful cadence, more in pauses than in words, and in a subdued dialogue which unties interior knots, to release a new awareness. In the third act the comedy is toned down, giving way completely to melodrama and pathos, as Amalia is rehabilitated and expresses her nostalgic desire to return to a state of peace and love. In general, De Filippo shows the individual, his conscience aroused by the overwhelming disorder in himself and others, aspiring to a new order, to friendship, love, and brotherly union.

Filumena Marturano

Millionaires' Naples! presents Naples during and after the war, its people struggling to survive conditions that they neither created nor understand. At the same time, it studies a way of overcoming estrangement and establishing solidarity, the only means humanity has of enduring. The play is important for showing De Filippo's optimistic side. Along with the next play, Filumena Marturano (1946), it shows the author at the height of his power as a realist.

Immediately after Millionaires' Naples!, De Filippo wrote Questi fantasmi (Those Ghosts!). But he was uncertain what would be the public response to a play with a gloomy atmosphere, a pessimistic viewpoint, and— features unusual in that period of triumphant neorealism —a surrealistic structure, abstract concerns, and metaphysical qualities. Therefore, he wrote the more realistic Filumena Marturano, which he planned to substitute for it, in case Those Ghosts! was poorly received, and thus keep the theater season going. Those

Ghosts! was very successful. Filumena Marturano was staged on 9 November 1946 at the Politeama Theater, Naples, and on 9 January at the Eliseo Theater in Rome, where it enjoyed its first great success with a non-Neapolitan audience (5). Since then, it has been interpreted by the best stage actors the world over and occasionally has run for years.

In this play De Filippo fully realizes his potential for creating complex and absorbing characters. Focusing on the status of a family conceived out of wedlock, he draws on his own experience in a fatherless family, producing a cathartic play (6). Throughout the drama the father is repeatedly subjected to De Filippo's reproof and comes finally to repent his lack of paternal responsibility. The closing lines have particular relevance to the author's life: "One son is like any other son. All sons should be equal!" Like two later works, Le bugie con le gambe lunghe (The Hidden Truth) and De Pretore Vincenzo, this play was written to call attention to the unfair treatment of illegitimate children and to encourage legislation to improve their legal status. The poignancy of the play, however, is due not so much to the dramatist's personal concern as to its simple treatment of a mother's selflessness in her determination to raise her children and give them legitimacy despite a hostile environment. The play remains one of the most satisfying works of the postwar Italian theater and the clearest confirmation that appreciation of De Filippo's theater does not depend on knowledge of the Neapolitan world or the acting ability of the author of his sister Titina, who inaugurated the title role. If we except the figure of the wife in Who is Happier Than I!, Filumena Marturano marks the first time De Filippo develops his social and psychological concern through a female character.

A character of great and complex vitality, Filumena epitomizes with simple forces sin and religious faith, poverty and generous sacrifice, the patience of the humble woman and the dignified revolt of a "liberated one," the throbbing jealousy of love and sublime maternal devotion, the rage of a commoner and the tenderness of a family woman. She is the mother figure so recurrent in De Filippo's plays, like Amalia in Millionaires' Naples!, Elena in My Family!, Concetta in I Won't Pay You!, and Rosa in Saturday, Sunday and Monday. But Filumena is the only female protagonist who not only

initiates action, but fully participates in it. In the
isolation and the sense of morality and idealism she
portrays, she has affinities with many of the male protagonists. Indeed, her position in the family is initially comparable to that held by Gennaro Jovine, Luca
Cupiello, Alberto Stigliano (My Family!), among others,
since she too cannot communicate with her family. Yet
her plight is more serious, primarily because the members
of her family know nothing of her relationship to them
and, secondly, because her past as a prostitute has made
her an outcast in certain circles of society.
    Filumena's life has been a lonely one, spent entirely
in the service of her family. Her only comfort has been
in confiding in her aged companion, Rosalia Solimene, a
limited comfort, however, since Rosalia's social role is
that of a servant. She has not been able to confide in
her sons because that would surely have disgraced them
socially; and she could not speak to her lover, whose
only interest was self-gratification. Having become a
prostitute because of poverty, she keeps up a strenuous
fight against the society that wants to cast her aside,
convinced that her own human rights are worth respecting.
She does not beg our acceptance, much less our pity, for
she rises above easy sentimentality, indignantly denouncing injustice, hypocrisy, and egoism, and affirming her
own inviolable dignity.
    In its simplicity, the play has an almost classic
structure. Very few characters support the main action
between Filumena and Domenico, the two protagonists. The
action is not accompanied by lateral episodes intended to
present an overview, as in the first two acts of Millionaires' Naples!; rather, it proceeds by itself, often in
a sweeping manner, keeping within the realm of the family. The different levels of representation, the long
scenic space dedicated to background and prelude, to
situating the protagonist and his drama, the usual techniques of the naturalistic theater: all these are abandoned. Past events pertinent to the play are exposed
retrospectively, if at all. The spectator witnesses only
conclusions, discussions of the background, and the
conflict which they determine. The action develops out
of a contrast between, on one hand, the rancor of the
humiliated woman, the fury of the threatened mother,
the rebellion of the scorned commoner, and, on the
other hand, masculine egoism, the hatred of the trapped
lover, the sarcasm engendered of revenge.
    Filumena is no longer young. She is a middle-aged

woman who sees herself abandoned for a much younger rival by Domenico Soriano, the man to whom she has dedicated herself entirely for twenty-five years and who now seems to consider her an object to be thrown away after use. The passion of the woman-mother who believes in herself and in her rights rebels against this unexpected treatment. The action begins in medias res. Pretending she is dying, Filumena has obtained from Domenico a marriage in extremis. Now she leaps out of bed and, revealing the trick to him, firmly seizes the reins of the household. In a vigorous scene De Filippo sculpts the characters and establishes their relationships, forging a precise correspondence between ideas and gestures, impassioned senses, and vocal outbursts. Domenico, humiliated, slaps himself repeatedly and rails against Filumena. He cannot accept the fact that a wealthy and well-born man like himself has been made a fool of. But this very exasperation makes him appear weaker than his antagonist, who lets him pour out his feelings. Filumena is and will stay stronger. With a tormented look on her face, the "mask of a past of fights and sadness," deathly pale partly because of her recent pretense and partly because of the storm she knows she has to face, she looks like a "wounded animal ready to pounce" on the foe who has exploited and betrayed her. She has the energy and resourcefulness of the commoner who faces instinctively the necessities of life, accepting it for what it is. Not caring about the consequences, she reacts ready and sure of herself, revealing to Domenico the existence of her three sons. With a passion both delicate and excited, she recalls her mystical encounter with the Madonna and her acceptance of her mission as a mother. For her, it did not matter from which union her sons were conceived: they had a right to live, and without the humiliation that goes with illegitimacy. Despite her solitude and lack of resources, then, she drew on an instinctive morality and chose not to abort. Her words, revealing her inner world and reaffirming her faith, have a high eloquence because they gush forth from sincere and profound feeling; they are rich in theatricality and flow spontaneously, giving a certain freshness to the character's dramatic logic. Her offended dignity, her fear for the future, and her passion as a mother move her to speak:

> They must be told who their mother is. They must come to know all I've done for them. They should love me.

(Fervently) They mustn't feel ashamed when they go and ask for documents or show their birth certificate . . . they're not to be regarded as bastards! They too must have a family to fall back on and to rely on for advice, so they can let their hair down or let off steam. (Pause) They're to bear my name. [1:197]

In the second act Filumena receives the annulment papers from Nocella the lawyer. As in Millionaires' Naples!, here too the impact of the play depends on seizing the "pregnant moment," when the present can be shown to bear the past within it, when the inner existential condition of the characters is revealed so inescapably that their prehistory can be presented. As Filumena explains her circumstances, the roots of the misfortune which drew her to sell herself to man after man are forcefully exposed. The style is perfect in its distribution of gestures, pause, and tension:

(Pause) Mr. Nocella, do you know about slums? The ones at San Giovanni, at Vergini, at Forcella, Tribunale or Pallunetto? Black, smoky hovels . . . there's so many people to a room that in summer it's so hot you can't stand it, and so cold in winter that your teeth chatter. That's where I come from, from one such slum in the Vico San Liborio. As for my family, there were so many of us we lost count. I don't know what's happened to them and frankly I'm not interested. All I can recall are sad, hungry faces, always at odds with each other. You would go to sleep at night and nobody ever said goodnight. [. . .] And the heat. At night, with the door shut, you couldn't breathe. We'd sit around the table . . . there was just one big dish and heaven knows how many forks. I may have imagined it, but I felt that every time I dipped my fork into the dish they were looking at me disapprovingly, as though I were stealing that food. [1:223-24]

In Filumena's paternal home overcrowding and hunger were insurmountable daily problems. The only solution that the poverty-stricken parents had available to them was to turn their children out as soon as possible.

In the fervor and sincerity of Filumena's denunciation one cannot help but feel how much the author's work arises from that deep pity and human solidarity reflected even in his earlier works, but now given a more eloquent tone and form. Filumena has acquired a new morality in her anxious search for purity. The spirit of the woman has stayed sane and noble even under the most degrading conditions. Her description of this past rises to a poetic re-evocation of her desolate resignation to dishonor, the squalid selling of herself from misery to misery, from man to man, to survive, and the silent anguish of the mother. One evening Domenico had told her, "Filume' let's pretend we really love each other!"; but after giving herself to him with true love, she was instead then paid as usual. She had bitterly written the date of that encounter on the hundred lire note and saved it. Now she throws it in his face as evidence that he is the father of one of her sons, saying, "There are things money can't buy!" Her sons were not born merely from a sexual relationship, but also from affection and desire. Implicit in her words and actions is the denunciation of the injustice of labeling the illegitimate, of attaching a stigma to their existence, of blaming them for something for which they are not responsible. Filumena gets around the law the only way she knows how, but De Filippo makes it clear that the law itself is wrong and in urgent need of re-evaluation and alteration, for, as Domenico himself comes to understand, "Children are children . . . and are all equal." When she refuses to reveal which son is his, Domenico finally surrenders and adopts all three, understanding that what counts is the truth of love; tired and a little confused, but satisfied and comforted, he accepts his paternity as a solution to his drama.

At the beginning of the play, however, he is a vain egoist, proud of his youthful conquests, unwilling to surrender to old age, as assisted by the law, he tries to trade the now-faded Filumena for a twenty-year-old. But little by little his heart is opened to the flowering of a belated paternal feeling. At the beginning his middle-class mask prevented him from understanding the sincere passion that animated his antagonist. Upset, with all the violence of his wounded pride, he refused the paternity imposed on him. But then Domenico's drama begins. Here the Defilippian male character re-emerges into the limelight, though he still remains inferior in stature to the female character. When the three young men arrive, it is he who opens the conversation, saying that the next day they will have his last name and therefore he hopes they will cut out that "Don Domenico" and call him "papà."

They reply that they will do so as soon as it comes spontaneously.

Fatherhood must be earned through sincere affection. And in fact that affection is visibly growing in him: he takes an interest in the young men and is moved by the thought that he is the father of one of them. De Filippo creates an attractive balance in the character between pathetic bewilderment and instinctive spontaneity. Domenico scrutinizes every attitude of the young men to discern in one of them some gesture or accent remembered from his youth. The scene is not one of mere silent scrutiny; the father in search of fatherhood relives the story of his youthful sensations. Ultimately, physical paternity loses its significance as Domenico decides to renounce his old self and accept the new feeling, accept in fact his emotional paternity. He has understood the difference between denying or ignoring the lives of others and making oneself a part of them; he has felt the need to forgive and be forgiven, to love and be loved.

At the end, Filumena's dream of a legally constituted family comes true and she becomes the traditional heroine of De Filippo's theater: the wife and mother around whom the lives of her family revolve. This traditional role is enough, ironically, to assure her a place in the society from which she has been excluded. Filumena has aggressively brought into being a family unit which is all the more important because it establishes the principles of brotherhood and social equality. Yet, in this play, as in Millionaires' Naples! and the later My Family!, among others, it is only the father-figure who can provide unity. In this case, however, the concept of the paterfamilias, so basic to the Italian family and society, is qualified: the father need provide only a name rather than guidance and authority. In order to achieve success Filumena has had to direct her efforts not toward her sons, who readily accept her, but toward Domenico, who alone can provide security, even though this security is legal and financial in nature rather than moral.

In this work De Filippo is not far from certain fundamental themes of his contemporary Ugo Betti (1892-1953): through the whole drama, as in the plays of Betti, the protagonists search for themselves, for their own dignity. They finally seize it, freeing themselves from their own egoism and pride in a final outburst of sincere feeling. The indignant, offended, vindictive Domenico and the aggressive, mocking Filumena of the first scene become more intimately sincere and more profoundly human in the last ones.

De Filippo's political and social concerns come across most strongly in Filumena's two long recollections of her past. These are not superfluous rhetoric. Rather, through them Filumena rises to become a symbol of enforced degradation and the will to persevere, to fight, and to sacrifice; in turn, through her resistance, society is put on trial. De Filippo himself has pointed to the presence in the play of symbolism and allegory. Filumena represents the eternal thirst for justice, while Domenico is the State, and the children the various social classes. With Filumena the masses become aware of themselves, their status, their rights, and the deceit of which they are victims; and with her they rebel, to shake the State out of its callousness, indifference, and defense of the privileged. In accepting his collective paternity, Domenico represents the State finding its own balance, and the source of its own progress, only in the equal participation of all societal roles, symbolized by the three sons, worker, businessman, and artist. The State must not neglect any one of them or banish them for something arbitrary like illegitimacy: "when they are men, either they are all children, or they are all enemies." The solidarity and understanding that Domenico comes to know by facing up to his responsibilities toward Filumena and her sons represent love among the social classes; it is the solution that Eduardo proposes and desires for Italian society after so many years of oppression, inequality, and social injustice.

This symbolism and social criticism obviously do not diminish the artistic value of the drama. In Filumena Marturano De Filippo avoids overelaborate structures, reducing the dramatic qualities of his theater to simple, fundamental terms, while maintaining a dignified, classic style. He uses the whole range of his expressive means—not only the dialogue, but also mimic devices, glances, pauses, and especially the stage directions—to give eloquent voice to the feelings, the profound anxieties, which move the drama.

Filumena Marturano's Failure on Broadway

De Filippo's rise to prominence in the international theater has come mainly because of Filumena Marturano. The Moscow journalist who reviewed his Russian performances in 1962 was not the first to call the Neapolitan actor-playwright a modern Molière. But, despite this broad appreciation and worldwide acceptance, Filumena Marturano has had two painful encounters with Broadway. Indeed, the first New York production of Filumena Marturano was a resounding failure. The play had been translated into English by F. Hugh Herbert, the American author of light comedies, under the title The Best House in Naples. The Mexican actress Katy Jurado made her American debut in the title role, and Reno Negri supported her in the role of Domenico. From the beginning the play was beset with troubles. Claude Dauphin, the director, resigned early in rehearsals, and Nick Mayo, the producer, took over the work of staging. The Best House in Naples opened at the Lyceum Theatre in New York on 26 October 1956, and closed after three performances.

Critics who viewed the play were unanimously unimpressed. They noted that the audience's laughter seemed nervous, not genuine; they criticized the international cast's unintelligible mixture of accents, and they felt the play was clumsy, repetitious, and woefully dated. Elliott Norton, in the 8 November 1956 Boston Daily Record, said: "Neither F. Hugh Herbert nor William Shakespeare could have transformed The Best House in Naples into a play of significance," while in the 27 October New York World-Telegram Tom Donnelly wrote that "plays like 'The Best House in Naples' should be not seen and not heard. . . . My final reflection is this: when is bordello-conscious Broadway going to give us a musical version of 'A House Is Not a Home,' with Miss Mae West presiding over the festivities?" Brooks Atkinson, in the 27 October New York Times, wrote:

> It would be interesting to know what sort of play the author, adapter, director, producer, designer and actors thought they were inventing and what were the hopes of the backers. For "The Best House in Naples" is about as pointless a comedy as Broadway has put on in the last fortnight. Let's not even go into the problem of taste.

And Robert Coleman wrote in the 27 October Daily Mirror:

> We cannot understand why Herbert should waste his gift on adapting such corny trivia as "The Best House in Naples," when he can pen such delightful originals as

"The Moon is Blue" and "Kiss and Tell." But if he wants to, it's his privilege. He's earned the right, via previous achievements, to have a brief holiday from merit.

Noting the inertia and sobriety of the first two acts, critics came down heavily on the acting, the direction, and the playwriting. The drama review headline of the Newark Evening News for 27 October read "Boring Bordello." The New York Morning Telegraph of 29 October called it a "rather dreadful play" and said that "'The Best House in Naples' needs cleaning." Critics disliked much of the stage business which Herbert added: the haberdasher's son who painted nude portraits of American actresses on his neckties, and the nurse's removing her sponge rubber "falsies" to prove that she is far from voluptuous. A representative comment by Thomas R. Dash appeared in the 29 October Women's Wear Daily:

> This is a farrago which jumbles together some maudlin sentimentality, some egregious buttock-patting, and many ribald allusions in a framework of a plot that is reeking of sin. . . . For the most part the playwriting is inept and ragged and is perilously close to the amateurish, despite the fact that the Italian author is one of the foremost of his country and despite the fact that the adapter is a man who should know his way around the stage.

The Variety review on 31 October placed much of the responsibility for the failure on the adapter:

> Maybe F. Hugh Herbert should go back to plays about virginity. . . . Although prudes could conceivably find some of this shocking, it is more apt to seem just sophomoric and tedious. It may be approximately as tasteful as dirty words scrawled on the back fence, but hardly a matter of morality. Just possibly, however, there could be ammunition for the grumpy observers who have always found Herbert, even in his fabulously profitable The Moon Is Blue, numbingly adolescent.

Probably few works have suffered more in translation than Filumena Marturano in this adaptation into English. The title which Herbert chose for it—The Best

House in Naples—alone suggests the wrongheaded change in emphasis and tone. Eduardo's original play was not intended to be, nor was it interpreted elsewhere as being, salacious. A comedy of character, Filumena Marturano is less concerned with sin than with redemption.

Eduardo himself has provided some clues to explain the first New York fiasco. After he had finished translating the play into English, Herbert sent a copy of his version to Eduardo in Naples for his approval. Unfortunately, Eduardo knew no English. To get an opinion about the merit of the adaptation, he sent it to a friend, Isabella Quarantotti, his present wife, who was skilled in English translation. After several days he telephoned her for her opinion and was quickly assured that the English translation was true to the original. Reassured, he wired his approval to Herbert. A few days later Ms. Quarantotti called to tell him that when he had called earlier she had not read the script, but had been too embarrassed to say so. Now her conscience had forced her to admit that her earlier judgment had been based solely upon the reputation of the translator.

His fears intensified by rumors of serious tryout problems, Eduardo hastened to leave for New York to consult on pre-Broadway revisions. Bureaucracy suddenly changed his plans. The playwright found that his passport had been inexplicably revoked. Seeking a reason, Eduardo was told that someone had reported him to the United States Consul in Naples as having shown sympathy toward Communism in his plays. He hopefully protested that, unless he could get to New York, a United States producer would lose much money. The protest failed to move the authorities. When the passport was finally issued, it was too late. He never went to New York. Nor did he ever discover who had reported him for Communist tendencies. But, as Eduardo himself has said wryly, commenting on a situation that in many ways resembles the plots of his own plays, "I would not like to think that the informer might have been one of my fellow playwrights" (7).

On 10 February 1980 Filumena Marturano returned to Broadway via London. Because of its success there, producers Danny O'Donovan and Helen Montagu brought Filumena to the St. James Theater. In London, using the excellent translation by Willis Hall and Keith Waterhouse, with direction by Franco Zeffirelli, and with

Neorealism

Laurence Olivier and his wife Joan Plowright in the leading roles, the production was a big hit for two years and won the Best Play of the Year award, the 1979 Comedy of the Year and the Best Actress award for Joan Plowright. The Broadway production had some new faces—Laurence Olivier became director, while Frank Finlay took his place in the role of Domenico— and the end product was as good as in London. The response of the critics, however, was something else, and the play closed after a month. In the 25 February 1980 Newsweek David Ansen pointed out that "despite its two-year success in London, Eduardo De Filippo's funny-sad confection . . . may prove to be too slow on its feet for restive Broadway audiences." In his 11 February 1980 review in the New York Times Walter Kerr attributed the failure mainly to an "imbroglio" of accents:

> At first, it only sounds curious. Mr. Finlay, a superb actor . . . is making use of an Italian accent thick enough to resemble a bowl of minestrone that's been left in the refrigerator for a week. He's good, mind you. Splendid, even. But he doesn't seem to have come from any neighborhood Miss Plowright ever inhabited or visited. She's using a blurtingly defiant speech rhythm undoubtedly meant to suggest her unhappy origins, but it still ripples off her tongue in a tune that is patently British. The supporting players . . . employ a wide, wild range of dialect sounds that would do credit to the Tower of Babel.

This time, however, there were some positive comments, though not enough to offset the bad ones and convince prospective spectators that the play was worth seeing. In Time Magazine G. Clarke wrote:

> There is a narrow line between sentimentality and mawkishness, and not many writers can walk it without falling into the swamp of syrupy sugar waiting below. . . . Eduardo De Filippo, the Italian playwright, is a rare exception. Filumena . . . may be the easiest, most companionable show on Braodway. It is warm, undemanding and, in its own modest way, always enjoyable.

In the Daily News Liz Smith called the play "just the kind of meaty comedy about sex, love, and life that Broadway needs. Frank Finlay will be a Tony Award winner for his sensational playboy-grown-older. Don't miss the delicious Filumena and her men." The Broadway audience will have to wait until next time!

Chapter Five
Reality vs. Illusion
A New Crisis and Encroaching Pessimism

Unlike the works discussed in the preceding chapter—
works written during a period of euphoria at the end of a
destructive war and an oppressive political regime—the
plays written at the end of the 1940s and in the early
1950s convey a mood of pessimism. While never completely
abandoning his preoccupation with the family, sensing the
stirrings of existential philosophy, De Filippo penned a
number of plays dealing with reality and illusion and
man's existential plight. The protagonist of these plays
is free of social or civic responsibility. Nothing stimu-
lates him or fills the emptiness that has come with his
new political freedom. He has no goal in life, no positive direction. Either he is bogged down by what has
happened during the war or he feels impotent to change
things. He is a man incapable of action, devoid of a
workable and realistic sense of life, and too much concerned about ethical conduct. Consequently, some of
these plays may be pretentiously philosophical and too
intellectually literary. The surrealistic atmosphere of
some scenes and the disquisitive nature of the dialogue
contribute to such an impression. In these and other
respects the plays reveal affinities with the works of
Pirandello and the "theater of the grotesque," an earlier
movement which set itself to subvert the dramatic structures and moralistic attitudes of bourgeois comedy. De
Filippo, however, fuses this kind of structure with the
portrayal of customs and manners so that the ambience of
lower-middle-class Naples, with its superstitions and
pathetic attempts at facing life from one day to the next
becomes the vital undercurrent of the plays. When he
fuses the pathetic-surreal tone with a comic-tragic-
realistic one, the sarcastic, hilarious premises of the
bourgeois comedy of adultery—intellectualized through
disquisitions characteristic of the "theater of the
grotesque"—become a tragic testimony to the daily suffering of a man faced with excruciating social and existential problems.

Contrary to what many critics say, then, De Filippo cannot really be labeled an intellectual playwright, interested more in the pursuit of ideas than in representing drama through living characters. Even in these plays, the characters cannot be regarded as puppets and therefore abstractions that lack flesh and blood. Even the protagonist, who resembles the Pirandellian raisonneur and at times presents the playwright's viewpoint and expounds his philosophy, is a man of flesh and blood: his suffering becomes the central concern and elicits a compassionate response. De Filippo does indeed explore such complex issues as the multiplicity of the human personality, the relativity of truth, and the difficulty, if not the impossibility, of establishing the dividing line between reality and illusion. However, his primary focus is on the characters who must deal with the effects that such ideas have on their lives.

The fact is that the De Filippo with the old-fashioned notions—that life has meaning, that if things go wrong the reason for the failure can be found, that meaning and matter may be adequately conveyed by language—is not out of tune with relativistic and existential thinking. Indeed, his thinking is on the same wavelength as that of the avant-garde playwrights. With these plays the theme of a disintegrating world begins to recur with a certain frequency. Nevertheless, these products of the intellectual crisis following the postwar euphoria cannot be labeled completely pessimistic. De Filippo is less concerned with hope or despair than with the need for people, individually and collectively, to understand each other's suffering and thus avoid increasing the victims' pain.

Those Ghosts!

De Filippo hoped that the Italian people had been sufficiently disillusioned by Fascism and the atrocities of the war to be able to exorcise the ghosts of past actions. However, he soon realized that nothing had changed. The country and the world were no less chaotic and blind. The theatergoer still had to become aware of his own condition. To give him that awareness was the aim of Questi fantasmi! (Those Ghosts!, 1946).

The main theme of Those Ghosts! is not really the poverty of the protagonist, the forty-five-year-old Pasquale Lojacono, though that certainly has a direct bearing. Rather, it is the more or less honest and courageous way he chooses to fight the continual assaults of misfortune. Pasquale Lojacono is another of De Filippo's resilient, shabby-genteel heroes. Forty-five years old, a failure at everything he has tried so far, but unbowed, ready to start over, he has been made the rent-free caretaker of a rambling sixteenth-century baroque palace which has been converted into an apartment house. The landlord's problem is that the place is known to be haunted, and nobody wants to move in. Pasquale has accepted the position, conquering his own lively fear of ghosts, and he hopes to set up a boardinghouse for paying guests in the eighteen-room apartment he has the use of. His duties—designed to prove to the neighbors that the house is once again inhabitable—involve making an appearance night and morning at each of the sixty-eight balconies and conspicuously beating carpets (or overcoats, since he doesn't own any carpets!) on the terraces on all four sides. We meet him as he is moving in his furniture, enough for four rooms, with the aid of the superstitious but calculating and none-too-honest doorman, Raffaele. Pasquale's nervousness upon entering the palace is so great that he hugs the live chicken he is carrying so tightly that it suffocates! Raffaele, who would obviously like to see the chicken in his own pot, remarks that no gentleman would eat a chicken that had not been properly killed. But Pasquale is not to be shamed and hangs the bird on a nail on the balcony, planning to cook it tomorrow.

The apartment is supposed to be haunted by the ghosts of a Spanish grandee and his lover who were walled up together there several centuries ago. Raffaele, who had already pocketed a number of items before Pasquale's entrance, warns him that one of the effects of the haunting is that everything disappears. It would, however, be a bad mistake to report the losses, since you never know what the ghosts might do to get their own back! After an encounter with Raffaele's crazy sister Carmela, whom Pasquale takes to be one of the ghosts, the porters arrive with a heavy wardrobe. They are followed by Maria, Pasquale's twenty-six-year-old wife. When Pasquale accompanies her offstage to show her the bedroom, Raffaele takes advantage of his being left alone to steal the chicken. When he leaves and the stage is empty, the wardrobe doors open and out steps the figure of a young man. We will later learn that he is Alfredo

Marigliano, Maria's lover. He places a bouquet of flowers on the table and a plump roast chicken in a drawer. He scarcely has time to get back into the wardrobe when Pasquale enters and sees the flowers. Since Maria has no idea how they got there, he concludes that they are a welcoming gift from the ghosts. As it is getting dusk, he goes out to buy candles, leaving Maria behind to be joined by Alfredo from the wardrobe. We learn that he has abandoned his wife and children for her a year and a half ago. The well-off Alfredo has decided to assist Pasquale in his dream of setting up a boardinghouse in the apartment. He offers Maria the roast chicken. When Pasquale unexpectedly returns, he is dumbfounded to see the figure of a young man standing stockstill in the corner by the wardrobe. (Alfredo had not had time to get back in!) To make conversation and put on a brave face in front of the "ghost," he asks Maria, noticing that the chicken has gone from the balcony, if that really is a roast chicken on the table. There is a long tense pause, with everyone rooted to the ground; then Alfredo, the benevolent "ghost" begins to tiptoe out, with a knowing smile and a half-bow of salutation and complicity, which Pasquale returns. When he has gone, Pasquale collapses in a heap, overcome by the fact that he has really seen a ghost! The curtain falls on act 1.

When the curtain opens on the second act, some time has passed, and the pensione Pasquale has dreamed of has taken shape, exactly in fact as Alfredo had described it to Maria in act 1! The "ghost" continues to visit daily, as Pasquale knows from the money he finds every day in the pajama pocket that is always hanging in the same place.

Pasquale sees no shame in accepting the spirit's generosity, and he remains oblivious to the open contempt of his wife who cannot believe that he has not realized the truth of the situation. Things change only when other "ghosts"—Alfredo's family—turn up and persuade the "ghost" lover to return to them. By now, Lojacono is dependent on the "ghost's" money, and, when the visits and the subsidies stop, he follows the stratagem suggested by the old professor who lives across the alley. He pretends to leave on a business trip, but instead hides on the balcony, hoping that in his absence the ghost will appear. Alfredo does in fact return, hoping this last time to persuade Mrs. Lojacono to leave a husband so contemptible as to take money from his wife's lover. She allows herself to be convinced and goes into the bedroom to get ready. From his position on the balcony, Pasquale sees the apparition and directs to him such a fervent plea that Alfredo realizes that he really does believe—and always believed—him to be a ghost. Pasquale pours out to him all the sorrow of a man whose wife is his whole life and who, unable to rise out of poverty, feels he is losing her. He cannot admit his failure to another man, but he can to a ghost. Alfredo responds by leaving both the woman and a bundle of money behind.

Tailored, like most of Eduardo's main characters, to the stage presence of the actor-playwright himself— something of an alter ego—Pasquale is the protagonist of the unemployed or underemployed Neapolitan petit bourgeois. In spite of everyday hardships, he appreciates life's small pleasures, like "na tazzulella 'e cafè," a little cup of espresso coffee he prepares himself in the traditional Neapolitan coffee pot and on which he delivers a memorable monologue. His napolitanità, and that of the other characters, is corroborated by his popular religious beliefs and superstitions about the souls of the dead and their apparitions.

Of all of De Filippo's protagonists, Pasquale is the one who evokes the most compassion, for he is never shaken out of his idealistic fantasy. He is not reinstated in the family structure, but continues to be despised by the other characters, who think him a willing dupe, while he makes no effort to counteract this opinion, as do Filumena and Gennaro. Closed in his private world, not only is he at odds with his environment, but he never becomes conscious of his isolation. In fact, the ending does not establish harmony in the Lojacono household, for Pasquale has revealed himself only to the ghost. Maria is never made aware of Pasquale's innocence, nor he of her guilt. The author's irony informs the conclusion as Pasquale, satisfied with the money he has received, even goes so far as to hope that the ghost may return in the future. As Ferdinando Maurino points out, the tragedy in the play is all the more poignant because it is felt only by the spectators or readers, who know the truth and sense the main character's betrayal and isolation (1).

In a way, this play continues the social themes of the preceding two works. Millionaires' Naples! showed how simple people are dehumanized, a family ruined, by strained social conditions. In Filumena Marturano the eponymous heroine has become a prostitute for her own survival and for the well-being of her family. In Those Ghosts! the petit-bourgeois protagonist has lost his self-respect because he does not have a job and is poor:

> If you knew how humiliating it is, and sad, for a man to have to hide his poverty and pretend to be playful, with a joke and a laugh . . . Honest work is painful and miserable . . . and not always to be found . . . Without money we become fearful, shy, with a shyness that is embarrassing, bad. [1:196-97]

The whole play is an illuminating image of postwar Italy and a ruthless criticism of Italian society, bogged down, licking its old wounds, and neglecting the renewal necessary after so many years of oppression, fear, and conflict. Eduardo suggests that society can change only through social reform and the modification of out-dated laws. That is why all the characters live and act in 1946 as though they were in 1846 or 1646, and why, too, the action takes place in a baroque building. They represent an anachronistic way of life, the Italian people's way of life, and Lojacono is right when he says at the end of the second act: "The ghosts don't exist, we have created them. We ourselves are the ghosts."

Above all, however, the play reflects problems of an existential nature. This play is far from sharing the neorealist concern with manners. In the opening scenes with Raffaele, the "super," we get a picturesque touch of Naples, with its misery and superstitions, but only so that we will know what the protagonist will be reduced to in the following scenes. The ghosts reflect inner fears arising from social deprivation and spiritual aridity. Pasquale's belief that he must make money in order to preserve his wife's love is another of De Filippo's accusations against society. Society has allowed money to take on an absolute value, as if we could dispel moral evil with material good. Pasquale and his wife can live with a ghost between them only because their union is flawed and communication between them has faded. Yet the denunciation, when it comes, comes not in the long disquisitions of the existentialists, but lyrically.

In this play De Filippo once again takes up certain elements of characterization which go back to the figure of Luca Cupiello, and even further back. Pasquale is one

Reality vs. Illusion

of his most defeated characters, defeated by poverty but not yet degraded, still believing in goodness and keeping hold of a love that he does not want to betray. He is a character with an enormous emotional burden, though he finds it more bearable to reduce his problem almost exclusively to economic terms or, better yet, to believe that his lack of economic success is the direct basis for his distress. Nonetheless, when his hope for economic success becomes desperate, he is prepared to believe in what his fears would have him take as ghosts. But this way of solving the problem only makes matters worse, since the others think that his belief in the ghost is a convenient pretense, judge him to be a cynic, and despise him. When he asserts to his wife that what he does is right and that "he knows his business," these words take on a different meaning in Maria's poisoned mind. The result is painful to the reader, who knows the truth. As Maurino says, here "we have a prismatic reality; for if Pasquale doesn't attain a metaphysical make-believe, he nevertheless believes . . . in something that is not. He . . . is surrounded by a world of fiction, or perhaps even of fairytales" (2).

But Pasquale is pushed to believe in the ghosts not only by the fears caused by poverty, but also by his degrading and discouraging condition; by the extortions, the hypocrisy, the intrigues of those around him; and by his consequent loss of faith in man and his institutions. Thus, the ghosts embody his fear in the face of an uncertain future and the impossibility of winning respect in his milieu. As with primitive beings, in this atmosphere his fears become personalized. The situation, initially Neapolitan and Southern Italian, little by little is transcended. In a sane world no one would believe in ghosts as such. But in a world like Pasquale's real fears beget real ghosts. By agreeing to live in the "haunted" building, Pasquale initially triumphs over these fears. For a moment, at least, the ghosts do not exist. However, as soon as life's problems seem to be unresolvable, not only do the castles in Spain collapse, but so does the will to find a way to face hunger and everyday problems: all the fears which had disappeared return, and with them the ghosts. It is exactly in this blending of real fears and unconscious terrors that we find the emotional basis of Lojacono's credibility. This new development renders the character not only believable, but deeply human.

This play's evident affinity with Pirandellian theater may account for its portrayal, through Pasquale Lojacono, of the soul's eternal, restless, tragic search for a good which cannot exist in the absolute. However, this affinity is due less to direct influence than to shared themes and a common regional spirit. De Filippo's play is no intellectual dialectic, but a warm effusion of feelings in which the Pirandellian disquisitions about truth and pretense, illusion and reality, are replaced by a Neapolitan way of life which reflects the same relativistic, existential problems. De Filippo succeeds in keeping the local and historic reality which conditions his characters; he does not hide it under a universalized representation of anguish. Pirandellian characters try with agonizing desperation to escape from life because they understand how impossible it is to live there. Lojacono listens to the voices of those who love life.

Thus, it may be more accurate to see the play as De Filippo's updating of traditional materials. The theme of the individual coming to grips with the ghosts of his imagination can be found in many pulcinellate. In a scene reminiscent of the commedia dell'arte, which is at the same time an obvious parody of Pirandello's Six Characters in Search of an Author, the members of the "ghost"'s family come to implore Pasquale to show himself a man and send home the deserter of the conjugal bed, but he takes them for the protagonists of the bloody seventeenth-century love tragedy supposed to be at the base of the building's haunting:

Armida.	(Speaking dully) Sir, you see in me not a woman, in these figures not a family . . . You see five ghosts!
Pasquale.	Please be seated.
Armida.	Thank you. (After sitting) I died a year and a half ago.
Pasquale.	Oh, that recently.
Armida.	These two adolescents . . . (Aside, to the daughter) Blow your nose, you . . . And you . . . (To the son who is seized by a facial tic) stop it, control yourself . . . You're doing it deliberately! . . . (To Pasquale) He's so contradictory . . . These two adolescents, I tell you, have been nipped in the bud. (Speaking more strongly, with a

tragic overtone) I was killed in the moment
of loving, in the instant in which the
vibrations of my heart, of my soul, of my
senses . . . you follow me, touching the
acme of fulfillment, you understand, complete bliss . . .
Pasquale. Exactly in that moment? What a pity!
[1:179-80]

Pasquale believes he is witnessing a supernatural event,
and he is enchanted by it; to see better, he gets up on a
chair, on the table, watching like "a spectator who has
paid for a ticket." From punchline to punchline the comedy builds to whirl, and naiveté, pretense, desperation,
and loneliness are combined. The humor in the early
works stemmed above all from unpleasant situations and
misunderstandings and was resolved in gags and jokes with
a vaudeville flavor. Here it has become more subtle and
more painful, for it reflects a more tragic condition.
At the base of the misunderstanding in this scene is not
just the ignorance of the husband who is being cuckolded
and is acting like a fool. What counts theatrically is
really this enchanted man who believes he is helping
souls who want to return to life. And here is the irony:
he lives in a world of ghosts, and the ghosts want to
return to the world of the living. Mistaken identity, a
very common device with De Filippo and one of his attach-
ments to the old theater, acquires new meaning through a
character with a very modern psychology and in a new
situation. The easy laughter caused by Pulcinella's
misunderstandings becomes a caustic laughter evoked by a
self-gratifying idealist moving in a world of fear, mistrust, and deprivation.

The Big Magic

In La grande magia (The Big Magic, 1949) De Filippo
again develops the theme of the relativity of truth and
the falseness of certain middle-class, solidarity-
destroying conventions. Intentionally polemical, he
expands his earlier attack on those who judge the world
from an absolutist point of view and play a game of lies
and pretenses. He ridicules those who, trapped in absurd
situations, attach themselves to illusions in order to

survive. But here he adopts a new tactic, suggesting that the world is a stage where reality and illusion are indistinguishable.

The play opens at an Italian seaside hotel where Otto Marvuglia, a "professor" of magic, is performing for the guests. For a price, the magician agrees to play a trick on a jealous husband, Calogero Di Spelta, by making the man's wife vanish so that she can slip off for fifteen minutes with her lover. In fact, his wife Marta escapes from the sarcophagus in which she is placed through a small door and goes to meet her lover who is waiting with a motor boat to take her away forever. When Calogero insists upon having his wife back, Marvuglia questions him about her, revealing the depth of his suspicion and jealousy, then hands him a small box, informing him that his wife is now inside. The magician tells Calogero that he, the husband, is the only one who can make his wife reappear by opening the box—but only if he has implicit faith in her. Calogero stands transfixed. Should he open the box in spite of his suspicions and risk losing her forever, or should he reveal to the eager jeering audience, by not opening it, his misgivings about his wife's faithfulness? Calogero puts the box under his arm and returns to his table to watch the rest of the performance.

When, in the second act, Calogero shows up at the magician's shabby apartment with the police in tow, Marvuglia must quickly renew his disciple's faith in the subjective nature of things and the reality of illusion. He persuades Calogero that everything is still part of a stage "experiment," that only a few seconds have elapsed since the performance, and that, like everyone else, both of them are simply links in a great chain of social conventions, a network of illusions, each person's game depending on the games of others. And so it develops that Marvuglia and Calogero live the next four years together in symbiosis, the resourceful Marvuglia keeping up the framework of psychological and moral illusions, Calogero paying the bills. Eventually, Marvuglia takes pity on Calogero and urges him to open the box and end the losing game. But Calogero is determined to win. He will open the box only when his faith is complete, and that moment is drawing near. He now realizes that there had been no real communication between him and his real wife, that he had wanted to possess her like an object:

Reality vs. Illusion 101

My wife is enclosed inside here. And I enclosed her
here, in this box! I had become unbearable, egotistical, indifferent: I had become a "husband." . . . I
no longer paid her compliments. I never gave her a
tender word. We couldn't be frank . . . with one
another. We were no longer lovers! But now I believe
. . . I have faith. [1:446]

By coincidence, Calogero's wife suddenly arrives,
wearied by four years of extraconjugal life, and
Marvuglia waits for the opportunity to bring the game to
an end. Calogero is poised ready to open the box: "One,
two . . . and three!" But, with the unpredictable con-
trariness of life, Marta enters a moment too soon, with
the box unopened and Calogero's faith still untested.
Otto would like to see the game end as it began, with
Marta's magical reappearance. But Marta does not want to
cooperate, and instead she confesses to Calogero her
betrayal of him, her disillusionment, and her repentance.
For Calogero, to recognize her adultery would be to
destroy the illusion which has cost him so much, which he
has kept alive for four years as his defense against
reality. Consequently, he rejects her as a false apparition and takes up the game again, keeping the woman of
four years before, whose return he has anxiously awaited,
in the still-closed box. Only thus can he face the world
as a hero.
 The play hinges most directly on the conflict between
the individual and society, a conflict caused initially
by Calogero's lack of faith in his wife and subsequently
by his stubborn belief in illusions. Somewhat in the
manner of Pirandello, the plays sends the spectator off
into a realm of metaphysics, to speculate about the
nature of truth or, perhaps even more, the nature of illusion. At the beginning, the game is simple, linear:
everyone performs magic, and nobody believes in it.
Indeed, there is no gimmick to it: explicitly, so that
no one will misunderstand, the magician explains the
phenomenon as a game of suggestion. The game soon
becomes a test of faith, but gets out of control as players and spectators find themselves playing by rules they
do not know: in this game, as in life, there are no
absolute rules. Man's condition is portrayed as the
result of a mental disposition, a way of seeing things;
social values, like moral values, depend on the faith one

has in them, on the importance the person and society attach to them. De Filippo suggests that man can have faith in his fellowman and believe in his essential goodness only if he can transcend the appearance and accidents that are merely attributes of a moment.

Overpowered by the cruelty of those around him, Calogero lacks this faith, and he succumbs to a society that defines a husband as dictatorial and jealous. Like Lojacono, Calogero finds shelter in the palace of illusions. Thus the pretense becomes a pattern of behavior, a pitiful way of safeguarding his most delicate feelings. To it Calogero attaches himself with the force of desperation, as the last possibility of life that remains. However, the two protagonists are in different situations and respond differently to their entrapment in illusion. Lojacono believes in the ghost in good faith because he hopes it will resolve his financial problem and therefore allow him to preserve his love for his wife and his esteem for his fellowman. But Calogero believes in the magician in order to deny the unpleasant truth and to defend himself against the ugliness of a corrupt, incomprehensible, pitiful world. His "way of behaving is not vulgar connivance or compromise, it is a desperate attachment to a hope, to an illusion which cannot collapse, which must not be allowed even to crack" (3).

As the play shows, Eduardo knows as well as Pirandello how to play tricks with shifting perspective on reality, how to explore the process of self-deception and illusion. Indeed, when The Big Magic was staged in Rome on 20 January 1950, the audience stood up at the end of the performance and shouted over and over, "Pirandello! Pirandello!" The play recalls Pirandello in its theme of reality and illusion, in its act and scene structure, and in the thoroughgoing sophistry which sometimes undermines the naturalness of the dialogue. The noisy, indiscreet characters of act 1 suggest the bourgeoisie of Right You Are (If You Think So), while the behavior of Calogero's family in act 3 recalls Pirandello's Six Characters in Search of an Author.

But the most Pirandellian feature of the play is Calogero's clear affinity with the protagonist of Enrico IV. In both cases sexual rivalry causes the character to withdraw from reality, so that time appears to stand still except for the graying of his hair. The repugnance that each feels for others he transforms into a desire to be as those others see him or want him to be. He wears

Reality vs. Illusion 103

the mask that life—the games of other people—imposes on him, and he rebels when those others want to take it away from him. Each man hides his bitterness behind the shield of illusion, walling himself off from cruel bystanders and harboring resentment against them. Each flees life in order to live, at once both conqueror and conquered, both in control and condemned to eternal isolation. At the conclusion of each play reality threatens to shatter the illusion, but ironically reinforces it and makes it permanent. For a moment just before the curtain falls, there is a manic ecstasy in Calogero's bearing which makes one wonder if he is not conveying the same message as Enrico IV and countless other Pirandellian figures: that a measure of illusion is necessary to make life tolerable. And just as in so many of Pirandello's works, so here illusion and reality are not ultimately contradictory, but combine to form a new reality. Even if the box does not contain Marta, it is not really empty. It contains a faith, a hope which helps to overcome the horrors of life. Without doing anything heroic, Calogero becomes the hero of his own life. Like Enrico IV, like Pirandello's Mr. Ponza and Mrs. Frola, Calogero derives salvation from illusion (4).

But here the similarity ends, for behind De Filippo's play is a heart pulsating with real life. Because it is sensitive to subconscious reality, it shows illusion to be truly painful. At its most intimate level The Big Magic has a regional base: blows to rouse the crowd, jokes from Naples' alleyways, visual effects from the Neapolitan popular repertory, tricks from the dialect comedy. The characters have a human fiber; their words are warm and spontaneous, characteristically intimate. As De Sanctis affirms, they "are drawn from that book of the street and home that we know already; and in their nothingness do they make one think of aristocratic solitudes or cerebral comments" (5). Indeed, it is Calogero's and Otto's scant cerebrality that above all separates De Filippo from Pirandello. Enrico IV is quite lucid. He knows he is not Enrico IV, he knows that the woman has betrayed him. His whole pretense is only a subtle, astute vendetta against her and against the world; he is the one in control, pretending to be crazy and determined to stop time. Calogero, however, though he has moments of lucidity, is always in doubt. More important, Enrico IV presents a closed situation, with a beginning and an end. The Big Magic, on the other hand, presents an open condition, one which envelops everyone. Calogero's condition reflects vast problems which transcend the personal one of jealousy. It implies that if he, and consequently the spectator, knew who had put him in the world, who had made him as he is, and how everything will turn out, both he and humanity would be better off; they would not be groping in the dark, and their social relations would be quite different.

At the center of the play is "the little magic," a string of tricks that is part of the vast network of tricks, present and future, which is life, "the big magic," every trick depending on an infinity of other truths. Each person has his own "box," but he must not look inside it. One could conceivably open all the boxes and perhaps find nothing. If in some we have love, faith, God, we should not try to open them. There is no absolute, universal, knowable truth. We do not know anything about God and our destiny; everything is relative, and if that is so, what does it matter to Calogero if his wife has betrayed him or not? It is enough to believe that she is there, in that box, in order not to accept defeat. Thus "the big magic" of the title comes to represent not a conjurer's trick, but rather life itself. Overcoming his sin of jealousy, Calogero succeeds eminently in the game of life, developing and understanding a faith far beyond the comprehension of Otto or Marta.

Still, Calogero is no champion of irrationality. Rather, he is a victim set on the stage to demonstrate an aspect of human frailty, and one which particularly intrigues Eduardo: the refusal or inability to face "reality." Indeed, Calogero is brother to many other characters in De Filippo's theater who cannot face life: Luca Cupiello, or the Domenico of the first two acts of Filumena Marturano—the Domenico of act 3 has found that flight from reality provides no answer. Eduardo tells us frankly that we need illusions when reality becomes unbearable, as it is for Calogero. However, he also tells us that we cannot alienate ourselves from reality, but instead must turn around and face it as much as we can. He wants us to look behind life's conjuring tricks and contemplate the blood and feathers at the bottom of the cage, the violence and injustice and vendetta and starvation. He seems also to be saying: look your world in the face; it can be apprehended; it can be lived with; it can, perhaps, in time, be changed. And his argument is given power by the awfulness of the world he

Reality vs. Illusion 105

depicts: the only persuasive optimism, like Gennaro's in Millionaires' Naples!, must after all be optimism in the face of overpowering odds.

This view is articulated by Otto Marvuglia, the other central character of the play, as he speaks to the waiter who assists him in his act:

> So you think the sea is vast. You poor, ignorant man. There was a time when I too thought exactly the same thing and I took a dive into the sea. The moment I was in the water, I failed to find enough room to move about freely. The whole of humanity had jumped in before me. One thousand pairs of hands pushed me back roughly, and I was, as it were, squirted back to shore. (Pointing at the auditorium) It's no more than a drop of water, my dear friend. [. . .] A mere drop of water in the center of darkness without end, darkness which persists even during those hours when we imagine the sun has done away with it . . . (Now turns to everyone generally and goes on with typical conjurer's patter) Yes, ladies and gentlemen, the sun may be beating down, but through it I perceive darkness. [. . .] But we could, oh yes: we could destroy darkness with what I call our third eye, if only it were granted to each and everyone of us to possess it. Yes, the third eye: the eye without a window, the eye of thought, the only eye I am now left with. [1:383-84]

In this confession Otto expresses his disillusionment with living in a world that had seemed so "large, enormous, surprising during his youth." He says these words before an imaginary sea in which the audience is immersed. The imaginary sea symbolizes life, while the audience represents humanity, plunged into the sea's darkness without boundary, at times lit up, but by a deceiving sun. The deception is easy to discover, but only with the eye of thought, which penetrates everything and rejects a superficial vision.

The Hidden Truth

The works of the late 1940s apparently spring from the deep moral disillusionment that followed upon the euphoria of the Liberation; they reflect the most negative moment in De Filippo's ethical and existential outlook. The title of the play Le bugie con le gambe lunghe (The hidden truth, 1947) is an ironic variation on the Italian proverb "le bugie hanno le gambe corte" ("lies have short legs"), that is, "the truth will out." Through unexpected turns of events, comic routines, farce, and open sarcasm, De Filippo presents a society once again imprisoned by outmoded moral values and social prejudices, a society which has little respect for truth and morality, which has made external appearances and hypocrisy a way of life; its people obsessively falsify their lives, denying the undeniable and inventing "lies with long legs," which everyone accepts and professes publicly to take as the truth. Obsessed with pride, self-interest, and pretense, each individual sinks deeper and deeper into dishonesty, denying the possibility of a common bond of trust, love, and communication with others. But in The Hidden Truth De Filippo's moralism is always successfully assimilated into the creative effort. His criticism does not stem organically from the play's action—that is, from the central character's condition of suffering and from the hypocrisy and attachment to convention that characterize those around him. The situation should evoke the spectator's indignation; instead, we feel that a thesis is being demonstrated, the playwright's opinions stated and illustrated.

The Hidden Truth explores the plight of society not through a single, representative individual (as in Filumena Marturano) or a family (as in Millionaires' Naples!), but through the daily vicissitudes of a group of families living in one tenement building. The central character, Libero Incoronato, is an "esteemed" expert on stamps and the faithful confidant of his neighbors. Candid and open about everything, he has the task of showing those around him their deceptions. He alone seems "proud of the misery" in which they all live, while the others play a game of appearances to hide their poverty and to preserve their material interests and moral decorum. Even illegitimate children pay the price: at the center of the play is the problem of their ill treatment by a hypocritical society which, rather than place the blame on those responsible, resorts to lies and pretenses. These people accept the fictions less out of a need to protect the innocent than out of a basic desire to keep up social appearances. In fact, as the characters march through Libero's apartment, telling their

Reality vs. Illusion

stories and asking advice, they all reveal their obsession with financial and material security as a means to a socially acceptable image.

Libero is deeply saddened by this continual display of dishonesty and reprehensible maneuvering, and he decides that if his neighbors are going to regard him as a jerk, he might as well capitalize on it and condemn their lies with an even bigger one. At the baptism of his neighbor Olga's many-fathered child, he announces that he has saved up a small fortune over the years and that he plans to marry a chaste young heiress from the North. His fiancée is Graziella, an ex-prostitute. He has been forced to keep his relationship with her hidden until after his sister's engagement, but now he can no longer bear to be suffocated by convention. His announcement does not stem from the same hyprocrisy as prevails around him; he is not hiding behind the ridiculous mask demanded by external proprieties. Instead, he deliberately puts on the countermask of social protest. For him, Graziella is no pariah, but a good person and a victim of prejudice; she deserves acceptance at least as much as the others do.

The crackle of scenic effects from the commedia, the comic stratagems from the Neapolitan farce—still workable in Those Ghosts!—and the multiple intrigues, all take on a vaguely surreal, abstract quality in The Hidden Truth. No more do the characters have an affable humanity and profound suffering, rather they are chiseled with a certain bitter coldness. This stylization of comedy and character is of a piece with the abstract moral criticism, allusive in the first two acts, expressed openly in the bitter philosophy of the last act. The distressing melancholy of a good man's isolation in a world of egoists and blind custodians of appearances, never receives sufficient delineation; and the doubts that stem from a common human condition, the inability to attach oneself to a faith, the creation of a Kafkian atmosphere of absolute incommunicability, all remain rather vague and inadequately realized on stage (6).

The structure of the play is dualistic. On one hand, there is the hero of uncorrupted dignity, aware of how the war has radically changed the course of life and left all kinds of suffering in its wake, how too it has destroyed forever the artificial conventions of a society that has suffered humiliation and defeat. In opposition, there is the comic-grotesque "chorus" who persist in living according to the same old conventions and resolving problems through the same old pretenses and compromises. But, in this, De Filippo's most dogmatic play, the two sides are set up one against the other, and the author's didactic intent expresses itself in contrived harangues. Libero, the playwright's mouthpiece, emerges as the lone righteous man, "free," as his name implies in Italian, from the external and insincere chains of social convention which imprison others. De Filippo vents his bitterness also in his presentation of the "chorus," especially Libero's brother-in-law, Roberto, with his petty domestic concerns, and the clerk, Benedetto Cigolella, and his wife, who provide both easy laughs and a boorish, farcical confirmation of the general corruption and scandal. This attitude is underlined in the stage directions and shows up above all in the open sarcasm with which De Filippo treats the relatives who come to the baptismal reception, a sarcasm which becomes even more bitter in its contrast to the festive occasion and the humor of the guests.

Perhaps this is why Olga's transformation, her discovery of new value through the cathartic experience of motherhood, seems so little motivated. More successful in human terms is the treatment of Graziella, who, having redeemed her errors through the pain of losing her son, retains a sane scorn for pretense and convention and shows an unsuppressible need for love in a society that often loses sight of all human values and all human dignity. Most successful of all are the traditional mishaps, which, in addition to covering hypocrisy with ridicule, create tension and vivacity. But the dramatic technique lacks the usual full support of the language. From Those Ghosts! on, the language of the plays changes, still continuing to express the atmosphere of the lower middle class, but moving away from the Neapolitan dialect of the people and approaching the spoken language of the middle and lower middle class. In The Hidden Truth, however, the ongoing realistic faithfulness which underlies this choice is complicated by the moralism and the abstractness of concept and tone. Therefore, even the language experiences a moment of crisis, losing its communicative freshness.

Perhaps the play is limited by the way De Filippo chooses to direct his criticism against social ills. In Those Ghosts! the focus is on the individual whose freedom of action is limited by social convention. In his

Reality vs. Illusion

society, Pasquale cannot confess his sense of failures—
failure as defined by that society and by his own wife—
to any living person; only by believing in ghosts can he
confess, and accept the providential economic assistance.
But in The Hidden Truth the focus is rather on the
society that defines, accepts, and perpetuates the inhibi-
tions that alienate the individual. The grotesque situation has been made universal, and from it arises the
protagonist's sad humor and even his open sarcasm, which
is lacking in Those Ghosts! But, perhaps as a result
of this shift, Libero comes off as simply too good. He
has none of the weakness, the patience, the comprehensive
wisdom of Gennaro in Millionaires' Naples! nor, like
Pasquale, is he a defenseless victim calling for our
compassion and sympathy. He is clear-sighted, detached
from the situation, ironic in his attitude toward the
words and actions of those around him—perhaps a bit too
rigid in his detachment as he proclaims his indignation.
Especially near the end, his disdain proceeds more from
the author's moralistic impulse than from any struggle
with society's corruption.

The Voices Within

De Filippo's pessimism about human nature, so apparent
in The Hidden Truth, is intensified in the next play,
Le voci di dentro (The Voices Within, 1948) (7).
Taking his approach from the postwar theater of moral
inquest (Ugo Betti and Diego Fabbri), he again portrays a
society that lacks faith in men's ability to support one
another. Through its device of the supposed murder, The
Voices Within intends to reveal, in the words of the
title of the famous French film, that We Are All Murder-
ers or, at least, all guilty, as many of the plays or
moral indictment suggest. Once again, a family is taken
to represent society as a whole. Each of the four members of the Cimmaruta family is prepared, simply on the
basis of a neighbor's dream, to believe that another
member of the family is a murderer.

Alberto Saporito, the protagonist, who, with his
brother Carlo, carries on the family business, decorating
churches and making fireworks for feast days, has had a
dream—or maybe an hallucination, a vision from the realm
between sleep and waking. In any case, he is convinced
that his neighbors, the Cimmarutas, have murdered his

best friend Aniello Amitrano, so he reports the crime to the police, who quickly cart the entire family off to jail, only to be forced to release them almost at once for lack of evidence. Alberto continues to insist that he can find the evidence in the house, and a wave of suspicion sweeps over the Cimmaruta family. Whether there has actually been a murder has not yet been established, but the talk of one is enough to bring out the worst in everybody. Everybody searches frantically for the evidence which Alberto has dreamed of and which now is assumed absolutely to exist.

As the hate, jealousy, suspicion, and envy concealed behind the facade of an apparently united and harmonious family come to the fore, Alberto is terrified by the discovery of so much evil in ferment, and he decides that there was truth in his "dream," that he was not mad but had instead been listening to "inner voices." His uncle Nicola, an eccentric so disgusted with mankind that he has not spoken for over fifty years, communicating, on the rare occasions when he has something to say, by means of exploding firecrackers, makes him understand that the content of the dream was not unreal. Alberto next discovers that, when he was in danger of being arrested for falsely accusing his neighbors, his own brother, Carlo, had schemed to wrest the family inheritance from him. Overwhelmed by distress, Alberto apostrophizes his dying Uncle Nicola; but this time he does not understand the meaning of the distant explosions. The curtain comes down on Alberto and his brother with their backs to each other, silent, like two strangers. The spectator is left to guess at the protagonist's painful search for some feeling, even if it is only pity, which can break the loneliness, and to guess too at his tragic, futile self-questioning, his wondering whether the only possible solution is silence and rejection of the world, and his bitter certainty of the uselessness of every task and every reaction.

The Voices Within is De Filippo's most bitter, most cerebral and surrealistic play. However, although it is steeped in Neapolitan dream love and symbolism, the author does not evade reality. Indeed, reality remains his realm of investigation. In dealing with the theme of the multiplicity of the ego and the contrast between the "inner voices" and the exterior world of appearances, Eduardo presents the desperation of the Italians after the war, the feeling of loneliness, the impossibility of communication, of finding positive common values on which to build a better world: war created a state of insecurity, and it destroyed the ground for "mutual esteem." De Filippo confided to me in an interview that The Voices "is a fierce condemnation of the war and of man and his perennial sordidness; it demonstrates the abyss into which humanity has fallen after the calamity of a ruthless, bestial, useless world war." This time De Filippo intended to conduct his revolt silently because it is useless to speak when no one listens. His spokesman in this play is the enigmatic Uncle Nicola, who has given up speaking becaue humanity is deaf and wicked, and who expresses himself only by nonhuman means, through the explosion of the fireworks. He is isolated on his little landing at the back of the stage and goes to the balcony only to spit on the men below, men who are lost in their intrigues and daily masquerades. His strange method of conversation is an extremely happy invention which acts like a flash of light, illuminating the structure of the play as well as Eduardo's superb lyrical-dramatic temperament. Indeed, when this comedy was first published (in Dramma, 12 April 1949), the distinguished Sicilian poet Salvatore Quasimodo (1901-1968) rightly observed: "this curious colored Morse Code, with its choral function, is a powerful invention which encloses as it were in a circle the whole of comedy, where the ironic, the tragic, and the grotesque elements succeed each other in swift rhythm" (8). For this reason, most probably, the playwright reserved the last word of the play for this character, now invisible. After his death, toward the end of the play, we hear in the distance the firecracker conversation of the late Uncle Nicola to whom Alberto desperately turns for advice on what he should do. From the other world, Uncle Nicola replies in his usual fashion but this time Alberto, who has always translated easily before, does not understand. And once more Quasimodo rightly points out that "the force of the dialogue, its chaste vibration, tells us that we are far above the dense color of dialectical recitation" (9).

But despite the degree of his hermetic involution, De Filippo does not weaken his commitment or limit his denunciation by articulating it through a symbol like Uncle Nicola. Alberto serves as his polemical moral voice in the play. The character develops out of Libero in The Hidden Truth, who decides to emerge from his passivity as a witness and commentator and to act. With Libero he shares his misery and a sorrowful solitude. Confused, even paranoid in the first act, he slowly becomes an accuser of the world and of the forces that have driven him to act so strangely. However, in contrast to Libero, he is forced to include himself and his dishonest brother among the accused. Because of the atrocities of war, almost everyone has lost faith in his fellowman and acts in bad faith. This is why the Cimmaruta family goes to pieces. In the second act Pasquale Cimmaruta accuses his wife out of a combination of hate and jealousy. Then, in one of the most touching moments, which recalls Pasquale Lojacono's address to the ghost in Those Ghosts!, he confesses to Alberto his sad state as a man failed and betrayed. He does not curse, he does not yell, he does not threaten. Without fear of humiliation, he clings to his wife and opens up his heart:

> When the war was over . . . what with the heart trouble and with my arthritis . . . God knows what I suffered . . . I couldn't work any more. My wife, who once used to amuse herself reading the cards for her friends, now, as there was little money coming in, began to make a real job of it. There were customers in and out of the house all day long . . . mostly men. And I stood outside at the door. "Come along, come along, gentlemen! First come, first served! Madame Omarbey has been freshly illuminated today!" Some of them she kept more than an hour in her room. And I was outside there. [. . .] It's life that ruins men! I wasn't like this, Don Albe'. I've always been a good man, I still am. I can still feel the happiness and innocence of my childhood. [1:159-60]

Pasquale behaves like the protagonists of Those Ghosts! and The Big Magic. He finds himself living a divided life—on the one hand suspicious of his wife and fearful of becoming the laughingstock of the neighborhood, on the other hand collecting the profits of her trade. In the end, so he can live in peace, he deliberately suppresses his suspicions and continues to wear the mask of pretense.

 The motif of the dream first appears in Philosophically, then in I Won't Pay You, where the protagonist's dream of a losing or winning lottery number sets up farcical situations. But by 1948 it had acquired a more serious content, as a means of emphasizing a moral disparity.

Reality vs. Illusion 113

In The Voices the dream is the psychosis of war; it is
a result of the terror of the period, of the lack of tranquillity and the scorn caused by war. Alberto is not a
hypochondriac, but a visionary. Sunk in a world where
lies are daily occurrences, where stories are told about
cadavers being made into soap and candles, he lives in a
state of continual shock. He has lost faith and, like
the others, suspects everything and everyone. The dream
gives the suspicious form, the form of a conceivable,
appropriate crime. That is why, when Alberto accuses the
Cimmarutas of the crime, everyone believes it possible.

In the first scenes of the first act, the maid and the
doorman tell their dreams. Like Alberto's, these dreams
are symbolic interpretations of the surrounding reality,
though they also serve to prepare the surreal atmosphere
in which the drama unfolds. Maria's dream, of a white
worm, symbolically reveals the torment of a disintegrating humanity which shows no signs of recovering. The
worm with the black head and the umbrella, which gets
into church by crawling under the door and at the exit
gives her a revolver to kill a beggar, represents
Alberto's brother Carlo, who in the second act leaves the
house with his hat and umbrella, who goes to church daily
but leads a horrifying life. Carlo is the vilest worm;
he has within him the worm of jealousy, envy, hypocrisy.
And "disgusting worms" is what Alberto calls the
Cimmarutas at the moment of their arrest. Furthermore,
De Filippo seems to be suggesting that the Church has
failed because of her preoccupation with the abstract and
vague; instead, she should find God in the practical act,
in the encounter with man, in sincere social commitment.
Now if one goes into church as a "worm," one comes out as
an assassin.

Through the doorman's reverie, De Filippo approaches
the disappointment, deception, and resulting bewilderment
that the Italians experienced at the end of the forties.
It was a period for thinking bitterly about the promises
of April 1945, and the euphoria they had generated.
Realizing how he has been deceived, the average man retreats within himself, seeking in his memory the world of
infancy or adolescence, a remote past that can give him
again its consolation, peace, order, and harmony, none of
which the present, dryly skeptical and convulsed or incomprehensibly contradictory, offers. This condition explains why the doorman dwells on the beautiful dreams of
his youth, which opposes an honest, simple, and happy

time, unfortunately irrecoverable, to the "mistrust" of
the world he lives in as an adult. This juxtaposition of
past and present realities is also present in the speech
by Pasquale Cimmaruta which we quoted, and on him too it
has a desolating effect. These characters are aware that
something is morally wrong in their lives and reject the
notion that because they have lost the paradise of childhood they are irremediably condemned.

These two recollections of infancy, significant to the
moral content of the play, echo an important theme of Ugo
Betti's dramaturgy. The discovery of truth through criminal accusation and investigation is also a characteristic
of Betti's plays, even if De Filippo lacks Betti's logical structure and methodical, progressive development.
In Betti's Inspection (1942) as in The Voices the
arrival of a police inspector at the refuge of a fugitive
middle-class family provokes a series of horrendous
revelations. In both plays the wickedness and deceit
that smolder under the appearance of good-natured family
customs and friendly relations among neighbors are unmasked. Once souls are laid bare, no one is without
guilt.

Situations and themes reminiscent of Pirandello also
appear: the theme of the two selves, the two contrasting
consciences, one the mask of hypocrisy, the other the
repressed egoistic instinct; and the paradoxical contrast
between reality and pretense, reality and illusion, being
and appearing. The Pirandellian dualistic mode of representation emerges too: both the intuitive, emotional,
and subjective mode and the rational, critical, and
objective one, the latter predominating, taking on the
tone of bitter, ruthlessly burlesque irony which ruptures
the solid structure of the bourgeois play. But as Vito
Pandolfi succinctly states, De Filippo does not remain on
Pirandello's terrain:

> The substance of his plays has evolved toward a phase
> later and more timely than that of the contradiction
> between a man's essence, a man's knowledge, and the
> knowledge that others have of his reality. For
> Eduardo the drama does not consist in the impossibili-
> ty of finding a common language between two realities
> from which the logical link has disappeared, but in
> the impossibility of finding a common plane of good
> faith between two realities which have lost their
> moral connection. Whereas Pirandello's characters

yearn to find a suitable expression which escapes the
phenomenology of subjective impressions, Eduardo's
character yearns, in his struggle, to achieve a human,
sincere, honest understanding. (10)

In Pirandello's theater existence is painful mostly
because of an unchangeable destiny; in De Filippo's theater it is painful above all because of a social condition or a foolish choice. De Filippo's theater, then,
deals with unearthing the social and ethical truth of the
daily lives of common people. He does not concentrate
his prosecutory attention on the tragedy of the individual's encounter with his own self in a moment of painful
discovery—an inevitable, catastrophic encounter which
leads to intellectual, dialectical, and metaphysical
disquisition. Rather, he concentrates on the drama that
comes from the individual's encounter with society, from
the clash of human weakness and social injustice. Thus,
the play is not a pure invention of fantasy, though the
encounter may push the individual into a heightened state
of surrealistic tension, but is developed out of a situation that has moral implications very real for contemporary man.

But, notwithstanding this link with Pirandello and the
European intellectual theater, De Filippo has not succumbed to intellectualization. He seems less severely
affected than other modern writers by that heritage of
scientific empiricism and Cartesian dualism, the problem
of healing the schizophrenic division between mind and
body, subject and object. In part, that is because
certain prescientific or archaic attitudes are present in
his cultural milieu. Thus, while other writers find themselves exhausted or debilitated from struggling with the
autonomy of the intellect and the mind-body duality, De
Filippo can readily and frequently affirm the primacy of
the imagination—a power, that is, blending mind, body,
and affections. He has found it easier to retain a sense
of potential wholeness, the reality of moods, and the
tonal aspects of experience.

De Filippo never abandons either the verisimilitude of
everyday reality or the expressive elements of the popular Neapolitan theater. The main character is even now a
modern Pulcinella,

> a poor devil forced into the most reckless situations
> in order to make a living. Downtrodden and derided by

everyone, he is still capable, bitterly it may be, of laughing at them all. A character schooled, then, in the art of lying in self-defense, he is a clever swindler with an unbridled imagination. He lacks all desire to work and is resigned by vocation [. . .]. He is naive and shrewd at the same time, beaten by life and at the same time a winner because of his vocation as a dreamer, which always saves him in the end from tragedy. (11)

De Filippo's Pulcinella comes from postwar Naples, a city of a people plunged in misery, desperation, and rancor, in need of their illusions and of a feeling of solidarity —but also from the eternal Naples, with its passion for the game of lotto, and imbued with indolence, superstition, and cynicism. Thus, the theme of escape from unpleasant reality into the world of illusion, the fight to keep alive one's own reality, is the reflection of real experiences. Illusion is the simplest way to evade everyday misery, pretense the most convenient way to defend from violation of one's innermost feelings.

As in the earlier plays, in these later plays, too, a good dose of theatricality comes from the typically Neapolitan character of the minor roles. In The Voices Within among these characters there is the spinster aunt who takes care of the domestic chores in the make-do-and-mend spirit fostered by the hardships of the war, manufacturing soap and candles from the fat left over from the family meals and sewing provocative clothes for her "palmist" sister-in-law. There is the pleasant, garrulous, sleepyhead maid, a keen observer of her employer's daily life, who indiscreetly reveals the family secrets to the neighbors. And, last but not least, there is the doorman of the building, an interesting exemplar of a very colorful Neapolitan type, the providential factotum at the service of the tenants and always well informed of their health, manias, and moods. These characters are usually the antagonists, underlining and completing the action. They are the Neapolitan populace and the lower middle class: choral figures of the great stage of the streets, alleyways, and balconies of Naples, who chatter, confiding in one another, their confessions scarcely hinted. They recall, like a half-forgotten tune, all the sentimental nuances of the Neapolitan people, with their exuberant joy and their plaintive melancholy; they are the chorus of the ancient Neapolitan theater—the maids,

doormen, neighbors, friends, the vendors of the streets
and alleys, who create the chiaroscuro of the background,
as in the plays of Di Giàcomo and Viviani.
The rich humus of the plays is quintessentially Neapolitan. If it were merely a layer added on, the plays
would have degenerated into simple farces. However,
notwithstanding the theatricality and vivacity it generates, these last three plays do not have quite the
dramatic force of Millionaires' Naples! or Filumena
Marturano. Yet they do demonstrate a definite enrichment both in themes and the techniques of representation.
As he had done in Those Ghosts!, in The Big Magic
the author focuses on the painful drama of a main character affected by two kinds of suffering, one which results
from his discovering his own shortcomings and one caused
by a ruthless society which preys upon his weaknesses.
From this division comes a split in tone: an atmosphere
of sadness surrounds the central character who, because
of the sincerity of his suffering and his inability to
resolve his own dramatic situation, arouses the compassion of the spectator; while a note of irony, almost
mockery, even of bitter resentment, envelops the comic-grotesque world of the "chorus," unconscious of and
perhaps even responsible for the painful situation. In
The Big Magic the protagonist winds up believing in
magic not out of simple cowardice, but because to acknowledge his wife's unfaithfulness would have meant the
destruction of his vital affections—a tragedy for him—
and would have made him a laughingstock. He is victim of
social customs and convictions. In The Hidden Truth,
on the other hand, the comic-grotesque world is placed at
the center of the representation: a world of imposters,
of perpetuators of false conventions, haughty masks
worthy only of contempt. Rather than dominating the
action or being victim, with his sense of superior
conscience the Defilippian character assumes the position
of antagonist and demolishes the lies and hypocrisy of
those around him, denouncing their prejudices, egoism,
and impostures. In The Voices both the main character
and the world around him are at the center of the representation and both are equally developed. The main character, even though he continues to play the part of the
moralist, finds the will to act on what he observes; but
he observes too that he is not very different from the
others and is forced to include himself among the
accused. The result is a deep sense of collective respon-

sibility reminiscent of the plays of Ugo Betti.
In the plays that follow the action is developed to involve the chorus, which, representing society at large, continues to be the object of the author's irony. Nonetheless, the action still takes place within the family; it is concentrated on their private drama, and one begins to perceive some solutions. Eduardo no longer chooses to present his dramas in a symbolic key, creating a surreal, abstract, and hermetic climate; instead, he returns to a realistic presentation, now more rigorous than in the immediate postwar period. Psychological probing, coupled with subtle moral investigation, is more effectively blended into a purely Neapolitan atmosphere, both on the tragic plane and on the comic and the grotesque. In dealing with moral and social issues, De Filippo does not alter his realistic style in the direction of a programmatic Marxist realism. With spontaneity and sincere sensibility, he reflects the states of mind of the man in the street, concentrating on certain collective concerns of the period; and he does it with a new attitude that exalts man's trust in himself. This trust is necessary if we are to face up to and win out against the adversities of life and against the persistent fears evoked by a world in which peace and war have become indistinguishable.

Chapter Six
Family Drama

The Family

After two years of silence, from 1948 to 1950, De Filippo returned to the stage with his pessimistic disillusionment somehow moderated. Now he exalts man's trust in himself, seeing in it a basic way of confronting and conquering life's adversities. The source of this renewal of serenity is his closer examination of the family, always of interest to him and indeed at the base of his dramatic work. Through the family he expresses his principal convictions; and it is mainly and most forcefully in that context that he develops the theme of solidarity betrayed. For De Filippo, solidarity means a feeling of brotherhood, honest communication, and mutual assistance, both material and moral, which must be the goal of any collectivity, be it familial or social. This preoccupation with the family may be the result of his personal experience as a child lacking a father's guidance.

In his first work, <u>Pharmacy on Duty</u>, the family was seen as a kind of companionship which could lead to one partner's exploitation of the other and even to the disintegration of the union. In <u>Philosophically</u> this representation is tempered with the element of selfless love, previously unknown in De Filippo's theater. In <u>Sik-Sik</u> Giorgetta and Sik-Sik are parents-to-be struggling to provide a more secure world for their child. <u>Christmas at the Cupiellos'</u> suggests the need for a strong family relationship at the basis of society. <u>Millionaires' Naples!</u> reinforces the necessity of morality and proves that a solid family unit can be achieved under the most adverse conditions. In <u>Filumena</u> the situation portrayed is unique: not a <u>divided</u> family, but no family at all. At first, only the pieces of a family are present. At the end, the family can be forged only by the woman who has been totally dedicated to motherhood despite the hardships and sacrifice it entailed.

The family as a unit is subject to stress from various forces—war, corruption, poverty, pride, ambition, irresponsibility, the lack of genuine love, the attempt to break with the past—and De Filippo's approach to it becomes progressively more negative through Those Ghosts!, The Big Magic, and The Hidden Truth, his pessimism culminating in The Voices Within. The crisis very often brings about marital unhappiness which is revealed mainly through a disillusioned, middle-aged male protagonist.

 La paura numero uno (Fear Number One) is the first play in which De Filippo takes an optimistic view of the world through the family unit. There are some clear suggestions that man can face any obstacle if he is at peace with himself and able to establish a genuine love relationship with the members of his family. In the next two plays the new direction is clearly shown through moral pronouncements and contrastive structure. In the contrast between the negative side of the play, the pars destruens, the satire on the family's moral and social decadence, and the shorter pars construens, the phase of positive rebuilding, the spectator comes to understand the corruption of society, its need for salvation, and the way it can be saved. In My Family! and above all in act 1, the youngsters' language reflects the materialistic society of the postwar period, which seems determined to reject traditional civic and ethical values in favor of an egoistic pursuit of comfort. The result is a sharp, sarcastic documentation of the moral and social crisis of the contemporary "nuclear family," delineated especially in the relationship between fathers and children. This same satirical inquiry appears in My Love and My Heart, though with less drama and a more amusing irony. Here the relationship between brothers and sisters is shown to be undermined by egoism and hypocrisy, which are veiled in an ostentatious display of love.

 Even when, in later plays, the family would seem no longer to be a central issue—that is to say, no longer the only reflection of the individual's problems, for the conflict presented is now more specifically between the individual and society—in the background there is always the family as the microcosm of this society, suggesting that, despite all efforts to minimize its importance in our society, family structure should be preserved. Indeed, De Filippo constantly defends the sanctity of the family unit, for without that stable basis, there would be more corruption and solitude. However, this does not

Family Drama

imply that the dissolution of marriage should be opposed at any cost; on the contrary, when marriage is an impediment to harmonious family living, it should be terminated. Long before it was legal, De Filippo fought for divorce in Italy, and he himself went through divorce.

Fear Number One

In Fear Number One De Filippo expresses his trusting view of man and the world—recalling that of Millionaires' Naples! and Filumena Marturano—by combining everyday Neapolitan reality with surrealistic techniques which characterized the earlier, pessimistic plays. The mainspring of the play is Matteo Generoso's obsessive fear of a Third World War, a mental fixation recalling those of earlier dramas: the proliferation of false pretenses in The Hidden Truth, the suggestions, countersuggestions, and verbal illusionism of The Big Magic, the superstitions and ghostly apparitions of Those Ghosts!, and the menacing dreams and accusatory hallucinations of The Voices Within. Matteo's fear grows out of the memory of World War II, which will not allow postwar man to let down his guard; and he is kept in his disturbed state of mind by alarming and sensational news in the papers and on the radio, as well as by discussions among friends, who live under the same shadow. In this state of tension he lets every initiative fall by the wayside as he feels virtually paralyzed both in his family and business affairs. Matteo is finally cured when he hears a false radio report that the war has actually broken out.

But the fear of World War III is really only a topical element in the play. Underneath it is the drama of a father, Matteo, and that of a mother, Luisa Conforto. Mariano, Luisa's son and Matteo's daughter's fiancé, disappears on the day of the wedding, and when he reappears, he has a strange story to tell. The night before the wedding his mother Luisa had imprisoned him on the pretext that she was saving him from a possible army callup; only now had he managed to free himself. The wedding comes off a little later than scheduled, and Luisa returns home alone. She has lived in continual fear of losing her sole surviving son in some future war, just as she had lost her husband and her other son in the last one. She has told herself that she would not mind seeing him married to a good, fine girl like Evelina—until he tries to do so. Then, frightened at the prospect of losing him, she tried to prevent the wedding. Only now that every attempt to keep him for herself has failed does she resign herself to the fact. She proceeds to load the furniture with jars of jam and jelly she has put up. Now, sure that no one will take these away from her, she has the tranquillity she desired, and she pours out her affection on them:

> I've taken to these jams. I love them. As if they were my children. When I'm alone and I get a yen for a bit of cherry jam, I talk to it as if it were a living soul. [. . .] The jam is really mine and nobody can touch it. I have the key. And it's not a crime if I lock it up. [3:179]

Luisa's drama comes from her desire to possess her son as she possess her jams and jellies. Her absurd plan of walling up her son reveals an excess of maternal love to which any Neapolitan mother might fall prey (many did wall up their sons to hide them from the occupying Germans). Like Calogero in The Big Magic, she has to learn how to love wisely if she is to come out of her isolation. In fact, her attachment to her jams is precarious and finally unbearable. Only by reestablishing a true love relationship with her son and solidarity with her neighbors can she find coherence and harmony. Once she has done so, she shows herself tender and understanding with the fearful Matteo.

In some respects, this play recalls the Pirandellian ideas and techniques of previous plays. Especially noticeable is the idea of life as a game and the world as a show. In The Big Magic this idea is given body and form by, among other things, the brilliant show of Otto's conjuring, in which the spectator gets a backstage glimpse of all the mechanism of magic. As Bentley points out,

> to be told . . . that Otto had to convince Calogero of the reality of magic is very little compared to actually seeing Otto play his phonograph record of applause and persuade Calogero it is the sea. (1)

The same could be said about Fear Number One when Matteo is tricked into believing war has broken out: to

Family Drama

be told what happened would have meant very little compared with actually seeing the stratagem with the microphone enacted, and the comic sequence which follows. However, De Filippo's ruse is not just a device to show that illusion and reality are indistinguishable and that the world is a stage on which many plays are performed. In these games feelings are hurt and human relationships are betrayed. In such a world man has to find the moral courage in himself and then establish a sense of solidarity with his family and society if he wants to find a peaceful existence.

In the preceding plays De Filippo's habit had been to build the action on a broad, speculative subject, only to have it become incidental to his central purpose as the comedy progresses. In this play, however, the tactic has a deleterious effect. The fear of World War III activates the plot, but becomes obscured in act 3 by the emphasis on family relationships. The unifying theme of the play, the need for moral courage in establishing family and social solidarity, is projected through two different strains of plot, with different tones and different characters. The first two acts focus on Matteo, presenting the contingent events against a burlesque background. The third act, which deals with the vital problem, seems nonetheless to be somewhat disconnected from what precedes. Its tone is pathetic, tending toward the elegiac, as it focuses on Luisa.

This play shows an evolution in De Filippo's artistic development. The atmosphere is not so depressing as in the preceding plays. The Defilippian protagonist—destroyed by the enormity around him, impotent against a world of lies, bad faith, hypocrisy, and unfaithfulness, where war and peace seem so much alike—becomes aware that he must find within himself the capacity for living in harmony with others. "Everyone likes a little sweetness in life," and sweet is the peace that he reestablishes within himself; without it, one risks being an enemy and doing harm even to those one thinks one loves. This conclusion is prepared for in the first and second acts' detailed portrayal of the families' confusion and their comic fear of war, then conducted to the third act's bright, sentimental melody and touched by the grace of its smiling optimism. From the initial scenes which prepare us for Matteo's appearance, the humor is evident, and it is accentuated in the stage directions describing the comically excitable figure of Matteo himself. Comic

too is the excitement over the "outbreak of war," when
Matteo starts buying food by the ton. He regains his
normal dignity only in the third act, when Luisa becomes
convinced that peace is to be found within; then, accepting him as he is, and accepting herself too, she shows
him the importance of understanding—and being—oneself.
The dialogue, in the first act free and easy, more elaborate in the second, becomes reflective and intimate,
acquiring a more meditative tone, in the third. The
development of the theme requires the poetic union of the
two central characters and the two antithetical tones—
the farcical tone of the first two acts and the melodra-
matic one of the third—hand in hand so that the action
can shift from the external comedy toward the inner
issues. We may be left with a slight question in our
minds as to how successful De Filippo is in fulfilling
this intention.

My Family!

Singling out in the middle-class family—a basic
nucleus of human relations—the erosion of traditional
moral values in Mia famiglia (My family!, 1955) De
Filippo does not offer a concrete solution to the problem
at hand, but rather the wisdom of the past and the hope
of communicating this wisdom to others. In fact, financial strain is not responsible for the new family's moral
chaos. Material survival is no longer the central issue.
The Stigliano family belongs to the financially secure
middle class, in an era that no longer feels the direct
effects of World War II. The head of the family is not
unemployed like Luca Cupiello, Gennaro Jovine, or
Pasquale Lojacono. He is a successful radio announcer
who has been able to provide a comfortable home for his
family and enough money to allow his wife to gamble and
his children to engage in thoughtless frivolities. The
crisis, touched off by the violence of war and acceler-
ated by a fiercely materialistic mentality, has become
widespread, affecting the family as a whole. Indeed,
parents and children, young and old, find themselves
facing the same dilemmas, suffering the same anguish.
Although the adults are not immune, it is the young who
are especially attracted by the so-called new values—
easy wealth and "free" behavior. They are struggling to
find a road and a place in life in a time when all the

old certitudes have crumbled and the new ones are not yet built.

The Stigliano family is disintegrating because they have lost their hold on the traditional values. Eager for worldly pleasures and independence, the children Beppe and Rosaria have broken the bonds of family life. The mother too, wanting to be part of this new way of life, gives herself over to card games, losing money and jewels. She does not feel bound either to her children or to her husband; like her children, she rejects the simplicity of attachment to a job and to domestic life. The father, Alberto, who has cherished his offspring as his own self projected into the future, has given up the dreams of his youth and adapted himself to his career in order to make a decent life for his family. As a consequence, he cannot accept his son Beppe's aspirations for a movie career in Paris under the tutelage of an ambiguous figure who thinks he looks like a Greek god in a bathing suit. He cannot understand his daughter's lascivious conduct. Since he is aware of the scorn they feel for him and the way they have ignored his words for years, he has abandoned them to themselves. Lacking the fortitude of Gennaro Jovine in <u>Millionaires' Naples!</u>, to console himself in his loneliness he takes a lover. The situation becomes critical the day a group of the wife's friends arrive to make a scene, demanding that she pay a huge gambling debt. At the shock of the discovery, Alberto loses his voice and therefore his job as announcer. His inability to withstand the crisis mirrors that of Luca Cupiello. But Alberto turns out to be made of stronger stuff. Luca had been spared the truth about his family because of the fragility of his dreams. Alberto was aware of the problems facing his loved ones. His silence is an act of evasion caused, not by the pursuit of dreams, but by his frustration at not being able to communicate with his family. His silence is a positive act, for it gives him the time necessary to reexamine the validity of his principles as well as his position in the family. He can only be prompted to speak by an event that requires his authority and guidance.

His moment comes when his son, suspected of the murder of his Parisian protector, suddenly arrives home, distraught and exhausted. Hearing his story and believing him innocent, like Gennaro Jovine, Alberto finally breaks out of his isolation and calls the police. Then, in a long set speech he addresses his free-thinking, cosmopolitan children, defending the essential values of family life in a corrupt society, and fires at them a string of proverbs based on patriarchal, bourgeois moral wisdom. Then he suddenly stops, looks at them, and says:

> Aren't you laughing? Why aren't you laughing? I'm saying this old stuff and you're not laughing. I'm saying it, you're not laughing, and I'm not ashamed. That's important . . . that's quite important. It means that you tried to make me something useless, but you didn't manage it, and I thought I was dealing with people with a more up-to-date angle on things than me, and it wasn't true. Now that's important . . . that's a miracle! [2:299]

By reaffirming the value of traditional principles in which the virtue and unity of the family are of paramount importance, Alberto overcomes his isolation and asserts himself with his bewildered family, who now are at least willing to listen and be guided. Beppe, counseled by his father, allows himself to be arrested and is proven innocent. Rosaria, also trusting in her father, confides to him on her wedding night that she is not the promiscuous girl he thought her to be, but, like other girls of her generation, felt that she had to appear so in order to be accepted by her peers. This unexpected revelation shatters the last remnants of Alberto's wall of isolation. He now understands the reason behind his children's behavior and is even willing to share in the blame for their corruption. As Carlo Filosa has noted, Alberto achieves solidarity with his family by facing the reality of the moral corruption around him and actively challenging it, in order to replace it with a way of life that does not stray far from the principles that De Filippo had set forth in Millionaires' Naples! (2). At the end, through understanding, the errors of parents and children are overcome as, for both generations, is the old vision of the world. Its ways could become narrow-minded and backward if applied in absolute unyielding terms; but the ancient values are unsuppressible even in the face of new demands and purposes.

At the beginning of the play, the spectator is presented with a drama of the failure of paternal authority, the theme of the old against the young, youth in revolt, and, above all, the drama of the person who, old or young, parent or child, husband or wife, thinks he can

Family Drama

embrace egotistical ideals, ideals that would deny human needs and feelings such as spontaneous and sincere family affection. In My Family! all the characters think they can satisfy their own desires without considering those of others, and all fail. And, contrary to what many critics say, the paterfamilias, Alberto, is not placed above and apart from the others. He is not, as is customary, the playwright's spokesman; indeed, he has stepped down from the pedestal assigned to the traditional father figure, forfeiting his presumed superiority and infallibility. He is a victim of the same mistakes that lead those around him astray. He estranges himself from his family in the same way that the members of his family estrange themselves from him. He is not the weak but honest father of the bourgeois comedies. The characters' hostility arises from their mutual indifference and their own daily failures. It is a vicious circle: the more the individual estranges himself from the others, the more the others exclude him from their life.

Even in this play, the process of redemption can only begin at the cost of a personal trauma, yet it is an indispensable step if the character is to reach an inner clarification. As in Millionaires' Naples!, where the trauma of internment and flight had opened up Gennaro's eyes, while the danger of their little daughter's death makes his wife more aware, so here Elena must suffer the humiliation of her friends' revolt, face up to her husband's loss of his voice, and finally confront a son accused of murder before she can fully realize the collapse of their situation. Even Alberto, though always aware of the situation, can shake off his indifference only when his son is in danger.

In this play, as in so many others, the family is presented as a microcosm of society as a whole. In their affections and their tiffs, their sacrifices and their sacrileges, their confessions and their secrets, the family members reflect the external and internal processes of society. Since the family comprises not only social or economic values, but also more humanly sentimental ones, it lends itself to De Filippo's concerns, which are always more lyrical than speculative. It is not simply the institution as such that interests the author, but the inner feelings, man's relationships with his fellowmen, essential to him however much he may think he can do without them. The happy ending that crowns this play of caustic social criticism is meant to under-

line the validity of returning to certain fundamental
values, even though they be traditional ones.

The possibility of a complete spiritual metamorphosis,
of a pious and comforting fulfillment and redemption of
all the cruelty and pain of the earlier material, is
affirmed in the themes of this group of plays: man,
facing his own reality, must acquire an awareness of
himself and his own state and overcome it. Technically,
the first act, the whole first part of the play, is part
of the "sorrowful theater" of the years between 1946 and
1950—even if the misery and social despair are missing—
when De Filippo seemed above all concerned to render the
spectacle of individual and social collapse. In the
second part of the play, however, the emotional climate
changes and the sorrowful world is opened up to faith and
hope. All the characters develop in this direction. The
protagonist is initially a character similar to those in
the preceding pessimistic plays; alone, he entrenches
himself in his defeat, then, seeing himself as guilty
like the rest, he faces up to reality and takes up his
work with renewed faith. At first, the family members
find it uncomfortable to look at themselves as they are.
Nonetheless, little by little, they are redeemed.

The thematic development is also evident in the stage
directions and in the dialogue. In the first part's portrayal of the family's progressive breakdown, the directions, with their grip on the contingent, along with the
free-and-easy dialogue, pungent and bitter, provide the
satiric choral voice and the realistic presentation of
the contemporary world. In the process of interior clarification, which takes place in the second part, the stage
directions reveal the characters' inner lives, while the
dialogue becomes more reflexive, with warm speeches full
of human passion. And it is not a slow clarification.
In multiplying the scènes à faire, De Filippo also
multiplies the tension, the surprises, and the revelations.

My Love and My Heart

De Filippo again addresses the representative microcosm of the family in Bene mio e core mio (My love and
my heart, 1955). Through a deeper psychological analysis
of his characters, he further extends his study of the
deterioration of moral norms and reiterates the need to
preserve genuine relationships. The return of familiar

Family Drama

comic elements in a pessimistic story of emotional blackmail and exploitation of family ties produces a pensive, melancholy, psychological humor that does not, however, make his irony and sarcasm less bitter. Indeed, as with My Family!, the title itself is an exaggerated Neapolitan term of affection, often cited ironically to suggest the verbal pretense, the overstated emptiness of family affections, and the hypocrisy of those who, out of egoism, toy with the most delicate of sentiments, professing in words a sentimental attachment at odds with the facts.

The play opens with a scene as stirring as that which opens Filumena Marturano. Lorenzo Savastano, a picture-restorer, is discussing with the architect his plans for modernizing his old house in anticipation of his marriage. But his forty-year-old sister Chiarina, an unprepossessing spinster who shares the apartment with him, wants him to leave things as they are. In order to get her way, she steps out onto the windowsill and threatens suicide. To calm her, Lorenzo promises to give up his plans and leave for America, where he has been invited by a client to do some work.

When he returns ten months later, Lorenzo finds himself in the middle of a real mess. His sister, alone and still unresigned to being a spinster, has become infatuated with Filuccio, a young greengrocer in the neighborhood, and has gotten herself pregnant. Far from being dismayed, however, she is instead proud of her imminent maternity, although at times she cannot help feeling ashamed. Filuccio wants to marry her and has a plan for how he can support the family. He will open a bigger and more modern store on another property of Lorenzo's, which could easily be done if the place were given to Chiarina as part of her dowry. He claims to be too timid to approach his future brother-in-law, but his Uncle Gaetano, who keeps the family accounts, is ready to act as go-between. What follows is a scene punctuated by the wheedling refrain "my love and my heart," in which Chiarina explains the request to her brother in more detail. Lorenzo does not want to give in but he is assured that Filuccio really loves Chiarina and is prepared to marry her even without a cent, and will in any case hand over Chiarina's dowry to his needy old stepmother who takes care of his idiot brother. Lorenzo eventually promises to rent them the store and the apartment over it, maybe he will even give it to them outright once Filuccio has shown he deserves it. Before long, however, Lorenzo begins to discover the machinations of his "loved ones." In fact, Filuccio's stepmother Virginia turns out to be wealthy, young, and beautiful, and Uncle Gaetano would like to marry her. Filuccio has managed to forestall this by faking trances in which he speaks with the voice of his late "Daddy," imploring her not to marry. By this trick Filuccio has kept her huge fortune in the family without offending the uncle who does the accounts for both.

Lorenzo is as disheartened at their systematic, calculated repudiation of morality as he is attracted by Virginia's beauty. Accordingly, as deliberately and as methodically as they had done, he contrives his own trick. He asks Virginia to marry him, and she accepts readily. He then announces the wedding to the "loving" relatives in a manner that is a fitting answer to their own would-be deceits, telling them that he is giving the store and apartment to Filuccio and, as the young man had suggested, he has put the property in the stepmother's name. Like Libero in The Hidden Truth, Lorenzo destroys the immorality of others by turning their trickery against them, countering their stratagems with his own and putting an end once and for all to the cloying refrain "my love and my heart."

In this play De Filippo broadens the domestic theme by crossing the bridge from Lorenzo's family to Filuccio's, suggesting that if one could continue from bridge to bridge onward to infinity, one would find the same situation everywhere. In fact, he provides a pair of neighbors to confirm this thesis, combining them with other characters to make a little chorus. Indeed, the central theme of the play, that success is often based on astutely and hypocritically exploiting the affection of others, is presented through a situation that broadens little by little until it threatens to include the whole of humanity.

De Filippo does not limit himself to pointing out that evil exists. Rather, he attempts to pinpoint and unmask it behind the facade of a succession of deceptions and self-deceptions, developing the dramatic situations through the irony with which he invests the psychology of each of the variously scheming characters. The real intentions and psychological structure of the characters are hidden behind a veil of words and come to the surface only gradually, so that the spectator's surprise is continually renewed and the dramatic tension maintained

Family Drama

until the third-act resolution. A case in point is the figure of the spinster sister Chiarina. Her long-repressed femininity intensifies her loneliness, her awareness of her fading youth, and her vulnerability; she thus displays an ambivalent combination of spontaneity and self-interest. Her maternal feeling (which was also a significant factor in the psychological makeup of Olga Cigolella in The Hidden Truth) adds interest to her character. As Mario Stefanile remarks on the effect of her pregnancy on her personality:

> There is no more room for prejudice, no honor to defend, no concern for what people will think or say. This is the finest and convincing moment in the play, this awakening of Chiarina—who has gone from virginity to imminent motherhood, and pregnant and alone, is in love and unafraid. In no time she remakes her life on the basis of this truth, a truth which in her blossoms from a physiological to psychological fact, so poetically rendered on Eduardo's stage. (3)

With her yearning and her pique, her daydreaming and her diatribes, her self-serving poses and her emotional intensity, Chiarina emerges as a great theatrical character. Little by little, her egoism and her generosity both work their way free, only to be submerged again in her relations with the other characters. The spectator faces a succession of events in which the unforeseen dominates until the very last line.

This kind of theatricality, on the other hand, is typical of the Neapolitan theater, which in many respects can be traced back to the masksof the old commedia dell'arte. Indeed, the whole play is developed along the lines of the commedia scenarios. Pasqualino, the mentally deficient young man, with his moronic humor and jests, is cast in the mold of the zanni. And Lorenzo himself, when his sister wants to jump from the window, points out the affinities of the scenes to those of the old theater: "Here we are, playing Pulcinella, Turzillo, Coviello, Chiachieppe." Not only does he recall all the most colorful masks of the commedia dell'arte, but he also links Chiarina's behavior to that of the characters in the popular farces of the San Carlino Theater: "If you step out of the window, a scene from a San Carlino farce will end up in tragedy."

The play's links to the old comedy are evident even in

the stage directions. At one point, De Filippo compares the behavior of Filuccio and his uncle to that of the commedia masks, showing his awareness and obvious pride in this vein of his humor. By inflating certain patterns of behavior, he pushes the play's framework out of proportion, altering its dimension and focus. He thus confirms what the French philosopher Henri Bergson said about caricature, that it reveals an aspect of the author's psyche, marked as it is by "insensitivity" and "ulterior motives." Caricature enables the dramatist to express in veiled terms his own feelings of superiority. The caricaturist, Bergson contends, like the puppeteer, can force his creature to express the most abrasive emotions under the guise of folly: "The art of the caricaturist lies in his ability to seize that frequently imperceptible movement, and to make it visible for all to see by inflating it" (4). De Filippo uses caricature to condemn a general evil and to express his own sense of revolt, his anger at society's hypocrisies.

At the same time, he manipulates his caricatures so as to intensify or slacken the play's pace and thus control its suspense. These figures are placed in an evolving dramatic structure drawn originally from the popular theater. In the early work and those of the immediate postwar period the misunderstandings, the intrigue, and the unexpected turns of events generated comedy and kept the action at a lively pitch. In the later works, however, especially from The Voices Within on, the intrigue assumes the symbolic value of the paradox of life; that is, it takes upon itself the task of revealing the incongruities or "deformations" of life in which the characters are involved. In this respect, De Filippo is both very traditional and at the same time very modern. His modernity consists, not just in the way he renders the inner complexities of life and the silent flow of conscious and unconscious thought and emotion in an outward form, but also in the way he handles the old plot devices, using them to express psychological dimensions of character. The dramatic turn of events is still there, but it is not obvious because it no longer has the old aim of holding the spectator's attention and making him react. The comic or dramatic turning points of the action have become inextricably a part of the mood, the psychology, and the overall problematics of the play, so that they remain almost unnoticed in the complexity of the orchestration. The same holds true for the characters. Now they are sharply delineated, given a more complex and mature psychology; at the same time, they are left almost to be intuited, through a network of subtle allusions. Finally, the comedy little by little has become more intimate and pondered; it has developed from a comedy of cases and types to one of ideas, taking its place as part of an in-depth treatment, rich in humanity and moral and social implications.

Saturday, Sunday and Monday

Sabato, domenica e lunedî (Saturday, Sunday and Monday, 1959) stands as the culmination of all De Filippo's observations concerning the family in the Italian South (5). In it he incorporates his most fully developed and refined depiction of the family ethic, fleshed out with its characteristic feuds, petty jealousies, misunderstandings, and rituals. Indeed, the metaphor that informs the play, the Sunday dinner, at which the members of the family gather to reaffirm their solidarity, is treated as the supreme ritual of Italian family life. Around this ritual the play revolves, and its disruption at the end of act 2 indicates De Filippo's loss of confidence in the viability of the family unit as he saw it in the 1940s. Although the family appears as a thematic element in subsequent plays, Saturday, Sunday and Monday proved to be De Filippo's final tribute to family solidarity.

The members of the Priore family are well-to-do, with a promising economic future; yet their domestic life is permeated by the ill will of a thousand small grudges, bitternesses, and hates caused by daily misunderstandings. Above all, the intimate relations of the parents, Peppino and Rosa Priore, have been deeply undermined by a growing resentment. Even the relations among father and children and grandfather (a former hatter who insists on grabbing the hat of every visitor to the house and attempting to renovate it) suffer, while the presence of Don Peppino's bachelor brother and widowed sister does not make family life easier.

This by no means exhausts the family roll call but it gives some idea of the range of personalities, and De Filippo's mastery in organizing so many rebellious temperaments into a coherent action. Two things keep the development on the rails: the build toward the weekend climax of Sunday dinner and the mystery of Peppino's taciturn detachment. These two elements coincide when, in the second act, during the solemn Sunday dinner Peppino reveals the cause of his hurt silence by publicly accusing his neighbor Luigi of seducing his wife.

In an English or American play this might be a banal accusation. Here it is not: it is a blow aimed at everything that gives cohesion to this society—the ties of marriage and old friendship, the ceremony of sharing food, everything that lies outside the weekly routine. How did it happen? We learn this in act 3, on Monday morning, when the daughter Giulianella explains that Peppino months ago inadvertently insulted Rosa's cooking and then mistook her resentful silence for a sign of her guilty infidelity. His own brooding uncommunicativeness was a vindictive consequence. Throughout the family we see similar opportunities for trivial resentments to smash relationships to pieces.

Don Luigi, the neighbor, has his own explanation for what happens in so many families on Sundays: it is the curse of the weekend. We slog through the working week hoping for some reward at the end of it, only to run into rows and black depressions on the day of rest. All life bogs down in deadly monotony. But we can overcome the loneliness and misery of daily life if we can avoid becoming slaves of habit, be open to self-criticism, maintaining respect for other people's feelings, and keep open a dialogue with others. In one of their private dialogues Peppino and his wife come to realize that their misunderstandings have their source in pride and in lack of communication, which in the depressed atmosphere of the weekend became overpowering.

This play is a return to the Neapolitan world seen from the familiar perspective of Millionaires' Naples! and My Family!, with the same realistic vision, but from a different moral angle. In those plays the disintegration of values was due in part to the confusion of the times. Here it is due to both moral degradations and psychological depression. This new perspective, however, reflects at the same time De Filippo's modernity. There is an unconventionality here that is not anarchy but a new gospel: family, marriage, and friendship should not be clung to simply because of civil or ecclesiastic laws or of blood ties, but should be a spontaneously felt inner need. Marriage, above all, should not be an artificial, unbreakable chain, but a union that is natural, free, not imposed from the outside, and that can be dissolved whenever love no longer exists. Neither laws nor social propriety should be allowed bo change its meaning. Love is not a possession, not a convention of the calendar, but a continuous spiritual conquest. When love ceases to exist, as happens for one of the characters in the play, the marriage contract should be broken. This is the reason that De Filippo presents Aunt Memme's revolt in positive terms.

Aunt Memme, Peppino's sister, is a sixty-year-old widow with a zest for life, a very agile mind, and sufficient financial security to permit her to live as she pleases. She has a passion for reading, is well educated, and is writing an autobiography, Yes, But You Need Courage, in which she recounts how in the past she was able to live her life free from hypocrisy and choose a lover who understood her far better than her husband. Because of her need for honesty, she found the courage to tell her husband, who fortunately understood and accepted the situation. Aunt Memme is an important character in the play—for the critic Fiorenza Di Franco, she is the playwright's mouthpiece (6)—because she articulates a basic concept in De Filippo's theater: when social conventions such as marriage victimize people, and women in particular, they are to be abhorred and rejected. As she speaks to her niece's future husband and expresses her creed, this marvelous old lady voices the author's contention that women must be allowed independence and individuality, even after marriage. The onus is not only on society, however, but on the women themselves, who should not accept a life of false domesticity which goes contrary to their real desires. Nonetheless, De Filippo is speaking only of those women who feel themselves imprisoned in marital and domestic life. Other women may be content to be housewives, like Rosa in this play. The possibility of happiness does exist within marriage; the successful couple of Peppino and Rosa provides a balance for those marriages that do not succeed. But the marriage contract is no guarantee that the relationship will be a lasting one, for Peppino tells us that in all relationships, "one needs courage . . . and purity of sentiments."

Saturday, Sunday and Monday is a delicate and living play. Its vigor lies mainly in the palpable humanity of the characters, whose psychological treatment, unspoiled by intellectual abstractions or moralism, allows them to show their sufferings, their anxieties, and their authentic desires. Although the author pays special attention to the two main characters and to the environment from which they emerge, he does not seem to me to create a "comedy of character" or a "comedy of place," as the critics Giorgio Prosperi and Nicola Ciarletta maintain respectively (7). In fact, the classic structure of the play and the symmetry of the three acts are necessary to the development of the themes and nothing else. In the first and second acts the ill humor and mutual resentment of Peppino and his wife are developed in the same progression. The first act, interwoven from small scenic fragments, opens in the kitchen of the Priore house, where Donna Rosa, on Saturday night, is preparing the ritual sauce for Sunday's pasta. With an occasional ironic jab, the action proceeds, lively and tight because of the mishaps, the contrasts, the tantrums, the suspicions fermenting in silence or manifesting themselves through innuendo, loaded allusions, hesitant and veiled words. The tension, which the silent presence of Peppino burdens to the point of breaking, bursts out at the end of the act.

In act 2, on Sunday, the clouds form and become larger, until they explode during the ritual weekend dinner. Jealousy, which has been growing in a crescendo of comic and grotesque scenes, makes communication even more difficult. In both acts the "sauce," the symbol of a life dedicated to the myth of the family, prepared on Saturday night and served at Sunday dinner, is the catalyst connecting the various scenes. In act 3 the action tends toward a gradual clarification, the dialogue taking on a more intimate tone, then becoming pathetic as husband and wife tenderly recall and comment on their past together, taking from it new strength for the future.

More than any other play, Saturday, Sunday and Monday illustrates the expansiveness of the De Filippo style, designed to give characters precedence over plot. The result of that design is to show people confined by the claustrophobic family world and pulling in different directions. The comedy generally comes where two or more egos collide. "I'm not going to be made to look like a fool in my own house," announces Peppino, donning a hat recently stretched by his father so that it almost comes down to his nose. His father's obsession with hats amounts almost to a sexual deviation. Ready to pat any

Family Drama

passing rump, he is absolutely riveted with desire at the sight of a girl: his eyes glaze over, the Old Bill moustache starts twitching, and out snakes a trembling hand to seize the prey. But there is more to the character than that or Laurence Olivier would not have chosen to play him in London. He too has his drama. He is an old man conscious of being left out and quick to anticipate rejection even before it is voiced; hence, his moods oscillate among deference, charm (when he has a willing audience), defiance, and hurt pride (standing like an ignored dog at the dinner table, stroking his stomach with hunger, but refusing to sit down until he gets his way).

After the war De Filippo's vision ranged from hopeful in the neorealist plays of the immediate postwar period, to pessimistic in the vaguely surrealistic works of the late 40s and the early 50s. In the later works analyzed here that vision acquires a more reassuring cast. In My Family! and especially in Saturday, Sunday and Monday De Filippo shows that he has regained hope in man's ability to control his destiny and make life less painful. Pessimistic resignation is completely dissolved in a vitalistic optimism which, in the remainder of his artistic production, will derive its strength mainly from his social commitment.

Chapter Seven
Theater: The Art of Social Awareness

A Renewed Commitment

The greater part of De Filippo's theater insistently focuses on social justice, or rather injustice: the plight of the illegitimate child, the oppression caused by certain institutions and social conventions, marital fidelity and infidelity, the social status of women, and, above all, the hard lot of the poor. As emphasized throughout this study, De Filippo's theater is on one level committed to curing social ills. Poverty is a hard fact of life, as is very often reflected in the setting of his plays and the living conditions of the characters, who are mainly from the poor and lower middle class. These characters have to endure many physical and moral hardships, which are felt at every level of social life—not sparing even the hallowed institution of the family, through which parents bequeath their destitution and despair to their children, along with the philosophy of survival at any cost and by any available means.

    The need for money and the lengths to which people will go to obtain it are evident in many plays. In Sik-Sik the magician is prepared to submit to painful humiliation and to place his pregnant wife's life in danger, just to make ends meet. In The Christmas Gift the two impoverished newlyweds sell their most valuable possessions to buy Christmas presents they could not otherwise afford in order to demonstrate their love for each other. In Those Ghosts! lack of money causes Pasquale Lojacono marital problems and makes him conquer his fear of ghosts to take up residence in a rent-free building. In My Love and My Heart sister is pitted against brother; in The Voices Within brother plots against brother because of their poverty.

    Throughout De Filippo's whole production the poor are seldom chastised for their wrongdoings. Like Saverio in Pharmacy on Duty, who forgives Enrico his obvious theft

Theater: The Art of Social Awareness

of a prescription, De Filippo, though aware of the wrongdoings of his less fortunate neighbors, is always careful to balance their misdeeds against the motives behind them, tempering his condemnation with a sense of pity. However, in the postwar works written up to the second half of the 1950s De Filippo shows an increasing commitment to change. Many characters attribute their pitiful conditions directly to their poverty or to events outside of their control and implicitly demand public recognition of their plight. Gennaro Jovine, Filumena Marturano, Pasquale Lojacono, and Alberto Saporito, in different ways from most of the protagonists of the prewar plays, are aware of their social condition and imply that, in another world, they could be better off. They do not yet have, however, the power to rebel or the courage to demand a forceful correction or improvement of society.

In the works written since the end of the 1950s the protagonists of De Filippo's plays, no longer satisfied with simply pointing out social problems, demand a solution. The characters' disaffection comes from the understanding that Italy's "economic miracle" of the 1960s and 1970s has not improved the social condition of the class they represent. Indeed, in the new consumer society the financially well-off, eager for more goods, exploit the poor even more than before and have become less concerned with moral values. De Filippo focuses on injustice in terms of the inequality of the social classes, particularly in terms of the exploitation of the poor by the rich. As a result, these later plays are sometimes criticized as offering ready-made social, political, and ideological solutions.

The Art of Comedy

On various occasions, particularly in interviews, De Filippo has explained some of his plays in relation to social conditions or historical events and has expressed his views on the social function of the theater. In 1965 he staged a play that could be considered a manifesto of his artistic principles and a mirror of his ripening social commitment. Basing his plot on Morulli's one-act I comici e l'avvocato (The comedians and the lawyer), he wrote L'arte della commedia (The art of comedy, 1964), a two-act play which recalls Goldoni's Il teatro comico (The Comic Theater, 1750) and Molière's Im-

promptu de Versailles. The play is a programmatic
declaration, a kind of "apologue" or moral fable on the
necessity, function, and importance of the theater in
society. Taking up the theme of theater versus life, he
suggests that theater is inseparable from social truth.
   The action of the play springs from the meeting of two
symmetrically opposed antagonists, the prefect De Caro, a
middle-class official of limited vision, and the head of
a group of strolling players, Oreste Campese. Campese
expresses some of the ideas that Eduardo had already
developed in a letter opposing censorship addressed to
the Minister of Entertainment in 1961: "The attempt to
substitute for what you call 'counterproductive' theater
a theater 'of pure entertainment,' alien to the problems,
anxieties, hopes, and concerns of humanity, and in particular of that portion of humanity which speaks our tongue,
would be tantamount to destroying theater at the very
roots" (1). Through his spokesman Campese, De Filippo
complains that government very often stifles the basic
principles of theater because through fear it compels the
playwrights to a kind of self-censorship. Only the most
courageous playwrights "succeed in overcoming such an
imposition."
   Since his views are not accepted by the Prefect,
Campese challenges him to recognize, among the people he
is scheduled to receive that day, any actors who might
come in disguised as someone else. The Prefect accepts
the challenge with the ironic remark, "feel free to send
over your 'Characters in Search of an Author'; they can
expect a warm reception" [3:437]. In a response that
reveals the changed position of De Filippo's theater with
respect to Pirandello's, Campese hastens to correct the
Prefect:

> No, your Honor. Pirandello has nothing to do with it:
> we are not dealing with the problem of "being and
> seeming." If I decide to send my actors over, I'll do
> so with the purpose of establishing whether or not the
> theater performs a useful function in its own country
> or not. They won't be characters "in search of an
> author," but actors in search of an authority.
> [Ibid.]

In challenging the Prefect to distinguish between life
and art, Campese sets the stage for the test of act 2.
   In fact, in act 2, the Prefect is unable to say

whether he has before him the real people or Campese's actors playing their roles. The first one to come in is the doctor from a nearby village. His situation is rather grotesque, but very real. He complains about the lack of appreciation or respect for his profession: each time he is successful, his clients think the cure is due to the miraculous intervention of a saint. He calls his situation a "real tragedy." One day he performed an operation in extremis to try to save a girl's life, but she had already died: "I was slitting the throat of a corpse. The curtain had closed unexpectedly, before it was supposed to." The people who had been watching attacked him as spectators do actors for a poor performance:

> They were all sitting still and quiet as if they were paralyzed . . . Then they started staring at each other and asking themselves, "Is that how it ends?" "Is it over already?" "But that's impossible!" "Oh, yes!" "Yes, yes, . . . it's over." And then came bestial yells: "Buffoon!" "Clown!" "You and all your colleagues are clowns!" "All of you play the role you have learned by heart, but you are murderers!" [3:444-45]

From the many theatrical images the doctor uses, the Prefect, like the spectator, is ready to believe that the man in front of him is one of Campese's actors; but no one can be certain. The confusion becomes greater with the arrival of the village priest. In every detail of his attitude and style of expression he adheres to the classical caricature of the amusing, rotund, small-town curé, which makes the Prefect suspect that he has to do with another skilled actor. The priest complains that he is tired of marrying couples just because they have to get married, and tired of keeping them together because there is no divorce. His protest is confirmed by the story of Rosetta, which clearly reflects De Filippo's support for the dissolution of marriages that no longer function to the mutual benefit of the partners. Rosetta, her lover Alberto, and Alberto's wife are all agreed that the only solution to their situation is divorce. The institutionalized church, however, refuses to permit such a final separation, even though individual ministers may not agree with the church's stand.

The situation is reduced to complete chaos by the

revelation that the person who had introduced himself as the pharmacist of the village "with a theatrical gesture" has swallowed pills claimed to be poisonous and died. When Campese appears and the Prefect begs him to admit that the man was an actor, Campese turns a deaf ear. A death in the theater, introduced to satisfy the demands of the plot, means that in some part of the world there has been or will be a real death; what is important are the circumstances and the causes of that death.

In the end, the mysterious knot is not untied. An atmosphere of ambiguity prevails, which involves the spectator as well as the Prefect. The spectator too will never know whether what he witnessed were the masks of reality or the masks of comedy, whether those tragic human case histories were the fruit of the actors' imaginations or cruel and distressing real-life experiences. What matters is the reaction that the spectator shares with the Prefect: his confusion at not being able to discern fact from fiction. As in Pirandello's plays, the curtain is lowered before the suspense dissipates. However, the context and the purpose are different: in Pirandello the suspense is metaphysical in nature, while in De Filippo it is moral and social.

De Filippo's insistence on the difficulty of distinguishing pretense from reality, both in life and in dramatic art, suggests that for this playwright art and life are reflections of one another. Art, which is as real as life, demystifies life. The theater is a mirror placed before individual and social reality, before life, to give it order and clarity, dramatizing its essential human elements.

To a question of mine on the meaning of the theater, De Filippo once answered that he believes that "the theater is the desperate daily effort in which man finds fulfillment in his attempt to give life some meaning." He says in this play through Campese: "It is not the action itself that counts. What counts are the circumstances, the particular conditions in the life of a person which allow us to clarify the reasons for that action." The theater, therefore, is not only or simply the mirror of everyday reality, but "the image of truth . . ., of a truth which has something prophetic inside it." Theatrical art is the result of a dialectical rapport between creation and reflection, the spontaneous and the rational. It has value insofar as it suggests or precipitates

a reaction and presents the visible history of an invisible moral and social present and future.
The representation of reality has always been important in De Filippo's theater. Yet the intention to teach through this representation is an element that has grown with the years. The dramatist's original priority was to amuse the public. Gradually this became less important as an end in itself; humor was given a secondary, but complementary role, and the stimulation of the public, moral reflection emerged as the central feature. In this De Filippo resembles many other authors of comedy as the examples of Molière and Goldoni will suffice to show. At the same time, the playwright discarded those aspects of the Neapolitan theater that he deemed irrelevant to modern society, trying not to break with the past, but to revitalize it, becoming himself "the son of Pulcinella" as the title of a later play suggests. Deeply rooted in tradition, De Filippo gives fresh treatment to traditional themes: the importance of the father figure, the integrity of the family unit, the corruption of society. Yet he differs from his Neapolitan predecessors in approaching these themes with a morally didactic intent.

The Top Hat

De Filippo again took up the themes of the social function of the theater and the indissoluble connection between theater and life in the one-act Il cilindro (The top hat, 1965). The play derives its title from the gentlemanly hat that an astute but unlucky man, Agostino Muscariello, inherited when the theater where he worked for so many years as doorman closed down. Now, unemployed and without a pension, he wears it in order to put on a proud face before the people of the backstreet he lives in. He shares a squalid apartment with Bettina, a former prostitute, and their tenants, a young couple whom they have taken in to help with the rent. Rita, the young girl, and her unemployed waiter husband are unable to pay, so Agostino has come up with a gimmick suggested to him by one of his stage memories. It works very well. The very attractive Rita, wearing only a short slip, attends to her toilette on a landing with a window on the street, enticing male passersby to come upstairs for rest and relaxation. As soon as the customer comes in and has paid, she bursts into tears, draws open the curtain, and shows her "dead" husband, laid out for the wake on the bed the customer was expecting to share with her! She explains how much she loved him and how poverty has forced her to prostitute herself. Rita's role-playing works well: the dismayed customer runs away, or, if he does not, Agostino enters wearing his impressive top hat and accusingly shows him the door.

The ruse works until one of the prospective customers sees through the trick. He ignores all protestations and offers to pay double, double again, for his satisfaction. Nor does he give in when confronted by Agostino or when the "dead" man finally gets up, outraged. Nothing can dissuade him from his goal. He climbs onto the bed and lies there waiting for Rita to keep her end of the bargain. After some hesitation, the prospect of such a large sum proves to be too much and the husband gives in and pushes Rita toward the bed. But the man is old and has fortunately fallen asleep, and when he wakes up, they make him believe he has already had his pleasure. He leaves happy, telling Rita he is willing to pay for her favors any time she wants and he is much admired for his persistence by the crowd of onlookers who have gathered.

Ironically, as the couple congratulate themselves on getting out of the bind with a substantial profit, an argument breaks out because the money is much more than they need to pay the rent. Rita thus discovers the falseness of Agostino, Bettina, and her husband, once the price was high enough. Only luck saved her. She decides, therefore, that if she must sell herself, at least let it be for a profit, and so she abandons the three of them to accept the offer of the rich old man, who seems to have the real "top hat": money.

Rita and the trio begin by playing roles for a living and end up living the roles. Life is a stage, and role-playing is as real as living: the two are inseparable. Like Pirandello, De Filippo sees human life itself as theatrical, aiming toward, and only realized in, the tragic epiphany. De Filippo's missionary impulse is channeled into a personal social vision. His view of things is pessimistic, he does not take his pessimism to the extreme, since he sees the possibility of salvation through social change. To be authentic, theater must have a social end: the correction of absurd social conditions.

Very often, as Rita's husband says, "life hounds a

poor man so, that in the end he has only two choices—to be a fake dead man or a real one." Few people commit suicide, but simulated death is not less fatal. As it is for these characters, life can be absurdly miserable. In such a world, a man may find an answer to his plight in deceiving his often no less poor and ignorant fellowmen; but that answer is a poor means of self-defense because in reality he can never win this way. What's more, Agostino succeeds in impressing only poor people with his top hat. When he is faced with rich and well-educated people like the old man, the "top hat" loses its suggestive power.

The Top Hat reveals the moral corruption that can stem from social injustice. The degradation of the victims of a society in which the needy and deserving are denied aid—the middle-aged Agostino, a veteran of two wars is now left without any pension—and in which those who want work, like Rita's young husband, can find none, is undeniable. But the degradation of those in power who perpetuate such a state of affairs is no less real. In this work, which shows De Filippo's pessimism at its most bitter, the author makes an implicit accusation against those in authority who, with their enigmatic and awesome powers (symbolized by the top hat), work for the rich, oppress the masses, and prevent them from recognizing certain elementary truths of social justice. In the twenty years that have elapsed since, for his black-market bread, Gennaro Jovine played the role of a dead man in Millionaires' Naples!, the social conditions of the Neapolitan masses have not changed. Only their cynicism has grown, and the urgency of De Filippo's social commitment has thus become more pronounced and direct.

The Role of Hamlet

De Filippo had dealt theatrically with the theme of the unity of theater and life in a prewar one-act play, La parte di Amleto (The role of Hamlet, 1940). As one might expect, in this early work social commitment is not one of his main concerns. A play in the tradition of "theater on theater" and something of a caricature of the theatrical world, The Role of Hamlet portrays a rather common state of spiritual wretchedness and narrowness found in the private as well as the artistic life of some theater people.

The events unfold on the stage before a performance of Hamlet. At the center of the action is the pathetic figure of a veteran provincial actor, almost seventy, who, forced by time and changing tastes to give up acting, has become a stagehand in order to make ends meet. Given half the chance, he is always ready to relive a few moments of his former greatness; but the actors are even more cruel than the audience which forced him off the stage. On this occasion, the leading actor has been fired because of a fight with the leading lady. The younger actors make the old actor believe that he has been chosen to stand in for the leading man in the role of Hamlet, and they even give him Hamlet's costume to wear. When he is told that the leading man will again be playing Hamlet, theater and life become as one: the moment of disappointment crushes the illusions of the old man, who had been expecting to play a character himself proverbially disappointed and disillusioned.

With this play, De Filippo opens yet another window on the nature of theater as life. What is portrayed is the dramatic clash of opposed values: art as dream and art as craft, the actor as artist and the actor as a man with daily needs, the theater as spectacle and the theater as an attempt to represent life. This last issue—of interest also to Pirandello—has constantly concerned De Filippo. For him, theater abolishes the distinction between art and life; art is seen as an aspect of life, and the theatrical presentation as no longer separate from life, but intimately fused with it. But what interests De Filippo most is the process by which the personal thoughts, feelings, and life experiences of the author or the actor find external expression in dramatic action. This is the concern reflected in The Role of Hamlet. In The Art of Comedy, however, the text and therefore the production are, and must be, socially committed; only thus can theater keep its original and most important function in society.

Chapter Eight
Plays of Social Protest

De Pretore Vincenzo

Beginning with De Pretore Vincenzo (1957), De Filippo takes up as his overt and dominant themes the demand for popular justice and the condemnation of those powerful institutions that exploit the masses. Indeed, what emerges from a close scrutiny of his later plays is his militancy in exposing what he considers to be the injustices of society. Though not always optimistic about the results, he advocates change within the existing system through legal means—even if the constituted authorities are not always to be trusted. His comments on marriage may now seem dated, given the new Italian divorce laws. We should bear in mind, however, that these laws have still to be socially accepted on a large scale, as is the case too with the status of illegitimate children and equality for women, at least in marriage. The unequal distribution of wealth and its consequences, however, are continuing, universal problems, and they attract the playwright's strongest concern.
De Pretore Vincenzo represents an important innovation in De Filippo's artistic development, both for its new solutions to formal and technical problems and because of the widening breadth of his social commitment. Forsaking the familiar domestic setting of the lower-middle-class apartment, he places the individual's fight against social injustice in a new context, against new backgrounds, giving his themes vast political resonance. His setting is still Naples, with the precarious circumstances of the Neapolitan people, who manage to survive even while being exploited. However, De Filippo expresses his social protest through a parable which universalizes their plight, thereby giving his play an epic dimension and subsuming history into the parable's meaning and forms.
When first performed at the Teatro de' Servi in Rome in April 1957, the play ran for only three nights before it was closed down by the police for allegedly slandering

Catholic morality (1). It was claimed that the play treated Paradise, God, and the saints in a less than reverential manner. In fact, despite the objections of the Catholic curia, in its defense of the poor the play is a warm, passionate treatment of basic Christian principles. The plot of De Pretore Vincenzo is drawn from the vast lore of Neapolitan literary and oral traditions which posit a special relationship between the people of Naples and the world beyond. One well-known dialect poem which treats the same theme is Ferdinando Russo's sentimental fairy tale "Un ladro 'mparaviso" (A thief in paradise). Another is the great Neapolitan poet Salvatore Di Giàcomo's famous work "Lassammo fa' Dio" (Leave everything to God). In the latter poem the poet imagines that God, coming down to earth one day and seeing it teeming with poor people, gathers them all together and carries them off to heaven, where, after regaling them with a sumptuous dinner, he closes their eyes in eternal sleep. One could in fact relate the blind man of Di Giàcomo's poem to the protagonist of De Filippo's play through the way each asks that justice be done when he arrives in Paradise. The theme had incidentally already inspired De Filippo himself to write a long narrative poem with the same protagonist (2).

The central character Vincenzo De Pretore believes that his unknown father must have been a rich nobleman and that he has unjustly been denied his "place in paradise." Ever since his adoptive mother Maria told him that he was of noble blood, he has been trying to solve the mystery of his birth. He thinks that perhaps his father was the "lord" of his native town, in whose palace Maria worked. He himself, however, had never succeeded in entering that palace. Pretensions to nobility are common in Naples, and Vincenzo, now a grown man and otherwise defenseless in the big city, supports himself by the only means at his disposal, stealing, while at the same time attempting to put on a front compatible with his noble origins. Vincenzo's elegance and gentility attract Ninuccia, whose pure love he accepts, unfortunately at the very moment the police arrive to arrest him for a recent theft.

When Vincenzo returns home after two years in prison, Ninuccia persuades him to ask the protection of one of the saints and make a kind of give-and-get pact with him. Touched by her naiveté and the practicalness of the proposal, Vincenzo adapts it to his own needs. His pro-

Plays of Social Protest

tector must be the most "powerful" and "influential." Therefore, he chooses Saint Joseph. When he finds an abandoned tabernacle dedicated to the saint in one of the alleys of Naples, he approaches and speaks to his chosen protector as "one man to another." By no means proud of the fact that the first time he was arrested it was for stealing an earring from a poor woman, Vincenzo now wants to be a thief with scruples and rob only those who will not feel the loss. In the next scene it is apparent that such occasions have come easily, and it looks as if Saint Joseph has accepted the deal. The once-neglected shrine glitters with rich thank offerings and has become a place of worship and related commercial activities. Vincenzo's robberies come to an end, however, when he is shot while trying to steal a few million from a banker.

Delirious, Vincenzo finds himself in a scene that recalls the entrance to the castle of the "lord," his supposed father, in his home town. Ninuccia, dressed like a "grand lady" just as he had always dreamed, appears and tells him that she is outside the gates of Paradise. She suggests he go in; but Saint Peter, the old gate-keeper of the castle, bars his way. In great dismay, Vincenzo asks to speak to his protector, Saint Joseph, who turns out to resemble his supposed father. Vincenzo accuses him of having broken their agreement, but offers him the chance to make it up by assigning him a place in the house of the "Lord." The saint fails to recognize him, but, at Vincenzo's insistence, he gets him an audience with the "Lord." In his presence, Vincenzo excuses himself for not having had time to prepare a "few nice words" to present his case, saying that he is sure that in the heavenly kingdom "conventional forms do not count":

The Lord.	Your name is Vincenzo.
De Pretore.	Yes.
The Lord.	And your last name?
De Pretore.	De Pretore.
The Lord.	Your father?
De Pretore.	(Lowering his eyes in shame.) De Pretore was my mother's last name . . . My father's unknown.
The Lord.	What does "father unknown" mean?
De Pretore.	I don't know myself. It's what they say when a child's mother was not somebody's proper lawful wife. [. . .] If only I'd

> had a father to send me to school! . . .
> I can't write . . . I can hardly read
> . . . You know how it is, Lord . . . I
> turned to thieving to make a living. So
> many people like me end up being thieves!
> [2:512-13, 514]

The "Lord" gives Vincenzo a place in his "kingdom." But as the light and the heavenly music fade away, the scene changes and we are in the "squalid little emergency room" of a hospital. De Pretore is at times conscious, at times delirious. The policeman watching him takes advantage of a moment of lucidity to ask him a few questions, coming eventually to the question of his paternity. Vincenzo goes again into a semidelirium and answers thinking he is still talking to the "Lord":

> De Pretore. (Annoyed by the repetition of that unpleasant question) I just told you. I confessed everything. (His breathing becomes increasingly heavy.) I told you that I was a thief and that they killed me this morning. Now I'm in your house . . . in Paradise . . . I have your promise . . . and I'm going to stay. (His face is twisted in a grimace of pain. Then he closes his eyes, his head slips down onto his right shoulder and he falls back on the pillow, dead.) [2:516]

De Pretore Vincenzo represents a novelty in De Filippo's development. The play is not divided into the usual acts and scenes, but into tempi ("parts") and quadri ("shots") as in the movies. Through these new divisions, especially the quadri, the author abandons the mainly realistic and linear representations with musical accompaniment. The play develops on three levels: the intensely realistic one of the first three quadri, first in Vincenzo's squalid room and then in the alleys, among the people and the "picturesque" life of Naples; next, the surrealistic level of the fairy-tale Paradise made up of images out of Vincenzo's infancy; and, toward the end, the realistic-surrealistic level of the hospital emergency room, when Vincenzo thinks he is still in Paradise. This structure effectively integrates the elements of the play's effusive lyrical themes. In

Plays of Social Protest

its staging of violent death and its portrayal of the teeming Neapolitan alleys, the play recalls many works by Raffaele Viviani. It certainly has affinities with Millionaires' Naples! in its background and the chorality of the whole, and with Christmas at the Cupiellos' in the candid sentimental climate and the lyrical fluidity. In its theme of the unjust treatment of illegitimate children it further develops the position taken in Filumena Marturano and later in The Hidden Truth, broadening the accusation of injustice to include all of society. At the end, the criticism becomes scathing with the indifference of the authorities to Vincenzo's death. Vincenzo was given no real choice in life; a victim of circumstances, he had no other means of survival but stealing. The cruel attitude of the police and medical staff is typical of society's general lack of concern for those it deems unwanted or superfluous. Even heaven is regarded with a critical eye. Its function here is to let De Filippo denounce the unjust treatment of the illegitimate from the point of view of the illegitimate themselves.

The author's criticism is also directed against the superstitions of Vincenzo and Ninuccia, who represent the millions of Catholics who conceive their faith as a hopeful complicity with the Unknown (symbolized by this or that saint) and who cling to their illusions in the hope of reaching their personal ends and interests. For De Filippo, obviously this is not true Christianity, but a paganized version. However, the significance of the play becomes profoundly Christian if one looks at it as a parable. The story of Vincenzo, the man who believes he has been deprived of his birthright and claims the right to be readmitted to the "paradise lost," is the story of all poor people. His attempts to return to the Eden which has been denied him, and from which others would like to exclude him for bad behavior, represent the search of every man who believes himself to be the son of God, the son of the Master, and therefore equal to all other men. Vincenzo clearly represents the disinherited classes in a world which the law protects the affluent at the expense of the poor. The dream of recovering a lost heritage, the myth of a lost "kingdom" to which we shall be restored, has been a powerful source of consolation and hope throughout the centuries. In playing out this myth, Vincenzo carries his fight even to the great halls of the palace of the Lord.

The conclusion is not inappropriate, as the authorities contended, but instead is the logical objective toward which the whole theatrical language tends, from the harmonious development of the levels on which the drama develops, to the treatment of the characters, to the action in general. As if through the movie device of fade-out, we pass from the world of everyday wretchedness to a fairy-tale world of dreams, whose symbols interpret a universal condition. The first three scenes present the protagonist's milieu, from which he emerges as already an outcast. In the later surrealistic scenes we pass into a supernatural world which is an extension and correction of the real world of the first three scenes. We are placed before a Paradise which takes its form from repressed desires and from everything missed in life; it is the indirect representation of frustrated hopes, unsatisfied desires, unfulfilled aspirations. The natural vocation of those here below who have nothing is to imagine the kingdom of hope as the counter-image of their worldly existence. The image of Paradise has therefore a popular character, it is the symbol of the desires of the poor. It is Paradise with a social edge, not the expression of religious irreverence, as the ecclesiastical authorities judged it.

Vincenzo himself is an emblem of human nature, expressing in his symbolic whim the hopes of all people who live in poverty. He is a vivid character who succeeds in conveying the profound significance of his drama. In the first three quadri he is seen against an authentic popular background. He is one of those likable rascals whose resourceful genius has its roots in a thoroughly Neapolitan imagination. He is the sentimental, shrewd, naive, and unfortunate, sharing the fanciful superstitions of the Neapolitan poor, who invoke the saints as protectors and accomplices in their vices, tipping them the wink and speaking familiarly to them man to man. In Paradise, even as he stands as a symbolic figure, expressive of the sorrow of a people caught in the meshes of a law not made for them, he retains the warmth of his humanity; ever the hero and the rascal, he remains in touch with the popular spirit.

Even the structure of the action reveals and dramatizes the central theme. All Vincenzo's efforts are directed at achieving the position due but denied him, but each of his projects is brusquely interrupted by an unexpected arrest. Beginning with a measure of serenity,

Plays of Social Protest

the action comes to a crisis at the end of the first scene, with the police bursting into the thief's squalid room just as Ninuccia abandons herself in his arms. This dramatic reversal gives the scene the violent, sensational, heartbreaking flavor of the finest dramatic sketches of dialectical naturalism. In the third quadro the action again begins calmly and again explodes in a crisis at the end, with Vincenzo suddenly wounded as he tries to carry out the most daring theft of his career. The pace is once again tranquil as the scene opens in "Paradise," but, after one lively squabble between Vincenzo and Saint Joseph and another between the two of them and the "Lord," finishes with the very short sixth quadro in the emergency room, where Vincenzo dies just when he thinks he has been accepted into Paradise.

De Pretore Vincenzo clarifies the nature of De Filippo's religious feeling and perhaps also the reason why he has so often been the target of the ecclesiastical authorities, even though it is hard to believe in their good faith. De Filippo is a religious man, but his religion does not consist of attending church services or believing in abstract dogma. It is a kind of humanism, a form of lay apostolate which in some ways adheres to the spirit that motivated Pope John XXIII and the Second Vatican Council: man finds existential values within himself, not outside, in abstract formulas. He must beware of abstract and vague ideals and find God in practical acts and personal encounters, in a sincere social commitment, in love for his fellowman.

Pulcinella's Son

In De Pretore Vincenzo the social protest was conveyed indirectly, through the purity and simplicity of a parable. In Il figlio di Pulcinella (Pulcinella's son, 1958) it is conveyed openly, through the free form of the commedia dell'arte as transformed by a twentieth-century sensibility. The play shows to what extent De Filippo has remained loyal to the old commedia through the years. Its protagonist is Pulcinella, the symbol of the commedia tradition in the Neapolitan dialect theater; and here he projects De Filippo's own personality and image into that tradition and theater, giving more than ample proof of the playwright's ability to carry the commedia forward in the twentieth century.

In many ways the play is a summing-up. Certainly it
is a summing-up of the commedia tradition in its most
classic function, as political and social commentary.
Through it, De Filippo gives one of his most telling
reflections of life in the Italian South as it has been
lived for centuries. The play treats the South's most
gnawing sociological questions: nobility versus servitude, feudalism, family solidarity, and political anarchy
and exploitation. Gennaro Magliulo considers the play
important for its synthesis of De Filippo's political
views (3). For Vito Pandolfi, "the political sense of
[Pulcinella's] parable is easily apprehended." "Behind a
succession of changing circumstances and humorous touches, its structure hides the bitter truths which it is
Eduardo's mission to uncover in the world he depicts
(which is also our world)." Pulcinella reflects "the
history of the Neapolitan people, who, in order to resist
(internally) the tyranny of their masters, have had to
don the mask . . . synonymous with pretense, dissimulation, and servility" (4). At the same time, however,
Pulcinella himself tells the story of the downtrodden of
all countries, as De Filippo himself clearly indicates in
his well-known dialect poem "Il paese di Pulcinella"
(Pulcinella's country):

> You know what Pulcinella says:
> That "country" means "world."
> He knows only that it is wide and round;
> He has no friends and no relatives . . .
> He knows the world of yesterday and tomorrow. (5)

In Pulcinella's Son, as in De Pretore, the forms
of De Filippo's naturalism, which have come to be associated with his wartime and postwar classics, undergo a
substantial change. In a method recalling twentieth-
century experimental theater, De Filippo lets the traditions of verismo and commedia dell'arte alternately
determine the play's superstructure. Thus he succeeds in
blending the real and the surreal, the past and the
present, the old and the new, the representation of
Neapolitan life and its symbolic interpretation from a
universal perspective.

On one level we have characters and situations that,
though comic, are basically realistic. Baron Vofà Vofà,
the representative of the upper-class nobility, is campaigning for office, and he is having a rough time pay-

Plays of Social Protest

ing for his campaign. His servants, house, and family are such a drain on his resources that he has persuaded his daughter Mimmina, though she is in love with the starving young painter Renato, to accept the suit of the much older but rich Nicola, a wealthy entrepreneur in fuel oil. On the second level we have imagery derived from a mixture of symbolism and surrealism, modified by structural techniques taken from Brecht's epic theater. Here we find the clown Pulcinella, who apostrophizes his soul (seen not as a cricket, as in Pinocchio, but as a lizard) in long dialectical monologues, commenting on his own past and present and those of the masses he represents. Bridging the two levels, Pulcinella is seen both in his own isolated world and in the practical world of the Baron. He is the dominant, most significant figure of the play.

When Pulcinella first comes on stage, the Neapolitan spectator cannot help noticing that his looks have changed. As traditional comic mask, his attributes and makeup are fixed and invariable, like the derivative puppet or marionette versions of his role, like Marcel Marceau's Bip, like a circus clown whose costume and makeup remain the same no matter who plays the part. But this Pulcinella has aged visible and his paraphernalia is visibly worn out. When, as is the custom, he lifts his mask so that the audience can see the actor beneath, instead of putting it back over his face, he takes it off altogether. The audience's expectations are thus partially disappointed, their conventional "safe" relationship with the role violated. Pulcinella thanks the applauding spectators, as he would in the commedia dell'arte, and immediately makes contact with a particular segment of the audience, assuming his role of representative of the people and directing his witticisms against the social class that exploits them. He makes his political significance clear from the very beginning:

> Easy, easy! Where do you think you are, at Portacapuana? This is a theater! . . . Who told you you could do as you like? Just look at the liberties they think they're entitled to for their two cents admissions! [. . .] Let the ladies and gentlemen in the boxes and orchestra speak. They've paid enough for it! What did you say? That there are people in the boxes and orchestra who haven't paid? What's that to you? They are the authorities and they have the right to speak

out just the same; especially in fact when they haven't paid. [3:22-23]

Pulcinella, the subservient but astute servant of the overbearing master, with his quick wit and ancient wisdom, his ever-youthful spirit, and his resourcefulness and adaptability, which allow him to accommodate himself to whatever way the wind happens to be blowing, reflects the unchanging life of the oppressed Neapolitan masses in their poverty and extemporaneous cunning, in their patient and unconventional vitality.

This twentieth-century Pulcinella is not so very different from his long line of ancestors. He responds to the call of Baron Vofà Vofà like a dog to his master. Like his predecessors, he inadvertently creates problems. The Baron has planned to distribute boxes of macaroni to the poor in order to get their votes; Pulcinella cooks it for his friends. The Baron had planned to have his picture printed on the campaign badges; Pulcinella substitutes his own picture. And when the Baron makes a political speech, Pulcinella ruins the effect with his inopportune interruptions.

But Pulcinella's Son is not just an affectionate homage to the moribund commedia tradition, like Petito's Palummella zompa e vola (Palummella jumps and flies), the play with which De Filippo opened the newly rebuilt Theater San Ferdinando in 1954. Instead, it is a daring, difficult, and fascinating attempt to enliven the old zanni and place him, with all the burden of his history, in the present. Finding inspiration in the old pulcinellesque farces, De Filippo focuses on the most ruthless of them and creates a political fable. In fact, this play is no tear-jerking slapstick representation of the damned of the Neapolitan earth. On the contrary, in it the author comes out against the condescension, paternalism, and colonialism of the ruling middle class and against the political servility of the Neapolitan masses.

It addresses a challenge particularly to the younger generation, who De Filippo hopes will create a new society disinclined to hypocrisy and compromises. As Di Franco observes,

> each of the social classes is personified by one or more characters of the [older] generation, to each of whom is opposed an exponent of the new generation. Thus, the De Pecorellis couple is juxtaposed with

their daughter Mimmina; Nicola Sapore, the exponent of the bourgeoisie, is placed next to the painter Renato Fuso; Pulcinella, the eternal sumbol not only of the Neapolitan masses, but also of the masses of the world, is contrasted with his son John. (6)

De Filippo seems to imply that in their revolt the young are trying very hard to teach their elders a lesson. Mimmina rebels by running away with the painter. She has realized that things can be different and better without hypocrisy and the lust for power and materialistic satisfactions. Living with Renato, she has found a true human relationship, and she has seen how easy it is to live on very little with the person one loves. She wishes her parents could also know these realities. Similarly, John, the young Pulcinella, does not want to help Pulcinella with the campaign. He cannot live by his father's intrigues and flattering lies. Having been deported from America for his outspoken views, he tells Pulcinella what he thinks of him, maintaining that he will live without the mask he has inherited.

Pulcinella's limitations are all too apparent. He is at the same time a generator of farce and of tragedy. He knows he is a slave and says so, but he does not attempt a single act of rebellion. Neither the external temptation of an emancipated, changing world nor the political ideals of the different parties have any meaning for him. His misunderstandings are simply comic mistakes; they are never deliberate attempts to sabotage the electoral campaign of his master. Like his people, he has not acquired a civic and political conscience and would not know how to live without a master. When his own conscience, the lizard, would like to tell the truth, he brushes it aside. But he no longer has the strength to hide the truth of his misery. He confesses the pain he suffers and declares himself a servant, at anyone's beck and call in return for a bowl of soup. He wears the mask because it is his emblem, but the mask no longer has the duplicity and the capacity to surprise that were its charms and its defense. It does not even have the ambiguity of the old mask of the Neapolitan theater, which presented the two faces of the people, the foolish side of the servant and the wise side of the rebel. Pulcinella's way of living openly reveals De Filippo's contempt for this aspect of the Neapolitan populace—a people thoroughly alienated and passively acquiescent to myths and ancient prejudices, a people incapable of higher aspirations to liberty and human dignity.

But De Filippo reserves his bitterest satire for the world of Pulcinella's "friends," who exploit and oppress the people Pulcinella represents. That world is the political reality of contemporary Naples. The city's democratic illusions had lasted only through the brief insurrection after Mussolini's fall, quickly succumbing to hunger, corruption, and demagoguery. The period of the play is that of the corrupt industrialist and political boss Achille Lauro and his neo-monarchical gang, when people sold their votes for a box of macaroni or a pair of shoes, one shoe being handed out before the elections, the other only after. The pulcinellate of the commedia have been adapted to democratic satire of the rules of the various legal Neapolitan underworlds, which in the postwar period seemed to have taken over the political and economic destiny of the city. But the satire is broader than that, encompassing every variety of slavery and exploitation. Where there is no Lauro, there is the Mafia and racial prejudice, as John discovers in America; or there is organized exploitation courteously imposed by modern means. Despite this savage indictment, De Filippo is ultimately optimistic. Along with defeat comes hope for liberation, a hope blossoming out of the most dramatic and painful experience in the history of Naples. John demonstrates that the ideals of the tragic but splendid moments of the insurrection, the so-called "Four Days of Naples," are still alive. Indeed, the future of Pulcinella's son is the death of Pulcinella. He will fight for his own dignity and respect. He may be defeated, but he will survive and eventually prevail. The new generation which he represents offers hope.

Pulcinella and the characters around him, like those in the earlier De Pretore Vincenzo and the later Tommaso D'Amalfi and The Contract, do not elicit the compassionate involvement of the spectator, as did the protagonists of the earlier plays. The plane of encounter between character and spectator is less emotional, more intellectual, tending to a more openly political judgment. Pulcinella's Son recalls Brechtian theater in its montage technique, which juxtaposes purely fantastic parable with the explicitly symbolic, as well as in its active polemic and its critical attitude to sentimental and fantastic delusions. Especially Brechtian is the use of musical comment in the form of three famous

Neapolitan songs. "Vita d' 'a vita mia, te sto aspettanno" ("Life of My Life, Long for You") comments ironically on Mimmina's rejection of Renato's love for Nicola's money. "Chi ha avuto, ha avuto, / Chi ha dato, ha dato" ("What you've had, you've had, / What you gave away, you gave away") underlines Mimmina's indifference to a past characterized by sincerity and love. "E levate 'a cammesella" ("Take off your blouse") expresses John's contemptuous detachment from the old sentimentalism in favor of a more down-to-earth understanding of love, which, though more frankly sexual, is a no less deeply felt rapport. Clearly, the traditional source of material, the sentimental substratum, and the dramatic tone of the earlier plays have changed profoundly. However, we are far from the alienation in which Brecht developed his Pirandellian paradoxes. De Filippo's parable demands an evocative staging that fascinates the spectator, rather than compelling his critical detachment from the performance. Brecht's methods are not merely grafted onto a new tree. De Filippo's poetic temperament is wholly different, and thus his aesthetic conception develops on a different plane entirely.

Tommaso D'Amalfi

In these later plays poverty and social injustice are not regarded as part of some inexorable way of the world, but as stemming from the exploitation of the have-nots by the rich and powerful. The individual's impulse to rebel against his poverty is represented in De Pretore Vincenzo. In Pulcinella's Son the poverty and exploitation of an entire class and city are demonstrated, as Pulcinella is seduced into assisting the Baron by the promise of food and new clothing. The result of this exploitation is voiced in Pulcinella's attempts to justify his insatiable appetite. In Tommaso D'Amalfi (1965) De Filippo turns to an historical figure and historical events to show the roots of these conditions: in Naples the masses have always paid and continue to pay, but their exploitation has in the past and could again lead to rebellion.

Like De Pretore Vincenzo and Pulcinella's Son, Tommaso D'Amalfi takes place not in a family setting, but in the squares and alleys of Naples, where the people go about their daily activities. The scenes are put together like the tiles of a mosaic, forming an impressive picture of popular Naples. The play is rich in pantomime fused from a variety of elements: musical comedy, <u>opera buffa</u>, Neapolitan popular drama, <u>commedia dell'arte</u>, and epic theater. The influence of Brecht and some of his Italian followers, like Luigi Squarzina (<u>Romagnola</u>, 1959), is particularly apparent in the musical and choreographic stylization, which gives harmony to the episodic structure and comments upon its motifs. In the earlier plays the motifs were like melodies; here they dissolve in an epic chorus. Gone are the exaggerated comic characters of the earlier plays, with the exception of the slightly clownish figure of the Viceroy; gone too are the pathetic characters, the bitter caricatures, the sarcasm and the whimsy. The dances, songs, and musical commentary are the basis of the action itself, reflecting the spirit of a people who wax enthusiastic one moment and lose all courage the next, who weep and laugh at the drop of a hat, who rebel and are appeased, whose moods change momentarily.

The people are brought together in the single figure of Tommaso, called Masaniello, the illiterate fisherman whose popular movement almost succeeded in overthrowing Spanish rule in Southern Italy in 1647-48. As Defilippian protagonists go, he is quite unusual. He is not the brains of the people. Though their leader, he does not march as their head, but is a spontaneous product of their best instincts and their truest voice. Better than they are but not above them, he shares their enthusiasm and discouragement, rebellion and ignorance; he rises and falls with his people. Thus, he cannot have the complex psychology that characterizes the protagonists of the middle-class dramas, but rather the heroic character typical of the protagonist in folk-historical plays (7). His potential for introspective psychological complexity is for one thing reduced by the presence of the numerous minor characters whose choral function he must support. Thus, like Pulcinella in the preceding play—though unlike him in the way he represents the people— Masaniello seems a character already developed and complete from the outset. Instinctively honest, never to be tricked into compromise despite his ignorance, consistently incorruptible, he never experiences a crisis, and he dies for the well-being of his people, all of whom— poor men and women—flow in their own way into his character and drama. His story expresses all the contradic-

Plays of Social Protest

tions, aspirations, and impotent rage, reaching even to madness, of a mocked and abused people.

At the beginning, the stage throngs with people, expressing the communal mood of rebellion against the constituted authority which has gone too far in abusing its power. But their accents, protesting the pathos of revolt and the open desire for revenge, moderate to a tone of muted bitterness and discontent as the hopes of Masaniello and the people go unfulfilled. At the end what remains is the contrast between leader and followers, Masaniello's absolute commitment as opposed to their caution, indecisiveness, and willingness to compromise. Thus isolated, it is inevitable that Masaniello die at the hands of the powerful. In the last scene, as his disconsolate followers call him back, his rhythmically chanting voice is heard in the distance, giving lyrical expression to the eternal destiny of the Neapolitans and the masses in general:

> Let me sleep another hundred years,
> A hundred more . . . another thousand years!
> The more years you add,
> The more peace you give me.
> People!
> People with worn-out shoes, people hungry
>   for bread,
> People with bloodshot and streaming eyes . . .
> These miseries of yours, to whom will you
>   confess them?
> I die a victim, but who killed me?
> People!   [3:410]

After the gigantic effort he has undertaken for the good of his people, Masaniello is infinitely weary and invokes the peace of oblivion, implicitly reminding them that he was killed not just by his known enemies, but by them as well. Nonetheless, his heroic spirit is not dead. He shifts the focus of his lament from his own death to the condition of his people, warning them to mistrust those who will respond in his name when they invoke him:

> Hollow-cheeked people dying of hunger,
> When you call my name out loud
> And somebody answers "here I am" . . .
>   it won't be me.

> Beware.
> People!
> I hear the lamenting voices of mothers
>   and wives . . .
> I hear bloody tears coming from
>   jails . . .
> Time passes, time flies by.
> People!
> Do you hear the cannon?
> The harquebus isn't used any more.
> Now there are machine guns . . .
> And the gallows gloats,
> And the priest bestows his blessing.
> People!
> Do you hear the airplane?
> People!
> The sound of the machine gun goes
>   with the wind.
> People!
> Time passes, time flies by.
> People!
> And the gallows gloats.   [3:410-11]

The curtain falls and Masaniello's plaintive lament continues to linger in our ears.

If Masaniello embodies and, like the Greek chorus, gives voice to, the vicissitudes of a people, this eerie closing chant makes us feel the presence of a destiny that even in modern times has prescribed misery for the people. What becomes evident finally is that, like Brecht's plays, this historical-popular drama is written with the eye to the present. De Filippo is thinking of his own Naples, which knew five days of heroic insurrection in 1944 and which has since remained lethargic, in need of reform and help. Despite the fall of Fascism, nothing has changed. Neapolitans still sell their votes en masse to a party that does not represent them, showing themselves once again incapable of taking their destiny into their own hands and asserting their freedom. In spite of centuries of misery and exploitation, they still lack a profound class consciousness, their morale is sadly undermined by ignorance, superstition, and prejudice. They seem prohibited from breaking their chains by some historical law enthroning over them an oppressor who, since time immemorial, has used religion as an "instrument of rule," culture as a monopoly of the "superior" elite, and intelligence as a tool for exploitation. The analysis of the historical ills of his native city reaches across the centuries and seizes upon the living dynamics of a still-current reality.

In these later plays De Filippo shows a strong political commitment without openly espousing any ready-made political ideology. His is a pious and touching hope which is constantly being betrayed by his experience of the real world. He was able to escape despair in the late 1940s and the 1950s by focusing his disgust on the moral decay that followed the war. When he paints this pessimistic picture, he generally talks about "man" and the "world," and only implicitly about man in a certain political system. He never tries to suggest what the world should change to or how it could be changed. In this, of course, De Filippo is genuinely Marxist, for Marx and Engels themselves never presented a concrete picture of the world they wanted to create. They too were essentially critics.

The Local Authority and The Contract

In De Pretore Vincenzo, Pulcinella's Son, and Tommaso D'Amalfi, De Filippo had demonstrated a clear social commitment in a new theatrical form that moved beyond realistic settings and acting. This does not mean, however, that he had completely abandoned his personal brand of realism. In Il sindaco del Rione Sanità (The Local Authority, 1960) he goes back to realistic portrayal, in terms of both the setting and the psychological portrayal of characters. Once again, the outcome is not dogmatic. De Filippo is able to control the Brechtian temptation to didacticism.

Like his earlier plays, The Local Authority depends on the moral commitment and strenuous efforts of its protagonist to introduce a measure of optimism into its portrayal of a world of poverty and degradation. Don Antonio Barracano, saluted by his constituents as "mayor" of his quarter, one of De Filippo's many idealists, is committed to saving the poor and ignorant from the very sort of exploitation portrayed in the preceding three plays. If these people are forced to commit crimes, it is because it seems they can receive no justice from the law. To protect them, Don Antonio not only intervenes in their quarrels and forestalls bloodshed, but actually becomes a distributor of work and wealth. Resigning from the imperfect moral community at large, he has set up an alternative, a more practical and equitable system of justice in his own working-district of Naples.

In The Local Authority De Filippo explicitly indicates that the social conditions of the poor and outcast cannot improve unless basic changes are made in the present system in Italy. His belief is based primarily on his lack of faith in the adage that the "law is equal for all" and on the fact that the law is far removed from the daily life of the common man because it is controlled by the class in power. The play enlarges on themes already introduced in Millionaires' Naples! Economic chaos continues; in a dog-eat-dog world poor men are prepared to shoot their no less wretched fellows in the desperate competition for menial jobs. The ignorance that Gennaro in Millionaires' Naples! had attributed to Fascist rule has not abated after many years of democracy, and De Filippo, through Barracano, attempts to protect the people from its consequences.

Don Antonio's position becomes clear in the confrontation with two characters in particular: his indispensable colleague Dottor Della Ragione and his antagonist Arturo Santaniello. In the first encounter Don Antonio's idealism, his peculiar sense of mission, the social role he has chosen for himself, come through as he assesses the relationship that he has decided to give up their common ministry and leave for the United States. He is tired of the constant risks to which he subjects himself by acting outside the law and protecting people who persistently engage in criminal activities. In response, Don Antonio reminds him of the importance of their gospel:

> They're poor and ignorant underdogs, and society knows only too well how to exploit them. My dear Doctor, the whole grasping machine of what you call society revolves round and is fed by the crimes and felonies committed by these poor devils. Oh yes, the ignorant underdog is as valuable as stocks and shares. He pays dividends. Put one of the poor bastards beside you, and you're in clover for the rest of your life. But the underdog's got wise to the system. He knows that he can't get anywhere without money and connections. He says to himself: if I go to court to settle my case, even though I'm in the right, what if the other

side'd got money, the right connections . . . and three or four paid witnesses? Because, as you know only too well, witnesses are to be had for the asking. Provided the price is right, they'll testify to anything. (8)

Don Antonio's convictions become even more evident in his confrontation with Arturo Santaniello, for he is Don Antonio's living negation. Indeed, the two are perfect antagonists and supply the poles of equilibrium in De Filippo's confrontation or right and wrong. Whereas Don Antonio has distributed his wealth to his children so that they may enjoy it with him, Santaniello refuses to give his son a single penny from his profitable bakery business. Don Antonio is loyal to his wife and affectionate toward his children, while Santaniello is unfaithful and sets a deplorable example for his son. The two men are so different that they cannot find ground for reconciliation. The sacrifices and privations they have both endured, coupled with the challenges they have had to meet in their climb toward financial success have made them both equally if differently stubborn men each of whom can face the other without flinching. Arturo is perfectly aware that Antonio's authority in the neighborhood is strong only as long as it is accepted by the people it is supposed to aid. Hence, he is not afraid to oppose Don Antonio's will, even to stab him when the demands that he help his son become too insistent.

Santaniello is "one of those rich upstanding businessmen who confuse the holiness of work with the veneration of their vested interests and are willing to pay for freedom of action with a stifled conscience" (9). Considering himself an honest, law-abiding workingman, he rejects Don Antonio's appeal. However, in the context of the play, his respect for the law marks him as someone who knows how to use the law to his own advantage. He stands a good chance of being found innocent of the death of Don Antonio. Don Antonio's last act is to tell Doctor Della Ragione to falsify his report on the causes of death, reporting it as a heart attack, something the doctor refuses to do.

Many critics, particularly F. Frascani, believe this work will be recognized as one of De Filippo's highest theatrical achievements (10). As he points out, the issues are not presented and resolved in abstract discussions on stage. The issues are there, but they are generated by the events lived or re-created on stage, in a coherent dramatic concatenation. The play is unquestionably one of De Filippo's best. It treats the social relationships among individuals and the effects of government from above on them, without neglecting the intimate relationships within the family. In fact, the administration of public justice—denounced for its inadequacy, impersonality, superficiality, and corruption—is seen in relation to the administration of family justice, which can be just as bad. In order for human relationships to be harmonious at the social level, one needs, first of all, harmonious relationships on the family level. One of the major threats to that harmony between parents and children is financial dependency. For De Filippo, inheritance corrupts the family bond, and therefore its effects should be minimized or eliminated. To the baker Santaniello and his son, who are ranged against each other out of self-interest, Don Antonio delivers a moving speech on how he divided his property among his children when they were still very young so that they would not wish for his death in order to take possession of their share, but would be bound to him by genuine affection. As he had done in My Family!, De Filippo reaffirms his position that fatherhood must be free of egoism in order to avoid creating negative feelings in the children.

Economic interests too play an important role in destroying social relationships. Often the ruling social classes manipulate the law, so that false witnesses are not always distinguishable from true ones, "cads" from the "people in good faith." Only "the man who has his own saints" (that is to say, money) goes to "heaven," for he is the only one in a position to defend himself. Astutely interpreted, this kind of justice gives the strongest the opportunity to perpetuate and exploit illiteracy and ignorance. This explains why the lower classes develop a bitter sense of mistrust toward the state and toward the written code which gives them no satisfaction and which they do not understand. This is why they are driven to anarchical revolt in order to create a justice for themselves, according to an unwritten code of blindly felt loyalties, more moral than legal.

Don Antonio administers justice according to this kind of moral sense, according to an understanding humanity which takes societal victimization into consideration first of all. On the surface, this portrait of a man who

Plays of Social Protest

feels he can fulfill all the needs of those who do not have "their own saints in heaven" would seem exaggerated, and thus a serious shortcoming in the play. One tends to be skeptical of the idea that Antonio alone has been given the perception necessary to distinguish right from wrong. Furthermore, his justice seems too different from justice as it is defined in the larger society. It excludes the possibility that crime does damage to society in general, and it denies the necessity of rehabilitating the criminal; instead of incarceration, it prescribes damages to be paid to the injured party. However, upon close scrutiny it becomes clear that Don Antonio's utopian justice can function only in counterbalance to, and as a criticism of, the official juridical system; it cannot substitute for it. No matter how well-intentioned, human feeling, or mercy alone, is too arbitrary and personal a criterion in the realm of justice, and a man of reason like Doctor Della Ragione (as the name implies) is and must be opposed to it. His refusal to sanction Antonio's request that he falsify his report on the cause of death reaffirms the necessity of a less arbitrary justice. Thus, De Filippo implies, if laws are inadequate, they must be changed, not ignored; if people are degraded or treated unfairly under a certain system, it must be altered, not disregarded. The last word in the play is given to Doctor Della Ragione.

Out of the confrontation between these two systems of justice emerges an appeal to conscience, brotherhood, and comprehension for the exploited and persecuted poor. The play should not be interpreted as portraying a merely local, limited situation. Its theme—the profound desperation generated by poverty, superstition, and ignorance—has a universal relevance. De Filippo himself has defined the play as "a symbolic and not simply a realistic comedy," one that takes as its point of departure "real characters with their roots in everyday reality, but then abandons [that reality] to become divine and give to justice a precise and all-embracing significance" (11). With their rich humanity, the characters transcend regionalism and become emblematic of all the downtrodden people of the world who silently suffer the same injustices. Through Don Antonio's mission to the poor, De Filippo extends one of his many invitations to the ruling classes to get closer to the people and to understand and remedy their plight by practicing Christian principles.
In fact, Don Antonio is also an emblematic figure: the

redeemer who, through his mission of freedom and reconciliation, seeks to achieve a universal human solidarity and equality. And, like Christ, he is betrayed by the men he wanted to save.

Don Antonio Barracano is different from other Defilippian protagonists in that, from the beginning, he is sure of himself and of the situation around him. The fact that he is a victim (he spent time in prison for a youthful crime) has only made him stronger; his suffering has forced him out of solitude and into rapport with his fellowman, the poor whom he protects as he wars against injustice. He uses the story of his own misadventures to demonstrate, as did Gennaro Jovine in Millionaires' Naples!, that the guilt of a few is the consequence of everyone's injustices. He might appear to play out the drama of his destiny in too heroic a key; however, his intense commitment to justice provides a strong moral charge that runs through both the second and third acts.

Don Antonio's strong central position, essential to the thematic development of the play, cannot help but overshadow the secondary characters. Not even the wife, always so important in De Filippo's plays, has any place here. Nor do the other secondary characters, the popular Neapolitan chorus which adds theatricality and vivacity to the play, have any real autonomy; they are followers of Don Antonio and are illuminated by him. Such is the case with the lovers Rafiluccio and Rita, whose pathos is intended to cap the emotional appeal in favor of Don Antonio's struggle. Only the doctor, who does not share Don Antonio's utopian ambitions, acquires any stature. Though he understands the will for justice that animates Antonio, he concludes that that kind of will is not enough. As in De Pretore Vincenzo and Pulcinella's Son, the secondary characters do not constitute the usual comic-grotesque chorus; though they come from a world outside the polite spectator's ken, the criminal underworld, the bas fonds of Naples, their presence in the play is not inspired by comic intentions, hence the play lacks the hilarity of earlier works.

Growing out of the conflict between the individual and an unjust society, the play seeks to involve the spectator in an active way and to bring him to reflect on the action and on the sufferings of the characters and their origins in social injustice. The play thus functions to demystify life, to encourage the spectator to criticize the world in which he lives, and thus to attempt to correct the present, which is the product of the past.

De Filippo continues his attack on the injustices perpetrated by the rich against the poor in Il contratto (The contract, 1967) (12)—this time, however, by means of a kind of perverted Don Antonio Barracano. It is as if, with mocking irony, he wanted to show that, in a society that will practice love and charity only if promised some material reward, the only way to do good is through fraud. Only in this case by exploiting the fear of death can an opportunist change the scale of values and act, ironically, as a distributor of love and wealth.

The protagonist, Geronta Sebezio, has learned about life the hard way. As a young man, naively taken in by pious rhetoric, he had behaved strictly according to Christian principles, so much so that he had acquired a reputation for sanctity. Even after he had been betrayed by his own brother and by his young wife (an orphan whom he had taken pity on), he continued to turn the other cheek. One day, when his ailing half brother Isidoro had been given up for dead, Geronta was called in. When he entered, crying out "Oh my dear brother, raise yourself up. Come back to life," lo and behold, his brother did so! From that moment on, Geronta has enjoyed a reputation as a miracle-worker. The contract of the play's title refers in fact to a series of contracts that Geronta proceeds to make with credulous people who wish to be resuscitated after they die. The miracle-worker makes no charge for his services, but, in return for a second lease on life, he imposes on the beneficiary two conditions. He must vow to dedicate his life to loving and helping his neighbors and especially his own family, and he must agree to bequeath a third portion of his estate to a formerly despised and abandoned relative. Modestly, Geronta disclaims any real responsibility for the promised miracle. It will be the outcome of the "chain of love" created by the transformed life-style of the beneficiary. If, on the other hand, the chain of love is not forged—and here we have an echo of the condition imposed by Otto Marvuglia in The Big Magic upon Calogero Di Spelta, before he can open the box that is supposed to contain his wife—the contract will be rendered null and void. No resurrection will take place.
In the second act one of Geronta Sebezio's clients dies, and it turns out that he had become so sanctimoniously odious in his reformed state that the family is not at all sure they want him resuscitated. Neither, in their

greed, will they be happy to see the reprobate cousin, whom the deceased had taken into his house and written into his will, receive his promised third of the inheritance! Already the litigious relatives have stripped the house, spiriting away all the objects of value before the lawyers come to take inventory. When the miracle-worker arrives, scared of the dead man's reaction when he returns to life, they hurriedly replace them. It will come as no surprise to learn that the resentments, grudges, and jealousies within the family are so powerful and so obvious that the attempt at resuscitation fails. Geronta, however, is able to convince the relatives to offer Giacomino Trocina, the reinstated black-sheep cousin, a lump sum in exchange for his share of the inheritance. The cousin is by this time so terrified of the others that he plans to emigrate. In the last act, seated in state and speaking in a language larded with unctuous pseudoecclesiastical terms and phrases, Geronta receives each of them in turn. He persuades Giacomino that given the massive inheritance tax that will be levied by the state, he is better off giving up his claim, accepting a monetary indemnity, and leaving his hated relatives saddled with the taxes. Handing over the suitcase containing the 140 million lire agreed upon, Geronta remarks: "I have brought you back to life . . . What is a man without money? A body without a soul!" As he leaves for the Americas, Giacomino leaves with Geronta a full-length portrait photograph for his gallery, inscribed "To my brother Geronta, who brought me back to life." Once Giacomino has left, however, we learn from the next visitor that the sum agreed upon to buy him off was 300 million, so that the astute and scheming Geronta's unofficial "commission" amounts to more than half! The play closes with Geronta and his latest dupe drinking a toast to yet another "contract."

 The Contract resists all attempts to limit its implications to the secular humanism that is the main thrust of Defilippian theater. Geronta, in fact, is neither a typical exponent of his social class, nor an out-and-out philanthropist, nor a miracle-worker exploiting superstition and ignorance to his own advantage. He is, rather, an emblematic figure who gives the action the character of a parable. His dual personality, as ingratiating charlatan and as idealistic peacemaker and distributor of wealth, is only apparent. He embodies both the wisdom of the legendary ancient philosopher of the Sebete River (whence his name) and the goodness and generosity of a saint opposed by a corrupt society. Having learned the lesson of his youth, that in this society real love has been replaced by greed and hypocrisy, and that pure and honest people are overwhelmed by corrupt institutions, Geronta continues to do good, but in a completely different way. His contrivance is successful only because of the corruption around him: ostensibly, the resurrection fails because the thought of the inheritance—greed for money—makes love impossible. But for De Filippo, the resurrection that counts is that of the living dead, the outcasts who exist on the margins of society to whom Geronta gives a fresh opportunity to make good, a new lease on life.

This resurrection, in harmony with true social justice, implies a powerful condemnation of contemporary society for having made money its supreme value, a condemnation already apparent in The Top Hat, Pulcinella's Son, and The Local Authority. In The Contract, however, the attack is broadened to include the government and the Church. De Filippo told me in an interview that "the main aim motivating the men around Geronta without exception is to grab as much as possible; the principal activity of the State is to steal and oppress its citizens, while the Church betrays Christ's teachings by allowing itself to be involved in materialistic interests, very often antithetical to Christianity." Thus, he adds, when he plays the role of Geronta he takes "great pleasure especially in the last scene," when he dons a velvet cape and sits in the "golden armchair, representing a throne, and assumes the air of a man accustomed to having everyone bow down before him," preaching, "in a mocking tone, goodness and altruism." This is his "way of impersonating the Church as it preaches the exact contrary of what it practices daily," thereby perpetuating the crucifixion of Christ, the symbol of true love for one's neighbor.

The War Memorial and *The Exams are Never Over*

De Filippo's social criticism becomes more pronounced in these later plays as the author became more and more disenchanted with the sociopolitical deterioration of postwar Italy. The Brechtian influence is more noticeable because of the vogue that Brecht's theater had with

Italian playwrights in the 1960s and 1970s. Despite the
occasionally abstract nature of this dialectical approach, De Filippo has been able to maintain the freshness and immediacy of his ethical inspiration. Because
of his rich and varied stage experience, he has managed
to combine the new Brechtian elements with more traditional techniques derived especially from the native Neapolitan drama so familiar to him. De Filippo continues to
work in this vein in his last two plays, in which he
displays intense indignation with ivory-tower idealists
and the purveyors of false beliefs.

In his next-to-last play, Il monumento (The war
memorial, 1970), De Filippo openly criticizes institutions that fabricate ideals and beliefs in order to
further their own ends. As a result of this manipulation, many men, unaware, lose perspective on the reality
of their daily lives. At the same time, he gives artistic expression to the anti-rhetoric campaign of the young
pacifists and to the ideals underlying the peace movement
which swept through the Western world at the end of the
sixties.

The protagonist is Ascanio Penna, a national guard
reserve sergeant who sees his men massacred by the Nazis,
and runs away from his barracks to take refuge in the
hollow base of a bombed-out war memorial. Ascanio is
unable to face up to the fall of the fascist-monarchical
regime and the collapse of what he had thought of as its
high ideals, ideals on which he had been led to base his
life. Through the years, he remains enclosed in the base
of the monument, as it were in a stone page from a
history book, remaining faithful to the past. Here he
has the company of his longtime lover Sabina and of petty
pilferers, hucksters, and the like who collect there for
their questionable comings and goings. Ascanio welcomes
their visits because they provide him with an audience
for his stories about the "great" period of his military
service.

For twenty-five years the ex-marshal lives in the
refuge of his illusions. Then, one day, all illusions
and ideals are shattered as reality mercilessly intrudes.
In the name of progress and Italy's "economic miracle,"
a powerful company is granted an eviction order so that
it can raze the monument and construct a modern building.
The poor old man is harassed not only by the police
officers sent to enforce the eviction notice, but also by
his fellow "inmates," some of whom openly revile him
while others stand idly by. Ascanio is so hurt by all of

Plays of Social Protest

this that he dies of a heart attack. In a symbolic act of love and recognition, his friends wrap his body in a sheet and place it on the monument in place of the memorial's missing statue. For the few hours before the doctor arrives to ascertain the cause of death, Ascanio Penna will have had his monument; and when the doctor removes the winding sheet, he performs the ceremonial unveiling that, accompanied by official speeches and trumpets, inaugurates the statue of a famous man.

This false unveiling is appropriate to a false hero. For De Filippo, a hero is one who grapples with situations and sometimes overcomes them, not someone who collapses at his first encounter with the reality of the postwar world which he has systematically denied. Ascanio Penna is a wretched man and a victim of rhetoric. Still believing in the myths he was fed by the old regime, he refuses to live in a world that has changed. Guarnaschelli, one of the frequenters of the monument, characterizes him as a fanatic and expresses the key theme of the play:

> In today's world, when people are fed up with rhetoric, you are a character out of time, a museum piece. They screw it into your mentality so badly that no one can take it out. The time of heroism at any cost is over. The world is progressing . . . Today no one walks blindfolded. . . . I can understand the bitterness of a man who has seen all the myths he blindly believed in crumble, but I can never accept stubbornness. Blind stubbornness took the entire country into a frightful tragedy . . . The same stubornness has kept you inside here for years living like a mole. (13)

Ascanio is a minor Don Quixote who refuses to adapt himself to time, who survives without regaining his reason in the unfortunate duel with the Knight of the White Moon. As V. Talarico observes, "his is a folly which makes him symbolize, without rancor, without anger, the multitude of unfortunate people who do not have the strength to react even with a wry face and feigned submission" (14). De Filippo told me on 9 July 1980 in a personal interview that Ascanio is a symbol of vacuous blind militarism.

His could be the first in a long series of "real" monuments which are looked at not because of how they represent a person, but because of what the person has done and has been: monuments which don't create any myths, but demolish them; statues to look at not as works of art, but as the consequence of what has made living men into dead ones. With a real dead person above, a monument becomes a work of destruction, a way of making us reflect, and perhaps then we won't make war any more.

Such a monument also implies the destruction of all the incongruities that lead men to forget the value of life. This position seems close to Brecht's in his Life of Galileo—"Unlucky is the land that needs heroes"—and to Brecht's repudiation of heroic values as the rhetorical exoskeleton of economic interests, a point of view expressed in The Threepenny Opera (1931) and Mother Courage (1938-39). Ascanio's negation of the present is not a matter of political opinion or a question of rationality, but an individual choice which immerses him in absurdity and petty disputes and generates a subjective drama. Through this situation De Filippo condemns all those who evade the daily work of life and leave all responsibility to others. The only real monument anyone can ask for is the one he builds for himself in a world of inevitable changes. In such a world authentic values never change, De Filippo suggests, only rhetorical and false ones collapse; authentic values may change their appearance, but never their substance. For the poor wretch who insists on remaining attached to his illusions, we can only feel pity. Every solipsistic attempt to deny the continual flux of life must fail, to the advantage of those who regard life as a game of chance and speculation. At Ascanio's death, others are ready to use his place for their own gain, the low life collected around the monument swarms with opportunists. Guarnaschelli, for example, at once both Ascanio's "double" and his antagonist, publishes a right-wing newspaper at his own expense, one copy for each of his old rich aunts. By this means he keeps them in perpetual fear of communism and thus disinclined to take financial risks, so that he will inherit their assets intact!

Given its concern with social and political issues, The War Memorial might well have lapsed into dry didacticism. But by inserting the pathetic romance of Ascanio and Sabina, the vivacious repartee of the characters descended from the old popular Neapolitan theater, and

Plays of Social Protest

the popular songs suggestive of Brecht, De Filippo gives the play a poetry and wit that relieve any tendency to portentousness.

There is something new here in the technique of representation. In the preceding works there are generally two nuclei, one made up of the central scenes in which the characters are shown chained in a grotesque or humorous situation, the other characterized by the protagonist's critical reflection of his mode of existence. "The first," says C. Vallauri, "expresses the creative happiness of a world which is determined to stay serene in spite of everything; the second reflects the disenchanted bitterness of the author facing life's realities" (15). In this play, however, De Filippo has created rounded characters, fusing the protagonist's meditation with the vicissitudes of the other characters. Not merely does the central character lack a foil who would allow him to express the author's views, but in fact he remains in the shadows, on the outskirts of the action, with relatively few lines. His story is more "told" by the other characters than dramatically lived; he blends into the vague comic-grotesque chorus of derelicts that seems to dominate the action.

What emerges from a look back on these late plays is the playwright's progressive pessimism, little relieved by his few positive efforts to demonstrate the possibility of achieving a measure of fellow feeling. Repeatedly, the childlike qualities of a Luca Cupiello are shown defeated, and even exceptionally strong characters like Antonio Barracano are vanquished because their faith in human solidarity is not founded on fact. In The War Memorial society offers only two alternatives: the machinations of a Guarnaschelli, which make solidarity impossible, or the futile attachment to a past solidarity which time has colored with idealism. The dramatist's initial faith in the traditional values of simplicity, integrity, and the inner solidarity of family and society seems to have been destroyed, perhaps intentionally, in order to provoke the public to restore them.

In his last play, Gli esami non finiscono mai (The exams are never over, 1973), we find De Filippo at his most aggressive, fusing elements and techniques of Brechtian "epic theater" with those of the commedia dell'arte (16). As the play begins, the main character Guglielmo Speranza stands before the curtain and explains the rules of the game to the spectators. They will be his confi-

dants and his judges, and they will know that they are
facing a stage reality—this point the actor insists on.
In his "confessions" he will take them through fifty
years of his life, and he shows them three false beards,
one black, one gray, and one white, which he will pin on
his jacket in turn, as he passes through each age. As
the play proceeds, the actor forgets about the beards;
the convention is necessary only in the first scene, as
he shows us the young Guglielmo among his student
friends. The actor delivers his address to the audience
just as the traditional Pulcinella delivered his; but De
Filippo makes this device not just a rejection of the
illusionistic conventions of the naturalistic theater,
but a means of creating the "V-effekt" (Verfremdungseffekt, also called "alienation") and thus affirming the
didactic end of theater. In fact, in order to evoke a
more critical and intellectual response from the spectators, the actor De Filippo comments on his life both in
and out of character, relating his experiences to them
and begging them to watch and try to understand why the
events of the play happen to him. Music, singing, pantomime, lighting, masks, and rhythmic physical movement are
all handled in anti-illusionistic style, which may recall, for instance, John Osborne's The Entertainer, in
order to strengthen the effect of distance.

    For Guglielmo Speranza the exams are never over. In
1922 he receives his diploma, that "piece of paper" that
should have concluded his examinations and assured him
security and independence. But soon he realizes that
these examinations are the last ones only according to
the rules of that particular game. Over the years he has
to face one exam after another. He is the subject of
envious gossip; his professional success is attributed to
his father-in-law's help, and, while his wife's infidelity is forgotten, his own affair with the one person—
appropriately named Bonaria, Good-Natured—in whom he has
found understanding lays him open to vilification and
intrigue. Even his children, ironically named Fortunato
and Felice (Lucky and Happy), turn against him when he
wants to take a financial risk that might jeopardize
their inheritance. He is a victim of the worst deficiencies of institutionalized marriage. His wife and her
family feel no affection for him and no need to include
him in their lives. He is tied to them by convention
alone. The only reason his wife decides to leave her
lover and return to her husband is, as in The Hidden

Truth, her wish for social respectability. Guglielmo is trapped between his own love for his family and their lack of love for him. He cannot leave them, subjecting them to the social stigma that would entail, so, like Zi' Nicola in The Voices Within, he takes what seems to him the only avenue of escape from society's conventions and hypocrisy: he confines himself for fifteen years to a life of silence.

Finally, Guglielmo reaches Shakespeare's sixth age, that of the "lean and slippered Pantaloon," with the family fussing around his sickbed, unable to understand why he prefers the care of a veterinarian friend to that offered by three professional medical buffoons. When it comes, Guglielmo's seventh age, unlike melancholy Jacques's, is a spoof of death. He had asked to be buried naked "as he was born," but instead he is dressed up in a carnival tuxedo, his hair dyed black like that of Visconti's Venetian traveler, his lips and cheeks rouged, while the hypocritical "best friend" delivers the funeral oration. Under these circumstances, Guglielmo's choice and acceptance of death should be viewed as a triumph, a fact brought home to us as the "corpse" grimaces and giggles in the direction of the audience, submitting to his final defeat with a smile. As the priest who had wrung a last confession from him warned, other exams are waiting for him in the next world; but Guglielmo is not worried.

Guglielmo Speranza's vicissitudes trace the existential itinerary of Everyman; De Filippo suggests that our life, like Guglielmo's, is an uninterrupted series of examinations forced upon us both by the innate desire of man to know and question and by his eternal nosiness about his neighbor's business. The author is especially interested in denouncing the latter kind of "examination," and his protagonist's fight consists in defending himself against the intrusions of the offensively inquisitive. The play that results, while giving life to De Filippo's views, nonetheless has a serious shortcoming. As in The Hidden Truth, the situation here is presented too much in black and white—a characteristic this late play shares with Brecht's epic theater. Guglielmo is capable of love, and no one else is. While such an approach may make its point quite vividly, the public can hardly be expected to accept the idea that the protagonist has not one confidant or sympathizer, or that no one else has even one good quality. The play's modern feeling stems, however, from the way it touches our sensibilities like the sight of an oil slick on the sea or the plume of flame from a gasoline refinery or a well of toxic waste. In Eduardo's world one sees human feelings being burnt out. But all is not despair; Guglielmo is not named Speranza—Hope—in vain. His grim humor during the funeral comforts us, telling us that all is not lost despite the pettiness, mediocrity, and hypocrisy of our supposedly virtuous everyday world.

Chapter Nine
Conclusion

By scrapping whatever has no meaning for contemporary society and at the same time retaining certain traditional themes, Eduardo De Filippo has shown himself the natural heir of the Neapolitan theater and an international playwright as well. His vision is conventional to the extent that he strives for a world governed by moral values. However, his world is like that portrayed by many contemporary European and American playrights influenced by relativistic and existential thought: disintegrating and chaotic, crumbling both physically and spiritually. In My Family! even the children claim their existential freedom, their phrases echoing the sentiments of Sartre characters. The members of the Cimmaruta family in The Voices Within are divided one from another by conflicting versions of the nonexistent truth. The relativity of truth is the dominant theme in Those Ghosts! and The Big Magic.

What most concerns De Filippo, however, and what he represents constantly, often with excruciating sorrow, is the drama of the individual, man or woman, unable to face life in a corrupt society. Such a person can rebel, as do Gennaro Jovine and Filumena Marturano, or he can be destroyed, like Luca Cupiello; or, to forestall his destruction, he can escape into a private world. Luisa Conforto chooses to live in the past, surrounded by her accumulated possessions. Uncle Nicola retreats into a world of silence. Still more dramatic is Calogero Di Spelta's solution. Luisa and Uncle Nicola, while they may evade society, nonetheless accept its existence; but for Calogero everything becomes fiction except his illusions of unbetrayed solidarity. What is preserved in each case is the individual's morality and convictions—but only at the price of isolation. And this is true even though Gennaro Jovine, Alberto Stigliano, and Filumena Marturano are ultimately reinstated in society. As Domenico Soriano discovers in the final act of Filumena Marturano, fleeing from reality is no answer: one must endure and find the strength to face it.

De Filippo is constantly suggesting that man has to look behind the trickery and trumpery of life's surface and contemplate with a clear eye the violence, injustice, and vindictiveness that lie concealed there. His theater insistently focuses on moral corruption: hypocrisy and evil masquerading as good, egoism concealing itself as charity, the alienating influence of a depraved society, the disappearance of tolerance and respect for human dignity. But if life is a game, the individual should not be taken in by shady rules. As rules vary depending on the kind of game being played, so do De Filippo's ethical rules change from play to play. What stays constant is not a fixed moral standard, but rather the imperative to create an ethical code in the midst of moral anarchy.

From the early works—light farces, yet showing a deep sensitivity to human values—to the great neorealist plays of the immediate postwar period, which explore the drama of a humanity ravaged by war and poverty, to the last works cast in parable form and more strongly critical of society, De Filippo tries to make his audience respond to his vision of a world in which faith and human dignity are constantly betrayed. Fathers are set against their children, neighbors cheat one another, wives and husbands break their vows, and the culmination of all these betrayals, the most complete and treacherous of all, is the harsh reality of war. The betrayal of solidarity reverberates most strongly through social injustice: the rich use the poor to their advantage, while the government favors the affluent over the needy.

De Filippo's theater cannot be labeled social theater, since it is not exclusively or even mainly concerned with the class struggle or with the conditions of only the socially and economically oppressed. Nonetheless, he finds drama in the life and language of those living in poverty and victimized by social injustices. Social themes—the arbitrariness and inadequacy of the judicial system, the plight of the illegitimate, the oppressiveness of certain established institutions and social conventions, the unfair treatment of women, the exploitation of the poor—are De Filippo's main social concerns and are examined continually, whether singly or in combination. Except for a very few early plays meant essentially to entertain, the social message is a constant element, presented with increasing force in play after play. De Filippo is adamant in his belief that solidarity can be achieved and injustices overcome provided that

Conclusion

integrity and idealism can be found and fostered. And if well-meaning characters frequently meet with failure, this does not imply any pessimism about achieving that goal; rather, it serves to dramatize the cause and render the idealism more poignant for the audience, who should then be moved to act themselves.

In fact, in De Filippo's works there is an increasing commitment to improving society by arousing the audience. The last works in particular display the author's clear didactic intent through their overt sociopolitical commitment. Only in a few plays—I'm the Heir, The Hidden Truth, My Love and My Heart, and The Contract—can the author's concern for moral and social improvement be criticized as hindering his exercise of his considerable theatrical skill. Seldom does his need to ensure the clarity of his ideological message prevail over his sensitive portrayal of character or the rightness of situations and settings. In his better plays, on the contrary, it accounts for the depth of his inspiration and his thematic richness, the strength and even the vigor of his plots, the authenticity of characters and dialogue, the evenness of the irony and humor, and the sense of perspective evident in the dramatization of social problems.

In most of his plays De Filippo shows himself able to embody the simplest and most obvious truths about human nature in a totally integrated comic work. His devastating condemnation of people for their lack of morals in no way limits his rollicking wit. Because his characters reflect real people with specific feelings and convictions, people who transcend any didactic purpose, and because of the delicate balance of wit and thought and the integrity of artistic conception, De Filippo's drama has shown itself a model of the dialect theater, going beyond regionalism to take its place in world drama.

Following in the footsteps of such Italian playwrights as Ruzzante and Goldoni, De Filippo bears the special distinction of having reshaped the Italian dialect theater to modern needs and sustained its life well into the twentieth century. He has succeeded in creating a body of plays all his own and giving them the character of great art. Here and there he could very easily have fallen into facile sentimentalism or superficial mimesis of folklore and local color. But De Filippo is first and foremost a poet. Only a poet could have inserted into the midst of all the typical, picturesque local touches of Millionaires' Naples! the story of the war veteran, a story which takes the spectator back to similar episodes in famous classical comedies. Only a poet could have given Filumena Marturano that scene of "recognition by means of a song" which led one critic to say that with this play Eduardo had placed himself "du côté de chez Chekhov." Only a poet could give us the great window monologue in Those Ghosts! But only a true playwright could have found so constantly the proper measure, the perfect equilibrium, the precise balance between humor and sadness, happiness and grief, melancholy and the Dionysian spirit, ever present in the greatest comic poetry from Shakespeare to Molière, from Cervantes to Gogol.

Notes and References

Chapter One

1. This and the following quote are taken from a private letter from Thornton Wilder dated 9 October 1971 to the author.
2. Ibid.
3. Silvio D'Amico, Paloscenico del dopoguerra (Turin: Edizioni Radio Italiana, 1953), p. 189. Three dominant themes characterize pirandellismo: man creates both his personality and his life, ultimately becoming imprisoned by them; reality is relative, changing with the viewer; art is the ultimate reality, superior to life because of its permanence and yet inferior to it because of its immobility. Behind all these themes lie several basic conflicts: the conflicts between the primitive life force and life as conceived by man and society, between nature and form, truth and appearance, face and mask.
4. Vito Pandolfi, Teatro italiano contemporaneo 1945-1959 (Milan: Schwartz, 1959), p. 126. Giovanni Verga is considered the leading Italian verist and his one-act play, Cavalleria rusticana, is regarded as the most exemplary work of this literary current. For Viviani, see below.
5. Giulio Trevisani, Teatro Napoletano (Bologna: Mareggiani, 1957), p. 3. At the beginning of the century theatrical activities in Naples were vigorous. The bourgeoisie frequented a number of theaters, among them the Teatro Mercadante, the Fiorentini, the Bellini, the Nuovo, the Sannazaro, and the Politeana. Closer to the common people and situated in the "lower quarters" of Naples were such theaters as the San Ferdinando, the Umberto I, the Rossini, the Mercadantino, the Partenope, the Fenice, and most popular of all, the San Carlino.
6. Cf. Mario Corsi, Chi è di scena (Milan: Ceschina, 1947), p. 47.
7. D'Amico, Paloscenico, p. 169. The legacy of the commedia dell'arte tradition, incidentally, to Chaplin

and early film comedy in general is explored in David Madden's well-illustrated Harlequin's Stick, Charlie's Cane (Bowling Green, Ohio: Bowling Green University, Popular Press, 1975).

8. Vito Pandolfi, Spettacolo del secolo (Pisa: Nitri-lischi, 1953), p. 227.

9. Pandolfi, Teatro italiano, p. 130.

10. Eric Bentley, "Eduardo De Filippo and the Neapolitan Theater," Kenyon Review 13 (Winter 1951):121-22. When De Filippo performed on television for the first time, critics noted that the close-ups of the television camera added greatly to the impact of the performance, focusing on Eduardo's incredibly expressive face.

11. T. Cole and H. K. Chinoy, Actors on Acting (New York: Crown, 1970), p. 471.

12. His son Luca, also an actor, has confirmed this view, saying that "In our home, we do not talk of anything except theater. We live for theater. We breathe theater."

13. Cole and Chinoy, Actors, p. 471.

14. Ibid.

15. Mimî D'Aponte, "Encounters with Eduardo De Filippo," Modern Drama 16 (Dec. 1973):349.

16. 'O canisto (Naples, 1971), p. 72.

17. D'Aponte, "De Filippo," p. 348.

18. Cole and Chinoy, Actors, pp. 471-72.

19. Cf. Luigi Codignola, "Reading De Filippo," Tulane Drama Review 8 (Spring 1964):109. For more about the commedia dell'arte tradition, consult, among many works available, the following: Pierre Louis Duchartre, The Italian Comedy (New York: John Day, 1929), Konstantin Miklaslovski, La commedia dell'arte, ou le thêâtre des comediens itlaiens des XVIe, XVIIe et XVIIIe siècles (Paris: J. Schiffrin, 1927), Giacomo Oreglia, The Commedia dell'Arte (London: Methuen, 1968), and the many works of Allardyce Nicoll, such as The World of Harlequin. A Critical Study of the Commedia dell'Arte (Cambridge: Cambridge University Press, 1963). The character of Pulcinella (known in France as "Polichinelle," and famous in nineteenth-century England as the hero of the ever-popular Punch-and-Judy puppet shows, before he contributed his name to the title of a well-known humorous magazine) is an indigenous Neapolitan maschera or role, a wily but browbeaten servant distinguishable from the more recognizable Harlequin by reason of his greater submissiveness. The protagonist of a modern novel by

Carlo Bernari—Vesuvio e pane (Firenze: Vallechi, 1952)—his role was studied by the great Neapolitan philosopher and critic Benedetto Croce in one of his earliest publications, Pulcinella e il personaggio del napoletano in commedia; ricerche e osservazioni (Roma: Loescher, 1899).

Chapter Two

1. Eric Bentley, Kenyon Review, p. 119.
2. Letter from Thornton Wilder to the author dated 9 October 1971.
3. Eric Bentley, In Search of Theatre (New York: Knopf, 1953), p. 289.
4. Thomas Belmonte, The Broken Fountain (New York: Columbia Univrsity Press, 1979), p. 29.
5. Ibid., p. 7.
6. Ibid., p. 30.
7. Bentley, In Search of Theatre, p. 290.
8. Robert G. Bander, "A Critical Estimate of Eduardo De Filippo," Italian Quarterly 11, 43 (1967):44.
9. Mario Stefanile, Labirinto napoletano (Naples: E.S.I., 1958), p. 115.
10. De Filippo recounted his encounters with Pirandello in a symbolic letter, "Open letter to Pirandello," Il dramma, Dec. 1936. It was written just a few days after Pirandello's death (10 December 1936).
11. Corrado Alvaro, "Eduardo," Sipario 11 (March 1956):6.
12. Vito Pandolfi, "Intervista a quatr'occhi con Eduardo De Filippo," Sipario 11 (March 1956):5.
13. Eric Bentley, What is Theatre? (Boston: Beacon Press, 1956), p. 200.
14. Pandolfi, "Intervista," p. 5.
15. "Prefazione," I capolavori di Eduardo (Turin: Einaudi, 1967), p. vii.
16. Ibid., p. viii.
17. Ibid., pp. viii–xi.
18. Ibid., p. ix.
19. Cf. Corsi, Chi è di scena, p. 49.
20. I capolavori di Eduardo, p. vii.
21. S. Lori, "Intervista con il grande autore-attore napoletano," Roma, 7 May 1969.
22. Pier Paolo Pasolini, "Manifesto per un nuovo teatro," Nuovi argomenti 9 (Jan.-March 1968):13.
23. Thornton Wilder, from the letter cited in Chap-

ter 1, note 1.
24. Bentley, In Search of Theatre, p. 290.
25. Indeed, the translation into standard Italian of Filumena Marturano (a dubious enterprise from the start) was not successful and has never been restaged.
26. Desmond Morris et al., Gestures (Briarcliff Manor, N.Y.: Stein & Day, 1979) gives an excellent account of Neapolitan gestures.

Chapter Three

1. As quoted by R. Iacobbi, "Napoli milionaria!," Il cosmopolita, 1945; reprinted in English in a pamphlet distributed to the spectator of Millionaires' Naples! at the Aldwych Theatre, London, 1972. De Filippo's collected plays are published in two series: plays from 1920 through 1942 in one volume, entitled Cantata dei giorni pari (Cantata for even days); those produced between 1945 and 1965—with the addition of Non ti pago, which is dated 1940—in three volumes, entitled Cantata dei giorni dispari (Cantata for odd days). The latter group contains his most celebrated successes. Thus stated, however, the order is deceptive, since the first volume to appear was actually the initial volume of the second series, Cantata dei giorni dispari, which came out in 1951 without the indication that it was Volume 1 of a series and without the original dates of the plays. A second edition of the same volume, with play dates ranging from 1945 to 1948, bears the copyright date 1957, by which time the project of publishing his entire works appears to have taken shape. Volume 2 of Cantata dei giorni dispari, containing, in addition to two earlier works, the plays written between 1950 and 1957, came out in 1958. Volume 3, plays produced between 1957 and 1965, did not appear until 1966. The success of the first volumes of Cantata dei giorni dispari led to the publication of the collected early works, in 1959, under the derivative title of Cantata dei giorni pari. The titles—which have been criticized as being not especially descriptive and somewhat pretentious—are in any case ambiguous. The phrase "giorni dispari" can mean either the odd-numbered days of the month or the odd days of the week, considered in Italy to begin on Monday. Perhaps the distinction is unimportant, however, since, in either case, the implication is that the "odd days" are the unlucky ones (cf. our own Friday the 13th). The ti-

tle Cantata of Odd Days, given in 1951 to the plays dating from the immediate postwar period, referred to the misfortunes of Italy in that time. The "even days" of the title later attributed to the plays of the prewar Fascist period are an ironical adaptation of the former title and presumably should be interpreted to mean "the days when everything seemed to be going well."

2. Anton Giulio Bragaglia in Pulcinella (Rome: Casini, 1953) affirms that in the pulcinellata there is a preponderance of jest and movement over word: "it is a theater free of any rigidly schematic form and the major techniques employed were those of repetitions of situations and the use of double meanings attached to situations, words and events."

3. Cantata dei giorni pari (Turin, 1967), p. 20. Hereafter page numbers in brackets in the text in this chapter refer to this edition. Translations are mine unless otherwise noted.

4. Bander, "Critical Estimate," p. 9.

5. Robert W. Corrigan, Masterpieces of the Modern Italian Theatre (New York: Collier Books, 1967), p. 8.

6. Gennaro Magliulo, Eduardo De Filippo (Bologna, 1959), p. 35.

7. Vito Pandolfi, I contemporanei, vol. 3 (Milan: Marzorati, 1970), p. 363.

8. Luigi Ferranti, Teatro italiano grottesco (Bologna: Cappelli, 1964), p. 57.

9. Sergio Torresani, Il teatro italiano negli ultimi vent'anni (1945-1965) (Cremona, 1969), p. 242.

10. Simonetta Scornavacca, "La storia della 'Gente' attraverso l'opera di Eduardo." Unpublished thesis written at the University of Rome, 1970, p. 27.

11. In two other early one-acts—Quinto piano ti saluto (Farewell to the fifth floor, 1934) and Il dono di Natale (The Christmas gift, 1932)—De Filippo shows ability to give this intimate note a semimelodramatic cadence, more fully developed in mature works like Filumena Marturano.

12. The "presepio" or crèche, an elaborate re-creation of the scene of Christ's Nativity, is a feature particularly characteristic of the churches and homes of Naples at Christmas time.

13. Luigi Ferrante, Teatro italiano grottesco (Bologna: Cappelli, 1964), p. 31.

14. Sigmund Freud, The Basic Writings (New York: A. A. Brill, 1938), p. 77.

15. For the Pirandello story in English, see Luigi Pirandello, Short Stories, trans. by Lily Duplaix.
16. Carlo Filosa, Eduardo De Filippo: Poeta comico del 'tragico quotidiano' (Frosinone, 1978), p. 132.

Chapter Four

1. Alberto Lattuada in P. Leprohon, The Italian Cinema (New York: Praeger, 1972), p. 98.
2. As quoted by R. Iacobbi, "Napoli milionaria!" See note n. 1, Chap. 3.
3. Eduardo De Filippo, Cantata dei giorni dispari (Turin: Einaudi, 1967), vol. 1, pp. 124-25. Hereafter references in brackets in the text denote first volume number then page number. In this and the chapters that follow I refer to this three-volume edition. Translations are mine unless otherwise noted.
4. Giorgio Prosperi, "Napoli milionaria," Il tempo, 10 May 1971.
5. In 1964 the play became a film, Marriage Italian Style, directed by Vittorio De Sica.
6. Not until 1961 did Eduardo officially admit that his father was the actor-playwright Eduardo Scarpetta.
7. Cf. Federico Frascani, Eduardo (Naples, 1974), pp. 181-82.

Chapter Five

1. Ferdinando Maurino, "The Drama of De Filippo," Modern Drama 3 (Feb. 1961):354.
2. Ibid.
3. Torresani, Teatro italiano, p. 255.
4. Maurino, "De Filippo," p. 352.
5. G. B. De Sanctis, Eduardo De Filippo commediografo neorealista (Perugia, 1959), p. 45. Federico Fellini toys with the same ideas and for him the seedy stage musician or hypnotist is a recurring character.
6. Magliulo, De Filippo, p. 66.
7. The Voices Within served as the rough basis for the film Shoot Loud, Louder, I Don't Understand with Marcello Mastroianni in the leading role.
8. Salvatore Quasimodo, Scritti sul teatro (Milano: Mondadori, 1961), p. 46.
9. Ibid.
10. Vito Pandolfi, Teatro italiano del dopoguerra (Bologna: Mareggiani, 1956), p. 342.

11. Giorgio Pullini, Teatro italiano del Novecento (Bologna: Cappelli, 1971), p. 125.

Chapter Six

1. Bentley, In Search of Theatre, p. 289.
2. Filosa, Poeta comico, p. 290.
3. Stefanile, Labirinto, p. 122.
4. Henri Bergson, Le Rire (Paris: Presses Universitaires de France, 1960), p. 5.
5. The play was a great success in London, with Laurence Olivier and Joan Plowright, and a fiasco on Broadway.
6. Fiorenza Di Franco, Il teatro di Eduardo (Bari, 1975), p. 182.
7. Giorgio Prosperi, Il tempo, 7 November 1959, p. 3; Nicola Ciarletta, Il paese, 7 November 1959, p. 3.

Chapter Seven

1. "Lettera al Ministro dello Spettacolo," in Luciano Bergonzini and Franco Zardi, Teatro anno zero (Firenze: Parenti, 1961), p. 145.

Chapter Eight

1. Though not the official religion of Italy, the influence of the Catholic Church is very powerful. The theater in which the play opened was a former convent refectory, which gave the Roman hierarchy specious legal grounds for closing a performance they judged offensive to public morals. The title of the play, incidentally, De Pretore Vincenzo, is the name of the chief character, last name first, according to the formula by which he would be known to the authorities. To his friends and neighbors, the members of his own class, he would be known by his first name, Vincenzo or, more politely, Don Vincenzo.
2. "De Pretore Vincenzo," Il paese di Pulcinella (Naples: Casella, 1951), pp. 59-77.
3. Magliulo, De Filippo, p. 81.
4. Pandolfi, I contemporanei, pp. 368-69.
5. Le poesie di Eduardo (Turin, 1975), p. 129.
6. Di Franco, Teatro di Eduardo, p. 174.
7. Pandolfi sees the lack of both organic structure and psychological complexity as common weak elements of

this phase of De Filippo's production. I contemporanei, p. 369.

8. Three Plays, trans. Carlo Ardito (London, 1976), p. 29.

9. R. Tian, "Il sindaco del Rione Sanità," Il Messaggero, 8 February 1973, p. 6.

10. Frascani, Eduardo, p. 117.

11. Personal interview with the author.

12. Il contratto (Turin, 1967).

13. Il monumento (Turin, 1971), pp. 68-69.

14. V. Talarico, "Il monumento," Momento sera, 26 November 1970, p. 6.

15. C. Vallauri, "'Il monumento' di Eduardo De Filippo," Ridotto, Jan. 1971, p. 18.

16. Gli esami non finiscono mai (Turin, 1973).

Selected Bibliography

PRIMARY SOURCES

Cantata dei giorni pari. Turin: Einaudi, 1959.
Cantata dei giorni dispari. Turin: Einaudi, 1951, 1958, 1966 (3 vols.).
Il contratto. Turin: Einaudi, 1967.
'O canisto. Naples: Edizioni Teatro San Ferdinando, 1971.
Il monumento. Turin: Einaudi, 1971.
Gli esami non finiscono mai. Turin: Einaudi, 1973.
Le poesie di Eduardo. Turin: Einaudi, 1975.

Translations:
Filumena Marturano. In Robert W. Corrigan, ed. Masterpieces of the Modern Italian Theater. New York: Collier Books, 1967.
The Inner Voices. Italian Theater Review 6, 2 (1957):25-47.
Sik-Sik, The Masterful Magician. Translated by Robert G. Bander. Italian Quarterly 11, 43 (Winter 1967): 19-42.
Three Plays: The Local Authority, Grand Magic, Filumena Marturano. Translated by Carlo Ardito. London: Hamilton and St. George's Press, 1976.

SECONDARY SOURCES

1. Books
Antonucci, Giovanni. Eduardo De Filippo-Introduzione e guida allo studio dell'opera eduardiana. Firenze: Le Monnier, 1981. Introductory study to the theater of De Filippo with a survey of its criticism.
De Sanctis, G. B. Eduardo De Filippo commediografo neorealista. Perugia: Unione Arti Grafiche, 1959. Places De Filippo's major works in the context of the neorealist movement.
Di Franco, Fiorenza. Il teatro di Eduardo. Bari: Universale Laterza, 1975. A useful thematic analysis of all the works.

191

Filosa, Carlo. Eduardo De Filippo: Poeta comico del 'tragico quotidiano'. Frosinone: Casamari, 1978. The most extensive appraisal of De Filippo, the man and his works, from the point of view of his Neapolitan cultural and social background and his links with the popular Neapolitan theater. Very readable despite meandering argumentation, subjective judgments, and overlong quotations.

Frascani, Federico. Eduardo. Naples: Guida, 1974. Analysis of certain works within the Neapolitan social context.

Magliulo, Gennaro. Eduardo De Filippo. Bologna: Cappelli, 1959. Identifies many themes later developed more fully by other critics.

Mignone, Mario B. Il teatro de Eduardo De Filippo. Rome: Trevi, 1974. Balanced biography relating the man to the period in which he lived; followed by a comprehensive analysis of all the plays. The basis of the present work.

Pizer Coen, Laura. Il mondo della famiglia ed il teatro degli affetti: Saggio sull'esperienza 'comica' di Eduardo De Filippo. Assisi-Rome: Carucci, 1972. A perceptive, useful study of De Filippo's work in relation to the southern Italian family.

2. Articles and interviews

Bander, Robert. "A Critical Estimate of Eduardo De Filippo." Italian Quarterly 11, 43 (Winter 1967):3-18. A good brief introduction in English to De Filippo's theater.

──────. "Pulcinella, Pirandello, and Other Influences on De Filippo's Dramaturgy." Italian Quarterly 12, 46 (Fall 1968):39-72. Establishes De Filippo's links with the Neapolitan theater and that of Pirandello.

Bentley, Eric. "Eduardo De Filippo and the Neapolitan Theater." Kenyon Review 13 (Winter 1951):111-26. Presents De Filippo's theatricality through the "Neapolitanness" of the characters.

Cole, Toby, and Chinoy, Helen. Actors on Acting. New York: Crown, 1970, pp. 470-72. De Filippo's answers to questions pertaining to acting and directing.

D'Aponte, Mimi. "Encounters with Eduardo De Filippo." Modern Drama 16, 3-4 (Dec. 1973):347-53. Contains some of De Filippo's most important pronouncements on acting and directing.

Maurino, Ferdinando. "The Drama of De Filippo." Modern

Drama 3 (Feb. 1961):348-56. A perceptive analysis especially of Those Ghosts! and The Big Magic in relation to Pirandello's theater.

Mignone, Mario B. "Note sul teatro giovanile di Eduardo De Filippo." Forum Italicum 7, 1 (March 1973):9-22. Demonstrates the considerable social criticism in the early works.

Pandolfi, Vito. "Teatro di Eduardo: un terreno sconvolto." Il dramma 22, 16-17 (July 1 and 15, 1946). Casts doubt upon De Filippo's ability to separate his demands as an actor from those as a playwright. Strongly suggests that the actor is a hindrance to the author.

―――. "La tradizione popolare di Eduardo." Il dramma 24, 60 (May 1948):8. Establishes clearly some points of contact between Eduardo's theater and the Neapolitan popular theater.

―――. "Intervista a quattr'occhi con Eduardo De Filippo." Sipario 11, 119 (March 1956):5-6. The most quoted interview for De Filippo's views as actor and playwright.

Torresani, Sergio. "Eduardo De Filippo." In Il teatro italiano negli ultimi vent'anni (1945-1965). Cremona: Mangiarotti, 1965. An analysis of De Filippo's theater through a study of his protagonists.

Viviani, Vittorio. "Eduardo." In Storia del teatro napoletano. Naples: Guida, 1968, pp. 879-934. Analyzes De Filippo's theater in relation to the Neapolitan theater.

Index

Altavilla, Pasquale, 3, 16
Altieri, Enrico, 8
Alvaro, Corrado, 27
Always Say Yes! (Ditegli sempre di si), 59
Antonelli, Luigi, 11
Art of Comedy, The (L'arte della commedia), 49, 139-43, 146
Atkinson, Brook, 86

Bander, Robert G., 41
Barthes, Roland, 59
Belmonte, Thomas, 22, 23
Bentley, Eric, 14, 20, 21, 23, 28, 35, 122
Bergson, Henri, 132
Betti, Ugo, 11, 16, 84, 109, 114, 118
Big Magic, The (La grande magia), 6, 13, 26, 28, 46, 47, 62, 70, 99-105, 112, 117, 120, 179
Bovio, Libero, 41, 49
Bracco, Roberto, 6
Brecht, Bertolt, 32, 64, 155, 159, 160, 171, 174, 177
Brechtian elements, 18, 158, 172

Cantata for Even Days (Cantata dei giorni pari), 37, 38, 186
Cantata for Odd Days (Cantata dei giorni dispari), 186
Cervantes Miguel, 182

Chaplin, 4, 13, 19, 29, 183
Chekhov, Anton, 49, 182
Christmas at the Cupiellos' (Natale in casa Cupiello), 24, 53-58, 119, 138
Ciarletta, Nicola, 136
Clarke, G., 89
Coleman, Robert, 86
Commedia dell'arte, 3, 4, 14, 15, 19, 22, 24, 38, 39, 45, 131, 184-85
Compagnia del Teatro Umoristico i De Filippo, La, 10, 11, 16
Consiglio, Alberto, 10
Contract, The (Il contratto), 70, 169-71
Corrigan, Robert, 45

D'Ambra, Lucio, 11
D'Amico, Silvio, 2, 13
Dangerously (Pericolosamente), 43
Dash, Thomas R., 87
De Filippo, Peppino, 8, 10, 12, 26
De Filippo, Titina, 8, 9, 11, 12
De Pretore Vincenzo, 31, 79, 147-53
De Santis, G. B., 103
De Sica, Vittorio, 68
Di Franco, Fiorenza, 135, 156
Di Giacomo, Salvatore, 5, 6, 73, 117, 148
Di Napoli, Guido, 9

Index

Di Napoli, Vincenzo, 9
Donnelly, Tom, 86
Dostoievski, Theodore M., 59

Engels, Friedrich, 163
Everyman, 70, 177
Exams are never over, The (Gli esami non finiscono mai), 18, 175-78

Fabbri, Diego, 109
Fascism, 11, 12, 37, 38, 43, 51, 53, 57, 59, 67
Fellow with White Hair, A (Uno coi capelli bianchi), 60-61
Ferrante, Luigi, 58
Filosa, Carlo, 62, 126
Filumena Marturano, 5, 13, 23, 24, 35, 55, 70, 78-90, 104, 106, 117, 119, 179
Frascani, Federico, 165

Galdieri, Michele, 10
Galdieri, Rocco, 49
Gennariniello, 52
Gogol, Nikolai, 182
Goldoni, Carlo, 41, 61, 139, 143, 181

Herbert, F. H., 86
Hidden Truth, The (Le bugie con le gambe lunghe), 79, 105-9, 111, 117, 120, 177, 181

I'm the Heir (Io, l'erede), 64-66
I Won't Pay You (Non ti pago), 23, 27, 47, 62-64, 79, 112

Jarry, Alfred, 25

Kerr, Walter, 89

Lattuada, Alberto, 67
Local Authority, The (Il sindaco del Rione Sanità), 26, 70, 163-69

Magliulo, Gennaro, 47, 154
Marceau, Marcel, 155
Marx, Karl, 163
Maurino, Ferdinando, 95, 97
Men and Gentlemen (Uomini e galantuomini), 10, 42-43, 59
Millionaires' Naples! (Napoli milionaria!), 2, 20, 24, 25, 55, 57, 71-78, 80, 84, 106, 117, 119, 127, 134
Molière, 24, 61, 86, 139, 143, 182
Murolo, Enzo, 9, 16, 49
Murolo, Ernesto, 5, 6
My Family! (Mia famiglia), 24, 26, 70, 79, 84, 124-28, 134, 179
My Love and My Heart (Bene mio e core mio), 70, 120, 128-33, 138, 181

Naples, 3, 18, 20-26, 116
Neapolitan theater, 2, 3-7, 38
Neorealism, 67-68
New Suit, The (L'abito nuovo), 61-62
Nicolardi, Eduardo, 49
Norton, Elliott, 86

O'Casey, Sean, 35, 73
Old Gang of Thirty Years Ago, The (Quei figurini di trent'anni fa), 43
Olivier, Laurence, 89, 137
Osborne, John, 176

Pandolfi, Vito, 2, 7, 13, 47, 114, 154
Pasolini, Pier Paolo, 33
Petito, Antonio, 4, 16, 156
Pharmacy on Duty (Farmacia di turno), 10, 38-42, 43, 119, 138
Philosophically (Filosoficamente), 42, 43, 47, 112, 119
Pinero, Arthur W., 35
Pirandellismo, 2, 183
Pirandello, Luigi, 2, 16, 25, 26-29, 59, 61-62, 63, 91, 98, 101, 102, 114, 140, 142, 144
Pope John XXIII, 153
Prosperi, Giorgio, 77, 136
Pulcinella, 4, 14, 19, 24, 43, 115, 116
Pulcinella's Son (Il figlio di Pulcinella), 153-59
Pulcinellata, 2, 3, 38, 39, 40, 43, 57, 73, 187
Punch-and-Judy, 43

Quasimodo, Salvatore, 111

Resistance, 67
Role of Hamlet, The (La parte di Amleto), 145-46
Rossellini, Roberto, 68
Russo, Ferdinando, 5, 6, 148
Ruzzante, 181

San Carlino Theater, 8, 40, 64, 131
San Ferdinando Theater, 5, 12
Sartre, Jean Paul, 26
Saturday, Sunday, and Monday (Sabato, domenica e lunedì), 24, 79, 133-37

Scarpetta, Eduardo, 2, 4, 6, 7, 8, 16, 34, 43
Scarpetta, Vincenzo, 8, 9
Shakespeare, William, 182
Sik-Sik, the Incomparable Magician (Sik-Sik, l'artefice magico), 10, 44-49, 119, 138
Squarzina, Luigi, 160
Stanislavsky, Konstantin S., 18
Stefanile, Mario, 24, 131
Stella, Federico, 5
Strindberg, August, 31
Synge, John M., 35

Talarico, V., 173
Those Ghosts! (Questi fantasmi!), 4, 6, 26, 46, 50, 62, 63, 70, 78, 92-99, 107, 108, 112, 117, 120, 138, 179
Tommaso D'Amalfi, 31, 159-63
Top Hat, The (Il cilindro), 47, 49, 143-45
Trevisani, Giulio, 3

Vallauri, C., 175
Varpokhovsky, Leonid, 53
Verga, Giovanni, 2, 73, 183
Villani, Peppino, 9, 38
Visconti, Lucchino, 68
Viviani, Raffaele, 2, 4, 6, 7, 8, 16, 117, 151
Vladimir, Doronin, 53
Voices Within, The (Le voci di dentro), 6, 26, 46, 47, 109-15, 117, 120, 138, 177, 179

War Memorial, The (Il monumento), 70, 171-75
Who is Happier than I! (Chi è cchiù felice 'e

me!), 10, 27, 50-52, 55, 79
Wilder, Thornton, 1, 21, 35

Zavattini, Cesare, 68
Zeffirelli, Franco, 88
Zorzi, Lodovico, 19
Zurlo, Leopoldo, 43